The Adviser's Toolkit

giving legal advice

Elaine Heslop qualified as a solicitor in 1985 after working as a teacher, local government personnel officer and community education tutor. She worked for a number of years in a Law Centre® both as a solicitor and legal director, and is currently employed as a solicitor in Kent Law Clinic at the University of Kent. She also provides training and consultancy, largely in employment-related areas of law and practice. She has helped to develop a foundation degree in legal advice at the London Metropolitan University and has taught on a number of legal and skills-based courses including an MA in Advice and Paralegal Studies, the Legal Practice Course and the Bar Vocational Course. She is co-author of *Employment Tribunals* (Law Society, 2004) and a contributor to *Discrimination in Employment: law and practice* (Law Society, 2006).

The Legal Action Group is a national, independent charity which promotes equal access to justice for all members of society who are socially, economically or otherwise disadvantaged. To this end, it seeks to improve law and practice, the administration of justice and legal services.

The Adviser's Toolkit
giving legal advice

Elaine Heslop

 Legal Action Group
2007

Published in Great Britain 2007
by LAG Education and Service Trust Limited
242 Pentonville Road, London N1 9UN
www.lag.org.uk

British Library Cataloguing in Publication Data
a CIP catalogue record for this book is available from the British Library.

ISBN   978 1 903307 49 6

Typeset by Regent Typesetting, London
Printed by Hobbs the Printers, Totton, Hampshire

Preface

This book is timed to coincide with a growth of interest in and examination of the skills of the adviser in the context of giving legal advice. In the past few years there have been various initiatives designed to give more structure to the skills of advice-giving. The recent implementation of the National Occupational Standards in legal advice is at the forefront of setting out the standards which guide and inform those in advice-giving occupations.

There is a growing recognition that advice work skills in the legal context need more profile and credibility and that training and qualifications in these skills will enhance the work done by advisers to the benefit of their clients and will provide a more skilled workforce in this area.

This recognition is allied to moves to provide more diverse training and educational qualifications in legal advice and to begin to co-ordinate the education offered so that there is a clear map of advice-work training and qualification. In the meantime there is a range of courses and qualifications which advisers can pursue in order to acquire advice skills.

It is to be hoped that this book will complement some of those courses. It certainly endeavours to follow the pattern of many of the new National Occupational Standards as a guide and interpretation of how those standards apply in the workplace.

In addition many law students are now taking practical clinical approaches to their legal studies. They are learning practice skills, taking part in case work and learning how to advise and assist clients. Students who are taking their professional legal qualification courses are also being introduced to a range of client care skills in the context of learning to advise.

Advice work and legal advice work is being carried out across a variety of organisations. Some of these are referred to and described in chapter 1. Many people do not see themselves as 'legal advisers' whereas the work they do is in reality vital to individuals seeking v information and help about their rights in society. Others are providing an advice service having learnt their craft through experience rather than formal legal qualifications. Where advisers have obtained legal qualifications they will be looking wherever possible to practise and improve their skills of advice and client care. Hopefully this book will be of value to all of the above in addressing the basic principles of giving advice and devising tactics for resolving clients' problems.

Part 1 of this book provides an outline of the national map of advice agencies, giving an overview of how both a national and local advice agency operates and how each model functions in terms of their work and how they deliver and fund their services.

In parts 2–4 there follows a step-by-step approach to giving advice. This approach is underpinned not only by the standards and skills now incorporated in the National Occupational Standards, but also by what informs the practice of a solicitor or other legally qualified practitioner in terms of the correct professional approach to advising and conducting cases for their clients. The approach is not one of assuming a high level of legal knowledge or expertise, but rather the opposite; to open up good practice which has been operating in the legal profession for many years to a much wider readership. This part of the book also has a practical case study included to illustrate the skills and approaches which are being explained and discussed.

Part 5 provides an overview of the legal system and explains what the structure of our courts and tribunals are and how it all interlocks. Guidance is offered on how to navigate your way around the formalities of the court system, how to address judges and tribunal chairmen, who the court personnel are and how to behave and dress in court. These are all helpful if advisers are to have the confidence to use the court and tribunal system. This part also offers guidance on how to carry out legal research, what the meaning of 'case-law' is and how to find out more about the subject you are advising on in a variety of ways. Although the criminal legal system is outlined in this part, examples of the practice of giving advice are based on civil law topics, and the case study relates to civil rather than criminal claims.

Finally, part 6 gives an insight into two areas of social welfare law, employment and housing, in order to explain the case study appearing throughout parts 2–4 and to give the reader a 'taster' of these topics. The book does not pretend to offer any legal analysis in detail but both these topics are introduced in a general sense so that the reader will see the structure and approach inherent in each of them.

This book is written partly arising out of many years' experience
as a solicitor and legal adviser in an inner city Law Centre®, and more

recently in a University Law Clinic setting, and partly out of a desire to ensure that the essential skills that advisers are utilising when they engage with those that use their services are recognised and passed on to new advisers.

It is hoped that the book will not only be a useful handbook for an adviser but will also be an aid in fostering good practice, and encapsulating the skills the adviser is using in their contact with clients and others when working on resolving their legal and allied problems. There is a unique satisfaction to be gained from advising and assisting members of our diverse communities in obtaining their lawful rights, or a remedy where they have suffered injustice. Hopefully *The Adviser's Toolkit* will be a useful tool in this process.

Acknowledgements are due first to Esther Pilger at Legal Action Group for taking the leap of faith and encouraging the publication of this book, to Diane Astin for her insightful and thorough review and helpful comments throughout, to a host of colleagues whom I have worked side by side with in the advice sector, and to friends and family for their encouragement and support, in particular Bob Henderson and Louise Petterson.

Elaine Heslop
September 2007

Contents

APPENDICES

Advice frameworks

CHAPTER 1

Advice agencies and how they work

1.1   Advice or legal advice – what does it mean?

There is no single definition of the concept of advice-giving and the national map of advice agencies is wide ranging and varied in terms of who each agency targets as its service user group and how advice work is carried out.

Categories of advice-giving agencies

Signposting and information

There are many organisations which provide a service to the public in terms of advising and assisting them to obtain more information, access to a service or benefit, or advice about their rights or remedies. Not all of these organisations will regard themselves as giving 'advice' but see what they do as providing information or 'signposting'. Examples of such organisations are a reception service in a local authority office, or a local library. Any information which an individual is likely to act on could be regarded as advice, although the recipients of that type of advice will not always be described as clients, but sometimes service users.

Serving special interest groups

There are also a range of national organisations which exist to represent the interests of a specific section of the population, such as refugees, or workers from the European Economic Area (EEA), women, older people or disabled people. They exist to ensure that this sector of the population obtains any necessary support and recognition as members of our society. Many of these organisations have help-lines or advice-lines for those individuals the organisation is there to serve.

An example of such an organisation is the Disability Rights Commission.[1] A national organisation such as this will give out general information and advice about policies or services for the groups in society they serve and they will also have experienced, and usually legally-qualified, advisers or case workers who can in some circumstances assist individuals to pursue legal claims.

---

1   Note, however, that from October 2007 the Disability Rights Commission (DRC) will become part of the Commission for Equality and Human Rights (CEHR) which will continue with and expand the work already being done by the DRC.

Community advice organisations

Another category of advice-giving organisation is community advice organisations and networks. Some of these are part also of a national framework such as a Law Centre® or a Citizens Advice Bureau. Others are part of a Government initiative, such as Sure Start, a network of community services for parents. They may be part of a local authority's service delivery, such as a racial equality unit, or a tenancy or welfare benefits advice service. Community Law Centres®, and in some areas, Citizens Advice Bureaux, will not only provide advice on legal and legally-related issues for the local low income community, but will also represent clients in courts or tribunals. Law Centres® will also look to pursue legal cases which will benefit the wider community as well as the individual client.

Community centres and drop-in services

Finally, some urban and rural areas also have community centres which serve groups in the community: parents, various ethnic groups or young people. They may provide a social outlet, a drop-in service or meals. These smaller groups often survive on limited budgets and their funding can be quite precarious. They are likely to rely heavily on goodwill and volunteers. They nevertheless provide a range of valuable information and support as well as often advising on quite complex and important matters.

Staff profiles in advice agencies

Each of these types of organisation will be staffed by a variety of different individuals. There may be managers, supervisors, advisers, case workers, outreach workers, volunteers and receptionists. There may be other support staff doing secretarial work or accounts, finances, marketing of services or fundraising.

As an example of the varying approaches organisations take to organising their work and describing what they do, workers in an advice agency may be called 'case workers' where their cases are geared to monitoring the progress of the advice they give to an individual. He or she will be expected to resolve their problem themselves, armed with the advice and information they have been given by an adviser. Other organisations will employ case workers to conduct legal cases in court for clients in the same way as a solicitor in private practice will do. Both models are typical and equally valid and demonstrate the broad range of what we term advice work and how it functions in different settings.

The volunteer

One common element in virtually all models of an advice agency is the presence of volunteers. Volunteers have formed a vital part of the process of running advice services for many years. With the possible exception of the statutory sector (local authorities) that are more likely to employ students, trainees, or those on work experience programmes in advice-giving parts of the sector, the volunteer will be an integral part of the advice system.

Many organisations actively recruit volunteers and some run a specific programme of work and training for the volunteers they take on. In some cases the time the volunteer will spend with the organisation may be limited, either because the organisation encourages short placements only, or because the individual, possibly as a student, is looking for work experience on a short-term basis. In other cases a volunteer may stay for a long period of time working alongside paid staff, and be given specific tasks to do or areas of work to cover. For many students, voluntary experience can help with their career progression into law or advice work.

Although the presence of volunteers is a necessary and rewarding part of the system of advice we have, their high profile does in some respects reflect the lack of resources which many agencies have: they are needed in order to keep their services running. Another explanation for their presence is that the caring and giving nature of advice work will always attract people who are willing to volunteer to give up their time to become involved.

1.2   Models of advice agencies: a community or local advice agency

To explain in more detail how advice services function, illustrations are provided here, on pages 8–10 and 11–13, of two models of an advice agency: a community advice agency and a national advice agency. Both are in part based on real organisations or a blend of real organisations, and therefore, hopefully, typify the organisation described. They have, however, been given fictitious names and locations. Their history, structure and staff profiles are typical and help to illustrate what their purpose is, how advice agencies function, who works in them and some of the funding and developmental issues they face.

Both of these models represent a part of the voluntary sector, which makes up the bulk of advice services in the UK. The voluntary sector is largely made up of organisations outside the formal, statutory sector servicing communities. Voluntary organisations are often funded in part by central and/or local government or by government agencies or lottery or other 'community chests'. The rationale is that they exist to support, or sometimes even fill gaps in, the work done by Government to provide more inclusion for certain, often disadvantaged, groups in society. Advice agencies are a part of the 'not-for-profit' sector of service providers. Voluntary sector organisations are sometimes referred to as non-governmental organisations (NGOs).

1.3   Models of advice agencies: a national advice agency

A different model from the local community advice agency is the national agency which serves a special interest in the wider community and which will have as part of its function a commitment to doing policy work for that group in society, in order to effect change. Many of these national organisations will provide advice to individuals; some will do so via telephone or e-mail.

1.4   Governmental and statutory advice and support

Although most advice agencies are in the voluntary sector, there is also a network of Government advice and information services. There is also a variety of sources of funding for advice, some central government, some local and some larger charitable organisations. In terms of Government policy on advice and more specifically legal advice, there have been some substantial shifts in the recent past with a greater emphasis on wider access being offered by new 'providers' as well as traditional advisers such as lawyers and advice agencies.[2] This has been linked to how and where the government intends to fund advice in the future and is likely to lead to funding for some types of legal advice and representation being reduced and smaller local agencies offering specialist services being less likely to be able to continue.

A book of this nature can only provide a snapshot of how advice work is supported and funded in order to give a general 'map' of current advice provision in the UK. Some examples of central government involvement in the field of advice are provided below, as well as an outline of how local councils contribute to the provision of advice.

2   See eg, the Government's 'Carter Review': www.legalaidprocurementreview. gov.uk.

A community agency: the people's law clinic

The People's Law Clinic (PLC) is in a large urban area, called Maidchester.

History and purpose
PLC was founded in 1977 and has just celebrated its 30th birthday. It came about as a result of two solicitors in practice in the south of Maidchester representing a group of employees in a local garment-making factory who had complaints about working conditions and lack of pay. In the course of running a claim for them in the recently-established Industrial Tribunal, (now called the Employment Tribunal) the solicitors got to know a local trades union activist and two community workers who ran English classes for some of the female home workers. The case was successful and it emerged that there were many other sectors of that local community who needed help with their rights; tenants whose landlords were ignoring the recently-introduced Rent Act, employees who needed help with claims in the new Industrial Tribunals and citizens of ex-commonwealth countries looking for help in respect of their rights to settle in the UK. The solicitors decided to form PLC with a grant from the local council. They were joined by the trade union activist, the two community workers and a local immigration solicitor.

Constitution
From the start PLC was managed by a management committee who represented the local community served by PLC. There are also local Councillors opted on to the management committee to represent the interests of the local council, which gives PLC an annual grant for its running costs. The Committee was and still is responsible for ensuring that PLC properly fulfils its stated functions, is properly managed, and that the finances are properly applied and run.

Staff profile and workload
PLC has now grown to ten staff. The staffing structure is as follows:

- a director of the centre;
- a supervising housing lawyer;
- a supervising employment lawyer;
- a supervising immigration lawyer;
- three case workers, one in each of the above areas;
- a welfare benefits and debt adviser;
- an outreach worker for refugee and asylum support in the community;
- a job-share receptionist (two staff covering the full time post).

There are also four or five volunteers at any one time, each of whom works one full day a week.

The director is responsible for all staffing matters, for the smooth running of the service, for the finances of the centre and reports directly to the management committee. She also supervises the welfare benefits and debt adviser as this is her specialist field of practice. The supervising lawyers supervise those in their team who advise on the same subject. They and the outreach worker run telephone advice sessions each week and also take on legal cases for as many of these callers as their time will allow.

Cases are managed by the supervisors who meet from time to time to discuss risk management and quality control of the work. They also meet with the director to discuss the ongoing work and future plans of the centre and the finances.

The volunteers help the case workers and supervisors with the preparation of their cases, assist the receptionist and help to keep the information systems up to date.

Organisation profile and funding
The current profile of PLC has changed from how it was in the beginning. There are many more systems in place internally and more financial controls. The type of advice work and casework has not significantly altered from when the centre began as the same areas of legal need still exist as challenges in the local community.

There have, however, been changes in the community profile in that time. Now most clients in employment come from the retail sector, as the garment-making industry has largely moved away from the UK. Local issues concerning immigration relate to recently arrived asylum-seekers. In addition there is a growing community of EEA nationals who have housing and employment queries. Low income tenants can no longer afford to pay rents in most private tenancies as a result of the 'buy to let' market; instead it is more common to advise tenants on their rights in the public sector field, gaps in provision, overcrowding issues and disrepair claims.

The director monitors these changes and developments and uses them to plan for the future of PLC and to attract funding wherever she can to support the centre.

Staff and organisation development
The three supervising case workers are all qualified lawyers. The director has worked for many years as a welfare benefits adviser and then a manager in the voluntary sector. None of the rest of the staff has any formal qualifications in giving legal advice. Two of the case workers have university degrees in non-law subjects. The third has recently attended an NVQ course in advice-giving. One receptionist used to work as a legal secretary before taking a career break to bring up a family. The other has worked in a night shelter as a student before giving up her degree to look after her child.

continued

The director is more than satisfied with the calibre of her staff and ensures that they attend regular external training courses on their practice areas. There is also a good reference library shared with the local Citizens Advice Bureau. The staff of PLC also have access to the Bureau's internal reference sources. The younger receptionist would now like to train as a lawyer and wants to commence or complete a degree in the half of the week she is not working. Otherwise the staff seem happy to remain in place. The organisation will, however, need to change soon as funding sources are likely to be cut for some work and there is a new mental health annexe recently added to the local hospital. The hospital's patient liaison service has frequently requested help from PLC to represent patients at mental health review tribunals and to advise the patients on their rights and human rights neither of which the current staff is able to take on or have any training for.

Future planning
PLC receives a grant from the local council to cover its running costs. It also receives government funding to pay for the welfare benefits and debt advice role. Case workers can claim for the advice they do in part under the Legal Services Commission Legal Help Scheme. This goes in part towards salaries. None of these sources of funding is secure and all are currently under review by the relevant funding body. This, however, has always been the pattern since PLC was set up and the director is constantly looking for new or more permanent sources of funding. She hopes to develop the benefits advice and the outreach work to include work for mental health in the local hospital and in the community and to obtain funding for that new work.

A national advice agency: the Women of Age Centre

History and purpose
The Women of Age Centre (WAC) is a national organisation dedicated to age-related issues for older women. It is run from a small office in Maidchester. It was set up in 2005 in anticipation of the age discrimination laws introduced in 2006. However, it has a wider remit which is to provide advice to individuals and to monitor developments and lead on policy issues which affect older women. Advice is given on employment law, rights to health services, family and domestic breakdown or isolation, rights for older same sex partners and money advice, including pensions and benefits.

In common with many national voluntary organisations, WAC also aims to provide a resource for other advisers and runs regular training courses in these areas of law, with an emphasis on older women's rights. Its policy and publication activities, as set out in more detail below, makes it more than an advice agency. Such activities are, however, common for national agencies with charitable status, as part of their functions are to inform and educate in order to promote the needs of the particular disadvantaged group they are working on behalf of.

Although WAC is a relatively new organisation it was founded by a group of individuals with strong track records in working with women's organisations and women's legal rights organisations.

Constitution
WAC is run by a Board of Trustees approved by the Charity Commission and the central government funding body. The Board meet regularly and examine outcomes, trends and deal with any staffing or management issues. They exert more control over the running of the organisation than a smaller local advice agency management committee is likely to. The director of WAC is required to be available on a weekly basis for a rundown of developments with the Chair of the Board. The Board is responsible for the finances and the accounting procedures and for returns to funders and reports to the Charity Commission.

They also receive annual training on their role as trustees. They are all acting as trustees in a voluntary capacity.

Staff profile and workload
Currently the staff group is relatively small and is enhanced by the work done by volunteer advisers who conduct telephone advice sessions with callers. There is

- a centre director;
- a policy officer;   *continued*

- a publications officer;
- a training administrator; and
- a finance and marketing officer.

The director manages the entire centre's activities, oversees the development of the training, publications and policy work and liaises closely with the Board of Trustees on the day-to-day running of the centre. She also does regular external speaking at various events in order to promote the work of WAC.

The policy officer drafts policy documents and briefings in consultation with a range of linked organisations and also keeps a watching brief on any changes in legislation affecting this group in society. Papers and articles are then produced to support, challenge or campaign for changes in the WAC newsletter or in appropriate national publications.

The publications officer has set up a website, and an on-line advice service for individuals seeking advice. She also produces a monthly e-newsletter which has a circulation among advice agencies and community groups. She hopes to develop a monthly magazine or brief for older women on legal and health issues.

The training administrator runs a rota of volunteers who conduct telephone advice sessions from their offices, using advice forms designed by the centre. Advice forms are then analysed by the director to ensure quality and to consider needs and emerging trends.

The training administrator also sets up around six courses a year on different topics at various venues in the UK using some of the volunteer advisers as trainers.

The finance and marketing officer handles the finance relating to training and publications and supports the training administrator, the policy officer and the publications officer in marketing their activities.

Organisation profile and funding
Although the organisation is relatively new it has done a lot to raise its national profile. The director has appeared on BBC Newsnight in a discussion on the role and rights of older female workers in the workforce and the circulation of the e-newsletter has increased from 1,000 to 3,500.

The subscription for the newsletter brings in income as does the training. The organisation, however, still relies largely on government funding. The advice service has also increased with advisers as well as individuals seeking advice on a range of issues affecting older women, the most popular being pension entitlement and job recruitment concerns.

Staff and organisation development
The staff of WAC all have previous experience in their field, some in the voluntary sector and some in the commercial sector. The

volunteer advisers are already working in other advice-giving organisations and volunteer two hours a week to do the online advice service. The areas the director wants to develop, advice services and publications, will require an input of more staff. Ideally she would like to take on two part-time advisers with two different advice specialists to develop the advice work further and to enable telephone advice to take off. She would also like the publications officer to have some part-time administrative support to develop the briefing project.

Future planning
The Board is anxious that the organisation is not too reliant on central government funding and believes it is unlikely to engender enough income from training and publications to be self-sufficient. It would like the director to consider making funding bids in the private pensions market in an attempt to underpin the advice and information service WAC provides on pensions entitlement.

Legal aid

Since 1949 there has been a government-sponsored and funded system of providing free legal services to low income clients, usually referred to as 'legal aid'. Some features of how it operates will be discussed below. It is available to support certain types of legal claims or procedures on a means-tested basis. The government organisation which administered this system was called the Legal Aid Board for a number of years. It is now called the Legal Services Commission (LSC).

Since the LSC came into being in 1999 there have been considerable changes in the approach to what legal proceedings should be funded and the administration of the system by the practitioner whose clients qualify for that funding. Legal aid is often now referred to as public funding. There is a Community Legal Service which aims to be a national network of information about the availability of legal services in the UK. For more on this see the LSC website.[3]

Equality commissions

Up until October 2007 there were three Commissions which the Government funded and which existed to promote policy, legal change and equality for certain groups in society. They were the Equal Opportunities Commission, dealing with gender issues, the Commission for Race Equality dealing with issues concerning race equality, and the Disability Rights Commission dealing with rights for disabled individuals.

As a result of the passing of the Equality Act 2006, there has been a new Commission formed, the Commission for Equality and Human Rights (CEHR). The new commission, launched in October 2007, continues the work done by the three existing commissions and also incorporates issues in relation to religion and belief, sexual orientation and age. There is now legislation protecting the rights in all of these six areas and the CEHR works to support and underpin those rights. It is able to take on cases for individuals but usually only to challenge a key issue or principle or a public policy point.

ACAS

ACAS stands for the Advisory, Conciliation and Arbitration Service, a Government-funded national organisation which aims, among other things, to promote and develop good industrial relations. ACAS is available to provide a helpful advice service to individuals with employment-related problems. It will also provide formal arbitration in large-scale industrial disputes. ACAS officers are also given powers to conciliate in relation to individual employment disputes in the employment tribunal system and to promote settlements between the parties. There are ACAS offices in all regions of the country. Research is regularly carried out to show trends in various aspects of industrial relations, such as patterns of employment and how and why individuals use the employment tribunal system to resolve employment disputes.[4]

Government departments

A number of government departments provide useful information and support for advisers and individuals on the topic relevant to that department. The Department for Children, Schools and Families provides advice for parents and children and other learners on legal issues.[5] The Department for Business Enterprise and Regulatory Reform (DBERR) – formerly the Department of Trade and Industry (DTI) – gives advice and information and legal guidance to employers

4   www.acas.org.uk.
5   www.dfes.gov.uk.

and employees on various work-related topics.[6] In addition the sites provide information about their functions. Their advice and information is free but generally quite basic and is usually set out in a way that is accessible both to advisers and individuals with queries. The legal advice provides a useful framework of the topic being covered.

Local authorities

The importance of local authorities both as part of the national map of advice agencies, as well as a support provision for voluntary sector advice agencies, is not to be underestimated.

In many advice agencies, battles are being fought on behalf of clients in relation to housing decisions made by a local authority affecting those clients, or in relation to a local authority's employees' rights or their provision of education.

At the same time, a local authority may be providing funding for community groups or advice agencies, and may itself have internal advice services for certain groups, such as tenants or claimants of benefits. This dual function of supporter and adversary is often inevitable where local councils are dealing with large and diverse communities and is not an uncommon model. Many private companies will face challenges to their practices at the same time as using profits to become more 'green' or environmentally-friendly for the benefit of the wider community.

In local authorities there will often be a range of advice services which have arisen out of their statutory functions, such as the provision of housing. Not all local authorities employ advisers and some will instead provide information leaflets or signposting services to local advice agencies. In addition, rural authorities will have different community needs from urban ones. Examples of the type of advice services which might be provided by a local authority are:

- private tenants' rights;
- consumer rights arising out of trading standards enforcement;
- welfare benefits advice;
- advice on community care; and
- education advice or information arising out of education welfare service.

Local authorities' websites are the best way of finding out what advice services they might offer.

6   www.berr.gov.uk.

1.5   How advice work is funded

As already indicated, the voluntary or not-for-profit sector finances its operations by obtaining external funding and not by making profit. If income is generated by an organisation, for example by selling publications or running training courses, it will be used solely to continue the work of that organisation. Advice agencies will not charge for their services but will rely on a variety of sources of funding to maintain their service provision. An organisation which has recognised charitable status (validated by the Charity Commission) is required to ensure that any 'profit' is used to further the work or purposes of the charity concerned.

Although there are a variety of sources of funding for advice agencies in the voluntary sector, there are perhaps three or four key types of funding. These are:

- grants or subsidies from central government including funds which can be bid for for a particular purpose.[7] This source of funding will include National Lottery funding;
- local authority grants or partnerships;
- legal aid (or public funding); and
- small or individual project funding, usually from a central source.

Of these, the first two have already been referred to above and what follows is a brief overview of how the legal aid and project funding works.

Legal aid funding by the Legal Services Commission

In relation to Legal Services Commission (LSC) supported public funding of legal advice or a legal claim, the following aspects of this system should be noted:

- it is only LSC 'approved suppliers' who will be able to offer their clients with legal problems access to public funding to help with legal cases. These suppliers are likely, in the future, to be in the form of an approved local network or syndicate as outlined in the Government's Carter Review of legal services. They may be

---

7   An example being the Neighbourhood Regeneration Fund provided for out of the Office of the Deputy Prime Minister (now called Communities and Local Government) to fund projects aimed at regenerating inner city areas where for example there may be particular problems in relation to housing or the physical environment.

qualified lawyers or other models of advisers or advice-giving organisations;

- approved suppliers – currently, private solicitors or not-for-profit advice agencies approved to do publicly-funded work have the authority to means-test and advise low-income clients for a set number of advice hours or cases. This approach to carrying out publicly-funded legal advice and representation is under consideration by the LSC at the time of writing (September 2007);

- public funding does not apply to all types of legal advice and court proceedings. The most notable exceptions relate to advice on matters which are not the subject of court proceedings, such as drawing up wills or conducting residential house conveyancing. In addition, some court claims do not attract public funding; personal injury claims being one example. What is or is not covered by public funding will need to be known by an adviser joining an organisation where this source of funding is still in place;

- public funding is means-tested and the process for assessing who is eligible will need to be understood by an adviser working where public funding operates;

- public funding is usually in the form of a loan not a benefit. Where a court case is won and the client has been receiving public funding, they will usually be required to repay to the LSC some or all of their legal costs if they recover money. There are rules about how this operates and some exceptions to this requirement which advisers need to be aware of.

Project funding

It is quite common for an advice or community organisation as a result of working towards a better service to obtain funding to run a particular project. This funding will often be provided by government. In the outlines above of the local and national advice agencies there was reference under the description of their development and futures to additional projects, such as welfare benefits advice for mental health service users or better funded pensions advice for older women.

Where funding is obtained for projects such as this it is likely to be short term and will often need to be attached to a post holder in the voluntary organisation who will see that project through. This does, however, often mean instability in the organisation. It will be hard to decide if a new post should be made permanent or fixed term. Expectations created in the community served by the creation and development of the project will have been raised as a result of the activity and it may not be possible to replace that funding once it runs out or to continue with that area of work.

Nevertheless, advice agencies will continue to explore every avenue, often in the context of very precarious funding arrangements, to ensure that they survive and continue to meet the needs of the communities they exist to serve.

CHAPTER 2

Getting started: studying, qualifying and working as an adviser

2.1   Studying advice skills

Some readers of this book will be using it as a background to studying advice skills; others may already be practitioners. This chapter is
aimed both at those who may want to train and work as advisers and
at those who are interested in developing advice qualifications. It will
also provide a profile of the advice sector and who is working there,
which has been drawn from recent research carried out by the NOS4
project commissioned to establish the possible need for and design
of a foundation degree for the legal advice sector.[1] This was the most
far-reaching review of the profile of the legal advice sector carried out
in recent times.

Need to qualify as an adviser?

Many people think of qualifying to give legal advice in the context
of training to be a legal executive, paralegal or qualified lawyer. In
all these areas of study there is an element of practical training to fit
practitioners for the role of advisers in practice. Others who do not
wish to qualify or perhaps are not ready to do so immediately may not
necessarily see themselves as requiring any form of qualification as
an adviser in order to practice in this field. Certainly, as we saw in our
outline of the community law clinic in chapter 1, it is still possible to
become a case worker in legal advice fields without necessarily having
a legal or advice qualification.

There is no one qualification to qualify as an adviser or legal
adviser which is recognised above any other. There are a range of different courses or qualifications at different levels. In addition, not all
employers specify advice work qualifications as an essential requirement of an adviser post holder; many will be satisfied with background voluntary or other relevant or similar practical experience.

There is, however, a growing number of courses and specifically
degree-level courses aimed at giving qualifications in advice-giving
skills. Some of these are foundation degrees, usually two-year courses,
which will also count towards an honours degree in law if that is what
the student would like to do. There are, in addition, some higher education institutions where it is possible to obtain an honours degree in
advice linked qualifications.[2] Other courses will be at a different level

1   Published in July 2006. See www.NOS4Advice.org.uk.
2   See for example the LLB in Advice Studies at Staffordshire University: contact
    details in appendix B.

in the Higher Education qualification framework, such as National Vocational Qualifications (NVQs).

When foundation degrees were introduced in 2002, they were designed to encourage a broad range of practical, work-based subjects to be studied at degree level. They were also aimed at students outside the traditional concept of a higher education student (although many of these do take foundation degree courses) who might want to study flexibly or while at work. They have recently begun to be developed by some higher education providers in advice or legal advice.[3] Although it is perhaps too soon to judge, this may lead to advice qualifications becoming more recognised and to a more skilled workforce going into and developing within the advice sector.

Routes to study

There is a range of short courses which can be taken up to learn more about advice skills. Not all are mentioned here but this will give a flavour of the different types of course available.

Some providers of training courses will run short, one-day courses which do not lead to any qualification but are aimed as introductory courses or updates on an aspect of the law. The course content may include guidance on exercising advice skills but it will usually cover an advice topic, such as an aspect of housing law, with the skills of advising in that topic being a part of the content of the course rather than the focus of it.

Others courses might be short courses leading to qualifications by way of an NVQ. For example, AdviceUK,[4] a national organisation based in London, provides courses for those advising in the voluntary sector. Their NVQ level 3 courses in 'Learning to Advise' runs over thirteen days and is taken up by many practitioners.

A volunteer at a Citizens Advice Bureau will be trained by attending the volunteer training course which has status as an Open College Network qualification. It is possible for credits obtained from attending the volunteer training programme to be used towards the National Open College Network Intermediate Award in Developing Information Advice and Guidance Skills.

---

3 See for example Peterborough Regional College's Foundation Degree in Paralegal Studies and London Metropolitan University's Foundation Degree in Legal Advice (from September 2007). See further, appendix B.

4 www.adviceuk.org.uk. See appendix B.

The National Occupational Standards

The development of the National Occupational Standards (NOS) in legal advice came about in 2006. They are recognised as part of the national framework of occupational standards. Nationally-recognised occupational standards mean that employers and educational institutions can work together to ensure that more areas of work and employment are recognised by reference to skills and learning needed to work within that sector, and standards can be set down and followed by employers and educational institutions within the relevant skills sector.

The NOS in Legal Advice are to be found in full on the Skills for Justice section of the Skills Sector Council which has also developed a detailed Toolkit for the legal advice sector on its website.[5] This means that they join a growing group of occupational standards approved by all levels of the education sector. Advice skills in the advice and legal advice sector have now been categorised and given formal recognition. Some of the Standards are reproduced in appendix C in order to give a flavour of some of the advice skills they prescribe.

Organisations and educational institutions will now refer to the NOS in legal advice in designing and delivering courses on advice topics and skills. This development will hopefully begin to address the current lack of a clear route to qualifying as an adviser on the basis that both employers and educational and training institutions will begin to use these standards as the approved benchmark against which advice skills will be taught and practised.

Learners and students will find that NOS in Legal Advice will now underpin many courses and qualifications, just as they have formed the backbone of much of the approach of this book.

2.2   Qualifying as a lawyer

For many, the experience of working in an advice setting, perhaps as a volunteer or a case worker whets their appetite and they plan ultimately to qualify as a lawyer. Others see working in that way as a route towards that ultimate goal. Many individuals who qualify as lawyers choose thereafter to work in the voluntary sector as advisers and case workers due to a commitment to the interests of the cli-

---

5   www.skillsforjustice.com/las.

ent group using free advice agencies and/or their own interest in or commitment to the areas of law traditionally practised in that setting. In any event a brief overview is given here of the routes to qualification as a solicitor or barrister.

Solicitor or barrister?

The decision to be made is whether to qualify as a solicitor or barrister. Each is a qualified lawyer. It would not be possible here to do justice to the functions of each branch of the legal profession. The main difference is that barristers' functions are largely in the arena of conducting court cases, and providing expert legal advice and opinions, with solicitors preparing for court claims with the client or assisting them in all the legal areas which do not involve court cases, such as the execution of wills or the buying or selling of property. Solicitors can now qualify to have rights of audience in the higher courts. More can be learnt about the functions of each branch of the profession from their professional bodies.[6]

Each route towards qualification involves a relatively lengthy and expensive process. Solicitors' training and qualification requirements are prescribed by the Education and Training Section of the Solicitor's Regulation Authority (SRA). Barristers' routes to qualification are set down by the Bar Council.

Educational qualifications: solicitor

Before embarking on any process of qualification as a solicitor, enquiries should be made as to what type of educational qualification will be needed. It is not necessary to have a law degree, as non-law degree students can take a postgraduate conversion course: the Common Professional Examination (CPE) or the Graduate Diploma in Law. However, since the pattern of degrees is now much more varied than it was, care should be taken to ensure that the type of degree held is at the right level. In addition, if someone does not have a university degree or, for example, has educational qualifications which include a study of law, they may be able to count these. If, for example, they are a qualified paralegal or legal executive they should enquire of their respective professional bodies or the SRA as to how these may count towards qualifying.

6   www.lawsociety.org.uk; www.barcouncil.org.uk.

Educational qualifications; barrister

The Bar Council, which is the body regulating barristers' training and practice, requires entrants to its profession to have either a law degree at a minimum level of a lower second or a university degree in a different subject together with the postgraduate conversion course, the Common Professional Examination.

Vocational or training stage

Once the degree or postgraduate conversion course has been completed the student will then need to do a postgraduate practice course either to train as a solicitor (the Legal Practice Course (LPC)) or as a barrister (the Bar Vocational Course (BVC)).

Following that, a period of training in practice needs to be undertaken. For solicitors it will mean obtaining a training contract by working at a firm of solicitors (or a local authority or Law Centre® with a solicitor supervisor qualified to take on a trainee) for two years. The two years can be completed on a part-time basis and in certain circumstances relevant legal experience gained elsewhere can be counted towards that two-year period.

A trainee barrister, before they commence their Bar Vocational Course, will need to be taken on by one of the four Inns of Court. These Inns are in essence societies of which a practising barrister is required to be a member. The trainee will be taken on by one of the Inns (Gray's Inn, Temple, Lincoln's Inn and Middle Temple) before they are 'called' to the Bar as qualified. While they are studying for the Bar Vocational Course, they will need to attend their Inn for twelve qualifying sessions. These sessions used to be called 'dining' as the trainee would be required to eat a dinner in their Inn on twelve separate occasions.

Once the barrister has completed their Bar Vocational Course they will seek to become a pupil in a barrister's chambers (or another authorised training environment such as a Government department) where they will be required to be trained for twelve months. The training periods for both solicitors and barristers are paid but at relatively low levels. The SRA fixes an annual minimum salary for trainee solicitors.

The SRA, at the time of writing is reviewing its training process to see if it can be more flexible in how people may be able to qualify. The Bar Council has also indicated that it would like to examine ways of offering a more flexible route to qualifying. There are, for example, a growing number of individuals in work, perhaps as advisers or para-legals, who are working part time towards qualifying as a solicitor or barrister. This can take a number of years and may mean taking out loans or suffering many rejections to be considered as a trainee or a pupil before they are successful. Qualifying in this way should not be embarked on without careful thought. It is, however, partly with this model of student in mind that thought is now being given to more flexible approaches to qualifying.

2.3 Applying for work: routes into advice work

As previously indicated, not all employers in the advice sector will look for paper qualifications. Some will, while others may look for previous experience. They may look for experience as a volunteer in the advice sector or work experience in a similar field, such as social or community care. They may look for work experience in a local authority as an adviser or administrator in that subject field.

Where qualifications are needed, they may be linked to the requirements of funders of the organisation. For example, where free advice is offered under the LSC scheme of public funding in an organisation, case worker supervisors will need to demonstrate a level of skills and experience which is of the standard of that required for practising lawyers. For that reason qualified lawyers are usually sought to fill those posts.

Because of the lack of a clear pattern of qualification as an adviser, getting paid employment in the field may be a frustrating experience for some. There are many individuals who are not qualified lawyers and who do not wish to qualify but who wish to work in the advice sector. The best advice that can be offered is to build up a portfolio of the following experience.

Volunteering

Volunteering is now a very useful way of building up relevant experience to work in the advice sector, as well as a way of testing out your commitment to this type of work. If you are accepted to volunteer in a Citizens Advice Bureau you will be offered their Open College Network training course which will immediately give you skills and competencies as an adviser and help you towards any further routes towards qualification. Otherwise apply as a volunteer to any local or community organisation. This might include charity shops, community cafes or drop-in centres, church or other religious community activities, or any national organisation which has a shop or community centre or information centre in your area. Even if you begin doing work which is not advice-based, you will begin to experience working with and for individuals using community services. You may then progress to more face-to-face work. Volunteering is unpaid but expenses are often paid.

Legal advice organisations may have 'tiers' of volunteers. They may take on those with legal qualifications or experience to run advice sessions, as well as those who can assist with basic administrative duties, such as filing or leaflet updates and who will not need to have legal advice qualifications or experience. The second category will nevertheless have the opportunity to be a part of the work done by the organisation by assisting and observing.

Studying

Given the increasing number of courses now available which have advice skills as part of their content it is worth looking around to see if these will be helpful. Many degree or more advanced courses can be taken part time and over a longer period of time.

An individual who is volunteering and also studying may have a better prospect of getting paid employment for some of their week or once they have completed their course of study.

It is not possible to predict the type of qualification which an employer will prefer but someone who does not have 'traditional school leaving' qualifications (such as A Levels) can for example be given the opportunity to take a foundation degree which is now becoming more recognised and well known by employers. In deciding on the most appropriate course of study to take, it may well be worth scanning the job adverts pages over a period of time to see what qualifications employers look for when advertising for jobs in the advice field. Some may will specify an NVQ level of qualification, some may specify degree or above.

Similar work experience

Many people move around in the advice field from one organisation to another similar one. They build up experience in that field and work in different parts of it, perhaps moving from a local to a national organisation or from advice to policy work. This is partly because, as we will see in the next section, there is a fairly limited career structure in the advice field with most people earning and working at similar levels in most organisations. It is also because many people like that working environment and choose to stay in it.

There is also similar work experience which will be of assistance in developing a career in the advice field. Some advisers have worked in similar settings in local authorities, others in central government departments such as the Crown Prosecution Service or as court clerks or administrators. Others may have worked as lawyers or paralegals for solicitors, or may have experience in their field but in the commercial or private sector. Many jobs in finance such as insurance or building societies have information and advice aspects to them. The advice sector will always seek to ensure that job applicants can show a commitment to the type of client they serve, that they are aware of equal opportunities and of the work done within the advice sector generally to promote justice for all. Any relevant experience to show that commitment will be of benefit.

2.4   The nature of the job

As referred to in the opening paragraph of this chapter, recent research has provided a very useful profile of what it is like to work in the advice field. Profiles of who works, their career paths, aspirations and reasons for staying and leaving all appear as part of the NOS4 Project 'Foundation Degree Framework for the Legal Advice Sector'.

A number of national and some local advice organisations took part in the consultation process which led to the framework being published, and included in this was a useful outline of the profile of the advice sector nationally in the year 2006. Some of these features are summarised overleaf and may be of value for those in the advice sector as a pattern of their working lives as well as for those who might wish to become advisers.

The findings from this research helped its authors to recommend the idea of moving towards a more established pattern of training and qualification for those in the legal advice field. This may or may not happen in the near future and in the meantime the approaches to training and working in the voluntary advice sector can only be suggested in general terms and in line with the current somewhat uncoordinated framework of training and qualification in this field.

NOS4 Project: a profile of the advice sector in 2006: summary

Advice Agencies
There are 8,700 organisations in the UK that give legal advice. These
are made up of solicitors firms, not-for-profit organisations and teams
of employees in local authorities. Most advice-giving organisations
are quite small, 75 per cent employ 15 or less.

Demand
Demand for advice is growing as catalogued by the agencies who
took part in this research. This means that organisations are taking
on more staff where they can. At the same time it is not always easy
to fill vacancies and advisers do not always remain in post for long.
Recruitment is a challenge due to a lack of qualifications, skills and
experience on the part of applicants.

Type of work done
In the voluntary sector the type of advice work breaks down into
welfare benefits, debt, housing and employment. Less than half of
the not-for-profit organisations offered representation in courts or
tribunals as well as advice.

Profile of the workforce
The workforce is predominantly female. In the not-for-profit sector,
this translates into 71 per cent. In addition there are more older than
younger workers employed, with 40 per cent in the not-for-profit
sector over the age of 45. In addition 87 per cent are white with
different ethnic groups featuring as employees in specific regions of
the country. Three per cent of the work force are black, the majority of
whom are employed in London.

Educational background of employees
Fewer than 10 per cent have no formal qualifications. In the not-for-
profit sector 10 per cent of employees have law A Level. The majority
in the not-for-profit sector do not hold a qualification in legal advice
work.

Volunteers
Most volunteers are in Citizens Advice Bureaux. Generally in the not-
for-profit sector there are between one and ten volunteers working in
40 per cent of organisations.

These findings show that more diversity of age groups and more
men would make the advice sector a more balanced workforce and
that difficulties with recruitment and retention may be helped by a
more consistent approach to entry and qualification as an adviser.
It should be added that the way in which advice work is funded in

the voluntary sector means that salaries are not as high as in many other areas of public sector work and that career progression can be limited.

Other features of the job

There are features of the job of working in an advice agency that are common to many. Some of these have been hinted at in the outline of the model of a community law clinic in the previous chapter. Given the commitment that such an organisation will have to empowering a sector of society often disadvantaged in some way, the ethos of the advice field is one of inclusiveness.

Staff are usually valued highly within the organisation and efforts are made in recruiting staff and volunteers to ensure that the workforce is as diverse as possible. Many community organisations which serve clients predominantly from one ethnic group will aim to have staff or advisers who speak the language of that group or whose ethnicity is the same as that ethnic group.

Staff may work longer hours for less pay than in other sectors but are likely to have relatively generous terms and conditions of service relating to holidays, family-friendly leave or flexible working. Pay structures are usually fairly rigid with little capacity for progression up a given pay scale or opportunity to benefit from regular pay rises. Pay will always be a part of the equation in ensuring that the funding provided is sufficient to meet all the needs of the organisation.

It can often be the case that an adviser, within any limits laid down by good practice or funding restrictions, will have relative freedom to organise and shape the work that they do to the time and resources they have available to do it. Mention will be made of this in chapter 6 when looking at external influences which might be brought to bear on the adviser/client relationship.

Although advice organisations need to be professional in relation to the important service they provide to clients, many are, within that framework, relatively relaxed about dress codes or working structures. Many encourage teamwork and an open exchange of information to ensure that the best advice is given and that the best service is offered. Many will be flexible about staff's child-care needs where staff may need to bring children in to work on an occasional basis if there is no home support at that time. A positive and supportive working environment will usually reflect back on to the clients who are not therefore intimidated or discouraged from coming to the advice agency for help or assistance.

The adviser and the client

CHAPTER 3

You and your client: the relationship explained

3.1   The definition of a client

There are many relationships in our workplaces which we engage in. We work side by side with, and talk to, people doing the same job as we do; we encounter people in other related jobs at meetings or social functions. We also meet a range of people who come into the workplace to deliver goods, or provide support services. In the work context we are always receiving information from other individuals and also giving or taking advice from them, formally or informally, about our work and related aspects of our work. The passing around of such advice or information does not, however, make us clients of our work colleagues nor do they become our clients. Information and advice is also passed between an adviser and a client and so it is important to know the difference between that relationship and any other, and what the key features of that relationship are.

Key feature of a client: seeks advice and assistance using specialist resources

The word 'client' is now used much more widely than, say, twenty years ago. It used to be the case that only professional advisers such as lawyers, architects or accountants, had clients, while other organisations might have callers or customers. Nowadays it is quite common for anyone who provides a service for another individual or group of individuals to describe that group as 'clients'. Examples vary from businesses contracted to market a product for someone else to hairdressers seeing a high turnover of individuals each day and providing a service for them as their clients. This can sometimes be confusing for those new to legal advice as they may come into it with a range of perceptions as to what makes someone your client.

In the advice or legal advice field the word client has a specific meaning. A potential client will usually approach an organisation because it describes itself as offering advice or information in respect of a particular field of knowledge, which will assist the client in effecting change or resolving a problem they have in that area. The client will not have the key information or specialist knowledge necessary to effect that change themselves.

The individual seeking to become a client will require an adviser to take from them part of the burden of the unresolved problem. They will place their trust in the adviser, in that they will expect the adviser to meet their expectations as an expert or someone with acquired knowledge which will be used to resolve the client's problem. They will also place their trust in the adviser, expecting the adviser to act as their champion, achieving the desired outcome for the client, using their skills and knowledge in the process. They will expect the adviser to be non-judgmental and impartial in relation to what the client tells them. They will also form the assumption that the trust they place in the adviser will include a commitment by their adviser not to tell others what passes between the client and the adviser. To summarise, the new client is likely to come to you:

- assuming you have skills and knowledge to resolve their problem;
- trusting you as an expert in your field;
- trusting you to act as their champion;
- relying on you to be non-judgmental and impartial about what they tell you; and
- expecting you to keep their affairs confidential.

The adviser/client relationship is of course a two-way relationship and we will see in section 3.4 what the adviser will bring to the relationship.

3.2　Enquiries, matters, problems and cases

Before looking at each of the models of the adviser/client relationship in more detail, it may be helpful to clarify some different terms used to describe what it is the individual is bringing to an organisation when seeking their help. The terms 'adviser' and 'client' will arise in a number of different approaches to assisting a person who contacts an agency or help desk for assistance.

Enquiries

Many organisations where advice is given will also be able to assist those who contact them with enquiries. The nature of the enquiry may be to find out what help or assistance might be available for them in that organisation or elsewhere. It may simply to specify the type of problem that they have. It may be to give them information and guidance as to what their options are for taking a particular enquiry further. For example, an individual may come to an organisation and say that they have left their violent partner. They may be given information about their rights to seek help, the range of services they can obtain support from in that situation, such as the police, a refuge or

a lawyer. They may be referred to a solicitor for advice. Some organisations may refer to those enquirers as clients and will keep records
of enquiries. Other will refer to them as enquiries and may simply
record some aspects of the service they offered, such as where they
refer them on to.

Matters

The type of enquiry the client has will often be referred to as a matter.
This gives it a context – such as the client's 'housing matter' or 'welfare benefits matter'. This way of describing subject matter of clients'
cases has been used by solicitors firms for many years and it does
seem to be a useful way of 'pigeon-holing' different types of cases.

Problems

Within that framework the client will be seeking to resolve their situation. Within the context of their housing matter they need your help
because they are perhaps homeless. The concern they have in the
context of their welfare benefits matter may be that they have been
refused a benefit.

Moving on, the *fact* of their homelessness or lack of the benefit
will be referred to as a 'problem'. The word 'problem' in the context
of advice-giving may sometimes be replaced by other words such as
'issue' on the basis that calling something a problem perhaps denotes
fault on the part of the person with the problem. However, the word
'issue' may not always carry with it the seriousness of some unresolved problem which the client is carrying the burden of and is looking for expert help to resolve, and so the word problem will be used
for preference.

Cases

Once the problem has been formulated and it has been agreed that
the burden of it will be shared by the adviser, it will be referred to
by the adviser as a 'case'. As we shall see later, sometimes what the
client wants others to accept (that they are innocent of a crime or have
lost luggage through no fault of their own) will be referred to as the
client's 'case'. The adviser will be dealing with that as part of advising
their client as well as referring to the client's case as being the totality
of the client's problem and its need for a resolution. Where advisers

have a number of clients they are advising and assisting they will refer
to that as their 'caseload'. The adviser may offer advice only, in order
to enable the client to resolve their case themselves, or the adviser
may take certain limited steps to resolve a client's case, depending
on the nature of the service they are offering. Alternatively they may
'take on' a client's case. There are various models of an adviser/client
relationship in the advice sector as we shall see in the next section.

3.3 Models of the adviser/client relationship

It is important for both the adviser and the client to reach a clear
understanding of the point at which an individual actually *becomes*
a client. Under each of the models described below, organisations
may refer to those that they assist as a 'client'. There are distinctions,
however, between advisers who provide specialist information, those
who give information and advice relevant to the facts of the client's
case and those who take from the client the burden of conducting
their case, and who may also act as an advocate for their client with a
third party.

Different types of advice agencies will adopt a different approach
in the advice service they offer. In all models however, the adviser/cli-
ent relationship will have the hallmarks of offering expert advice in
a confidential setting. Examples of the various approaches to advice-
giving are outlined below.

Giving information or signposting

Some individuals may come to an organisation with all the expectations outlined above as to what they would like an organisation to
achieve for them, but may not be ready to become that organisation's
client. They may come to seek more information about what an organisation can offer them as a client. It may be explained to them that
this is not the organisation best suited to their needs and they will
then be given some 'signposting' information and directed to another organisation. They may be given leaflets or telephone numbers
to obtain more information about a particular matter. Alternatively
the organisation may be specifically set up to provide a signposting
service, giving its users (whom they may refer to as clients) specialist
knowledge or information designed to help move their query or problem along. This type of service is unlikely to lead to an adviser/client

relationship being formed although it is now an integral part of the map of advice-giving.

At this stage of offering help it will be important to deal with the individual's expectations. The caller or potential client will need to understand that at this stage the organisation is not providing them with legal or other advice designed to resolve their problem but with more information to enable them to make choices about how they take their problem forward. Many organisations have information leaflets which make this clear and information provided will in part be designed to help the client to decide if they need expert help and assistance and to explain how the organisation's advice-giving service operates. For more on signposting see chapter 14.

Giving advice but not taking on a case for the client: first tier advice

In the advice sector, advisers may work on more than one level in terms of the advice service they offer. One approach is to offer what is sometimes referred to as 'first tier' advice to callers or people who come to drop-in sessions or via e-mail advice services. An individual may tell the adviser in some detail what their problem is and in return will obtain advice on their specific problem.

The main adviser/client elements in that context will be that the adviser is fulfilling the client's expectations that the advice given will be accurate and relevant to the problem being outlined by the client. In addition the individual being advised will be entitled to rely on the accuracy of the advice given, subject to what the adviser has been told by the client. The individual will be given information about what active steps an adviser can take to resolve a client's problem, if any. These steps are usually limited to giving advice and recording that advice in a letter to the client. In the letter to the client the adviser will also outline to the client what steps that client can take to resolve their problem thereafter. They may also offer to write a letter to someone else on the client's behalf.

Taking on a case: advice and representation

Where the adviser agrees to take steps on behalf of a client and to share the burden of the client's problem, they will usually refer to this as 'taking on the client's case'. This includes giving advice in the way outlined in the previous paragraph, but there is the additional aspect of sharing the burden of the client's case and pursuing all necessary steps to resolve it on behalf of the client. This may extend to offering to represent a client in a court or tribunal in which case it could also be referred to as 'advice and representation'. Where representation is not part of the service offered, other substantial steps will be taken to resolve the client's case. A file will be opened, letters written and telephone calls made on the client's behalf and other steps taken, perhaps involving attending meetings or negotiating with the client's opponent or other individuals involved in the client's case. There is, however, no clear pattern; organisations may offer 'first tier advice' only or offer advice and representation only. Alternatively they may provide both models of advice-giving service.

A common route into an adviser taking on a case will be where an individual speaks to a receptionist on the phone and indicates specifically that they are seeking advice or assistance on a matter from a specialist adviser. The receptionist will then refer them for an appointment to an adviser. In the context of that first interview with the adviser they will become the adviser's client.

Alternatively many advisers make their own appointments to see someone whom they are willing or able to take on as a client, often arising out of a telephone call or a drop-in advice session.

Apart from the process of advising by telephone, where usually the advice is 'one-off', the client will be seen by their adviser face to face and certain information will be provided to them which outlines the basis of the adviser/client relationship.

The formation of that relationship should always be recorded in writing, with details provided as to how the two parties have agreed that the relationship will be conducted. A letter should record the creation of the adviser/client relationship, what its terms are and how it will be conducted by both parties. This is usually referred to as a 'client care letter' and an example of such a letter is on page 43.

Specialist advice and support: second tier advice

A 'second tier' service is normally advice and support offered by specialist organisations to those already giving advice. For example an advice agency may be giving housing advice but can turn to a more specialist service for further advice, support and information in relation to the advice they are giving to their clients.

3.4 Key elements of the adviser/client relationship

Introduction: in the nature of a contract

We have seen above the list of expectations which a client will bring to the adviser/client relationship. The client will bring these to their adviser no matter how seemingly inarticulate or distressed they are.

The adviser will ensure that there are key elements present in the adviser/client relationship, in order to meet the client's expectations and to ensure that the relationship is valid and professional. In addition, the adviser will be aware that it is a two-way process, and that once the adviser and the client are in agreement that the adviser will offer assistance, they will have entered into a contract in which there are obligations on both sides. Even if the client is not paying money to their adviser for the service they provide, the arrangement will still be in the nature of a contract with expectations as to how that contract will be performed by each party.

The overriding approach of the adviser to the adviser/client relationship, as we have seen, is to offer to share with the client the burden of their problem by offering to take an active part in attempting to reach a resolution of the client's case. The adviser will have the ability to give the problem a name, a legal context, where appropriate, to analyse it, and plan with the client how to resolve it. The adviser cannot take ownership of the problem away from the client, although many clients will want their adviser to just 'take over and sort it all out'. It is crucial that the burden is shared, with the adviser shouldering the responsibility of analysis, advice and taking steps towards resolution. The client will need to understand the analysis, act on the advice and take an active part in the resolution.

Adviser's primary functions

The adviser will ensure that the following elements are always present in the adviser/client relationship.

Taking instructions

The client will tell the adviser all they ask about the nature of their problem. This is known as instructing the adviser. However, the client will also ask the adviser to take certain steps on their behalf (such as writing a letter to the Benefit Agency). This is also known as giving instructions. The adviser will then be following the client's instructions.

Advising the client

Once the adviser is satisfied that they have understood the client's problem they will offer them advice. This can take a number of forms:

- analysing the problem;
- explaining what the law is;
- advising on the most effective way of resolving the problem – either using the law or taking a mixture of legal and practical steps;
- suggesting action which the client him or herself can take to resolve the problem; or
- suggesting action which the adviser is prepared to take on behalf of the client to resolve the problem.

Taking steps to resolve the problem on the client's behalf

Following on from the advice given, the adviser will be authorised to take certain steps on the client's behalf. This may include writing letters, speaking to agencies, landlords, employers, or solicitors representing others. Many outside agencies will expect an adviser to produce written authorisation from the client to speak and act on their behalf to that agency. In the context of conducting court proceedings a solicitor will refer to themselves as 'going on the record'. In other words they are making a statement to the court that they are the authorised representative of that client for the purpose of the conduct of that case.

Acting in the client's best interests

This has a number of different elements to it. The most obvious one is that the adviser will always seek to resolve the client's problem in a way that is most helpful to the client. For example, if the client says that they do not want a local authority landlord to offer accommodation to them which is near their violent ex-partner, an offer of housing in that vicinity is unlikely to be in the client's best interests. The adviser will try to ensure that the client's best interests are served in negotiating an offer of suitable housing for them.

Being impartial

As well as being non-judgmental it is important for the adviser to ensure that they have no interest themselves in the client's case. For this reason it would not be usual for advisers to take on cases for their close family or friends as they may find it hard to keep a professional distance from the case.

Keeping the client's matters confidential

This is an important element of the adviser's commitment to their client and should be properly complied with. The client is entitled to feel that everything that passes between them and their adviser should not be repeated. Advisers may need to discuss their client's cases with others in their organisation from time to time, in order to share knowledge and experience of how to conduct cases. These conversations should be conducted in private, and clients' names, or the facts of their cases, should not be discussed in front of other employees in the organisation.

Having trust and confidence in the client

The adviser will make it clear that they are entitled to assume that the client is:

- telling the truth,
- is not deliberately withholding information which the adviser needs to know in order to progress the client's case, and
- is prepared to put their trust in the adviser's professional skills as an adviser.

At the same time the client should be able to assume that their adviser will treat their client with respect, will offer the services in the way and at the times set out in their correspondence to the client and will act responsibly and professionally on the matters which the client has entrusted to them.

All these aspects of the adviser/client relationship will be explored in more detail in later chapters.

Sample client care letter

The adviser who has entered into an adviser/client relationship in which they will advise and/or take certain steps on a client's behalf will confirm that agreement by writing a client care letter after the first interview, which records the key elements of that relationship and any initial steps to be taken by each party as agreed. An example of a client care letter is set out opposite.

East Lynne Advice Centre, 6 Yard Lane, Milestown M2 1ER
Tel 020 7661 1086

Ms A Client
2 Mile End Street
Milestown M1 2ER

30 August

Dear Ms Client

Re: Your Case – Lost Luggage on Holiday
Thank you for coming to see me on 28 August. You came to see me because your holiday insurer was refusing to pay you for the value of luggage which was removed by a person or persons unknown in a hotel lobby when you were checking into that hotel at the start of a week's holiday in Majorca.

Your instructions
You told me that you went on holiday on 1 August for a week with your two children to a hotel in Majorca; you were taken to the hotel by taxi. The taxi driver unloaded your entire luggage and carried it into your hotel, The Viramar. There was a long queue at reception and while you were waiting you were distracted when you leant down to talk to your five-year-old daughter. When you next looked part of your luggage was missing. You are quite sure it was all brought in by the taxi driver. You complained to reception and the manager of the hotel and they were very apologetic and said that it had happened before and that you would need to claim against your insurance.

You contacted your insurance company when you got home but they said that the hotel was liable and would have to meet your claims.

My advice
I advised you that you would need to carefully check the details of your holiday insurance to ensure that lost or stolen luggage was covered. On the basis that it is, which is your recollection, then I advised that a letter should be written to the insurance company to establish the details of your claim and to exercise your rights to have the claim met. If alternative approaches are not successful in recovering the value of your lost luggage you will have the option of pursuing a claim against the insurance company in the local county court as a 'small claim'. Prior to that you would like me to write a letter to the insurance company on your behalf formally putting the claim to them and exploring any options to recover the value of the lost items. I will write this letter on your behalf once I have seen your insurance documents.

continued

Next steps
You agreed to bring in a copy of the insurance policy for me to check over. Once I have done so I will either write to the insurance company as outlined in the previous paragraph or I will write a further letter of advice to you concerning their liability to meet your claim.

My role as your adviser
Please note that I am employed by the East Lynne Advice Centre and my work is supervised by John Carter who is the manager of that centre. I will be available to advise you at times agreed between us. Please note, however, that the Centre's usual opening hours are Monday to Friday from 10 am – 4 pm. You can usually contact me by telephone or via e-mail.

I will endeavour at all times to conduct your case according to your instructions and in the manner agreed between us. I will expect you to give me all information which I request from you as being relevant to the conduct of your case. I will also expect you to give me all relevant documentation. I will not keep your original documents but will copy and return them to you.

If you have any complaints about the way in which the advice centre or I as your adviser are looking after your insurance claim problem then please would you address these to John Carter at the address above.

Yours sincerely

Abbie Gayle
Adviser

Direct line: 020 7661 1088
E-mail : agayle@elac.org.uk

3.5   Ending the adviser/client relationship

Although this book focuses on the skills inherent in building up and developing a successful adviser/client relationship, it may be helpful at the outset to be aware of the traditional routes which lead to the termination of that relationship. The usual situations leading to a termination of the adviser/client relationship are where:

- the adviser has resolved the problem and the client agrees that no further action need be taken;
- the adviser loses contact with the client and cannot take their instructions any more;

- the client decides to stop instructing the adviser or changes to another adviser;
- the adviser is no longer able to continue to advise or advocate for the client due to a breakdown in the adviser/client relationship.

In all except the first of these examples the relationship will be terminated prior to the adviser resolving the case. The various ways in which cases are resolved will be examined in part 4 on case progression and resolution.

Losing contact with the client

Where matters end without a resolution, the adviser must initially satisfy themselves that this is what has happened and then go on to ensure that the termination and the reasons for it are clearly recorded in writing. Reminders should be written prior to termination, and checks should be made of the client's contact details to ensure that they are accurately recorded. The termination letter (see page 47) will confirm the lack of contact. It is also to protect the adviser in the unlikely event of the client complaining that the adviser has sought to terminate the relationship inappropriately or has acted improperly in the way they have advised or assisted their client.

Change of adviser

If there is a change to another adviser, the new adviser should contact the existing adviser with the client's authority to request the release of any copy papers or information which the existing adviser may have collected to date in relation to the matter which they are dealing with for that client. Obtaining the client's authority will involve the client signing a form in which they are requesting their existing adviser to hand their papers over to the new adviser. There may also be additional matters to be clarified between the client and the adviser or the two advisers in respect of the funding arrangements of that client's case. Referrals to another adviser are also discussed in chapter 14 at section 14.4.

Breakdown in adviser/client relationship

If a client states that they are unhappy with their adviser every effort should be made to explore the problem and resolve it. If necessary the adviser's complaints procedures should be used to assist. If the client nevertheless indicates that they no longer wish to use the adviser's services then this should be recorded in writing, together with a reference to any complaints procedure followed to try to resolve the problem.

Alternatively the adviser may have reached a point where they do not feel able to continue to advise or assist their client. This will arise where the adviser has decided that trust and confidence between the adviser and the client has broken down. This mutual relationship of 'trust and confidence' is a cornerstone of the adviser/client relationship as we saw in section 3.1 above.

The breakdown of trust could arise in a number of different ways. A client may:

- become abusive and unco-operative;
- fail to give their adviser key information or accept their advice;
- deliberately withhold or falsify information; or
- continue to complain and show a lack of confidence in their adviser.

These situations are thankfully rare but nevertheless will give rise to a need for the adviser to terminate the client relationship. This theme is returned to in chapter 10.

Sample letter terminating adviser/client relationship: no contact

Opposite is a sample letter terminating the adviser/client relationship where there has been no contact for some time and no resolution by the adviser of that client's case. It follows on from the sample first letter written to a client above.

Ms A Client
2 Mile End Street
Milestown M1 2ER

18 September

Dear Ms Client

Re Lost Luggage Claim: 1 August
I refer to our meeting on 28 August and my letter to you dated 30 August setting out my advice to you.

Upon receipt of my letter you telephoned me on 6 September and told me that you had spoken to your travel agents and that they had offered to settle your claim for £200.

I then wrote, as requested, to advise you on this offer by letter dated 8 September. I wrote further to you on 22 September and 4 October but have not heard further from you. I enclose copies of those letters.

On this basis I assume that you no longer wish the East Lynne Advice Centre to assist you with this claim and will therefore proceed to close my file. Your papers (consisting of our letters to you and copies of documents you showed me at our meeting) will be kept in our archive system for a period of six years.*

In the meantime I confirm that there are no charges for our services.

If you have any queries on the contents of this letter please do not hesitate to contact me

Yours sincerely,

Abbie Gayle
Adviser

Direct line: 020 7661 1088
E-mail : agayle@elac.org.uk

---

* Note that the limitation period for legal claims for breach of contract is six years. In other word the courts will be able to entertain claims that a person wishes to make in respect of a contract they have been a party to at any time within that limitation period. Since the agreement that the adviser and client have entered is in the nature of a contract, organisations who are insured to provide legal advice will keep client's papers for at least six years in case there are any legal claims made against them relating to the work they have done for their clients.

CHAPTER 4

The client

4.1   Features of the typical client

You may be reading this book as an adviser and you may also have been a client at some point in time. We will look later at the particular skills an adviser brings to the process of gathering information, and assisting and advising their client. At this stage, however, it will be helpful for the adviser to be aware of the different ways in which clients are likely to present themselves to the adviser or seek to communicate with their adviser. All these different approaches will need to be accommodated by the adviser.

Furthermore, many advisers are limited in the time they can offer to a client and this time limitation is all too often driven by funding. Funders will often dictate the amount of time an adviser is expected to spend reaching outcomes for their clients. So where a client has certain limitations or lacks these abilities, more time may need to be spent and this can sometimes pose difficulties for the adviser.

Relating to the adviser effectively

To help an adviser to conduct a case efficiently and within a limited time period, ideally a client will:

- keep to pre-arranged appointments;
- answer the adviser's questions promptly and fully;
- communicate effectively that they are in agreement with actions to be taken to progress the case, both by the adviser and the client;
- take responsibility for certain aspects of their case and see those tasks through;
- produce documentation which supports what they say about their case;
- have that documentation arranged in a helpful or ordered fashion; and
- be consistent in what they tell their adviser about their case or things that they have said or done in the past or that have happened to them.

Advisers will reinforce those expectations when they meet or write to their clients as a way of explaining to the client the best way of working with their adviser on a helpful outcome to the case.

Client differences

Nevertheless, many clients do not or cannot conform to these expectations and usually for very good reasons. For example, a client who has a mental illness may be seeking to enforce rights as a mental patient, and the features of their illness will be a relevant factor in running that particular case. These features may make the above objectives difficult to achieve for that particular client. In other circumstances features of a mental illness will have no bearing on their case, but will be part of the client and how they present themselves to the outside world. Such features will make it equally problematic for the client to meet these objectives in running the case.

Advisers will need to be flexible in dealing with their client's personal or particular circumstances as well as dealing with their client's cases, and part of the real key to being a successful adviser is being able to deal with your clients' differences in order to achieve an equally efficient and effective outcome for each client.

Anti-discrimination laws

Advisers will also need to be aware that in some cases they will be bound by anti-discrimination laws which now cover a number of areas in terms of the provision of public services. Advisers in the statutory sector and many organisations which have charitable status will be required to understand their legal obligation to provide services in a non-discriminatory way and, at the time of publication, areas of discrimination law protected in relation to service provision are race, religion and belief, sexual orientation, gender and disability. More can be found out about this by contacting the Commission for Equality and Human Rights (CEHR).[1]

General factors which may cause clients difficulties in effective communication

To assist the adviser in this task of flexibility in the face of their client's circumstances, some particular categories of client and their needs will be outlined below. However, it will sometimes be the case that the client who does not fall into one of those special categories will exhibit features which can have the effect of frustrating the progress of the case; forgetfulness, inconsistency and tardiness being just some examples. It should be borne in mind that once someone becomes your client they are not only continuing to shoulder the problem which is causing them to come to you for help but are also going to be in a state of anxiety and stress in relation to the conduct and

1   The role of CEHR is also discussed in chapter 1, page 13.

desired outcome of the case. They may also feel upset or angry about the stance of their opponent or their behaviour. They may be anxious about giving evidence in a court or tribunal. All these concerns are likely from time to time to lead to lapses in clear thinking.

4.2   Clients who are vulnerable

As referred to above, clients may be vulnerable, for example, because they have a mental illness. Alternatively they may have become vulnerable for reasons connected with their case, as a result of something that has happened to them. An example of this would be where their lack of housing or racial discrimination they have suffered has caused them great distress. The impact of this on how the client can relate to their adviser will be part of how the adviser deals with a client when setting out to resolve a client's problem. Whatever the cause of the client's vulnerability, they will need an adviser who is able to work with them.

A client who is vulnerable may not necessarily describe themselves as such to their adviser. The adviser may, however, note that the client is finding it particularly difficult to order their thoughts, or appears to find it difficult to understand what is being explained to them or advice which is being given. They may have difficulty in concentrating, recalling events or understanding documents. Advisers will need to pick up on these features and ensure that they are nevertheless equipped to advise and assist such clients in an appropriate and helpful manner. It will be the case that many clients who come for advice in areas of social welfare law[2] such as homelessness or debt will be severely disadvantaged and/or vulnerable.

First, the adviser will need to ensure that they can clearly communicate with the client. This issue is not about language (for which see below) but about whether the client is able to give clear instructions to the adviser and can understand the advice being given and the steps needed to be taken by both the client and the adviser to resolve the case. If as a result of the client's vulnerability it will not be possible for the adviser to communicate with and advocate for the client then they may need to seek another method of doing so. Depending on the nature of the client's vulnerability, the adviser may need to consider whether they can obtain assistance in effectively communicating with their client.

---

2   For a brief discussion of what is meant by social welfare law and the legal topics which are usually referred to a social welfare topic in the field of advice see chapter 20.

As well as establishing if it is possible to communicate effectively with the client, the key issue for the adviser to identify is whether the client is or appears capable of making a decision. Examples of this are:

- is the client able to recognise and describe their problem/situation in order to seek assistance in resolving it?
- Can the client explain to the adviser (even with the help of friends, carers or others) what their problem is?
- Can the client properly understand the advice given to them either face to face or by letter? If you ask them to confirm that they do understand how do you know this to be the case?
- Can the client take any necessary steps to progress the matter, eg find documents, recall incidents, and provide a statement?
- Is the client able to evaluate and understand the effects of taking the advice offered and are they capable of putting advice given into effect?

Lacking capacity

If none of these appears possible then it is possible that the client lacks legal capacity. The steps above are those which form the 'test' of whether a client lacks legal capacity and are set out in a legal decision which gave some guidance as to when a client may lack the legal capacity which would enable them to instruct an adviser and understand and act upon advice given.[3] In addition, in the Mental Capacity Act 2005, the test for assessing a person's *mental* capacity relates to whether they can take a particular decision at a particular time. It should never be assumed by an adviser that the client does not have the legal or mental capacity to instruct an adviser. There will be many instances where clients may have short-term illnesses, including unwell periods for those with long term mental illnesses, or life changing events which cause them severe shocks or set-backs and these events may temporarily affect their ability to relate fully to their adviser. This will not amount to lacking capacity. The law will always presume that an individual does have capacity. The adviser will need to persevere with the feature of the client's behaviour which might make it very hard to progress their case before they decide that perhaps they do not have legal or mental capacity. In any event such a decision would also be made by the supervisor or manager in an organisation.

3   *Martin Masterman-Lister v (1) Brutton & Co; and (2) Jewell & Home Counties Dairies* [2002] EWCA Civ 1889.

If it does appear that a client lacks capacity, the adviser may find that the following approaches to advising and assisting the client will be utilised:

Power of attorney

Where clients lack mental capacity, a term defined in the Mental Capacity Act 2005, a power of attorney can be drawn up which is a legal document allowing others to speak and act for them in formal proceedings.

Lasting power of attorney

These are documents drawn up and registered in the Court of Protection (see below) for persons who are incapable of making decisions about their affairs. These replace the existing enduring power of attorney where an individual's property and financial affairs can be handed over to someone else. A lasting power of attorney will cover these types of decisions as well as those relating to the health and welfare of an individual. If someone wants to instruct you acting as an attorney for someone else, careful checks will need to be made that the legal requirements for drawing up and/or registering the enduring or lasting power of attorney have been complied with. For guidance see the Public Guardianship Office.[4]

Court of Protection

Where a client lacks the mental capacity to provide instructions, the Court of Protection (a part of the High Court civil legal system) can decide if this is the case and will take steps to represent that person's interests. The Court of Protection is due to be overhauled under the Mental Capacity Act 2005, with local courts being put in place. Its powers extend to appointing someone to represent them in court cases. The person appointed (usually a lawyer) is referred to as a 'Litigation Friend'.

Note, however, that there are some decisions which can never be made by another person on behalf of someone who lacks mental capacity. These include decisions such as marriage, divorce, sexual relations and voting.

---

4   The Public Guardianship Office is the administrative 'arm' of the Court of Protection and will assist in looking after the financial affairs of those not mentally capable of doing so themselves. See www.guardianship.gov.uk.

Enforced loss of capacity

It may be that the client has been placed in a position where they have been required to do something against their will. She may be a woman who has entered into an arranged marriage or who is a domestic servant being abused by her employers who is unable to leave. It may be someone who has learning disabilities who is being taken advantage of or held against their will. There are a variety of situations the adviser may encounter where a decision has been made to deprive a client of their ability to make choices or the capacity to act freely in certain circumstances. In this context the client will be asking the adviser to help them obtain a remedy which will include restoring their ability to act freely.

Support where the client has capacity

A more likely scenario will be that the client does have capacity but the adviser can enlist help and support in ensuring that the client gets the right level of service where they appear to have great difficulty in understanding, communicating or making decisions. Sometimes, an adviser may be able to obtain expert advice on the correct approach to take to communicating with their client where, for example, the client has a social worker or other outside support professional.

Advocates

There are networks of advocates in most regions of the United Kingdom, particularly mental health advocates. These individuals work for health trusts or voluntary organisations and can offer advocacy support for vulnerable clients; this support is likely to be to enable the client who is capable of making their own decisions to communicate more effectively. It may be offered at a time when a client is unwell on a short-term basis. In addition, aspects of the Mental Capacity Act 2005 which came into force in April 2007 provide for independent mental capacity advocates (IMCAs) available for those who lack mental capacity. An organisation like Advocacy Partners[5] will be able to offer information on this facility.

5   See www.advocacypartners.org.

4.3 Reading and writing

It may be the case that the only communication difficulty is that the client is unable to read or write. Clients may not always admit to this initially, saying that they do not have their glasses with them, or have forgotten to bring an important document to an interview. If the adviser does identify this as being a barrier to communication for the client and the client is happy to agree ways of dealing with it, the adviser will discuss with their client how this can best be dealt with in the context of advising on the problem. The adviser may discuss some or all of following approaches with the client:

- If letters are sent to the client by the adviser is there anyone that the client can call on for help in reading them?
- If there is no-one, or there is someone but the client does not wish others to be aware of the confidential matters they are seeking advice on, the adviser themselves may be the only person who can relay the content of letters to their clients, either in person or by telephone.
- It may assist for important interviews or discussions between the adviser and client to be tape-recorded and sent to the client to complement letters which the adviser will send out setting out discussions and advice.
- The client may not be required to write anything themselves as part of resolving the problem but, where it is a requirement for them to write or sign a formal document, there is a procedure for formal documents being written up by an adviser or legal adviser and then 'marked' by them in the presence of a witness. At the foot of the document will be a statement that the document is the client's in that it has been read out to them and that they are satisfied with the contents.
- A witness statement prepared in this way would then be read out by someone other than the client or their adviser in a court or tribunal (or just read over silently by the judge or tribunal members).

4.4 Children and young people

Legal rights and status

This book does not deal with family law, education law or criminal law, areas one might associate with the needs of child clients. There may, however, be circumstances in which an adviser may need to see a child or young person to give them advice. Examples are: young homeless persons or young workers seeking to enforce their rights.

There are specific rules about the way in which child clients of varying ages are dealt with in the criminal system which are beyond the scope of this book. In the civil legal system the age to be aware of is the age of 18. This is when the client will be regarded in exactly the same way as any adult client. Below that age, however, there are certain features to be aware of. For example, young people under 18 (referred to in legal terms as 'minors'):

- can claim to be refugees fleeing from a well-founded fear of persecution in their home country;
- can enter into contracts, eg to buy goods. Unless the goods bought are regarded as 'necessaries' (items the minor needs to live, such as food or clothing) a contract with a minor is not enforceable. Where the goods are regarded as necessaries the minor is required to pay a 'reasonable price' for them.
- can be employed and have specific legal rights at work.
- cannot become owners of property in law. They can have a form of tenancy with a landlord which is called a 'beneficial tenancy', where they have a right to live in and use the property. Once they reach the age of 18 they become legal tenants and are described as such on the tenancy agreement.

You may be approached either by a child or young person who is perhaps pregnant, vulnerable, homeless or has run up debts buying goods or using mobile phones or has a problem with a job. It may be that a parent, guardian or carer will be asking for your help in resolving the situation. Consideration will need to be given as to whether that child or young person, or the parent, should be seen as the client. Thought should also be given to whether the child or young person can give instructions and understand and follow advice and can lawfully exercise the rights they are seeking to exercise.

Once the adviser has satisfied themselves that they can continue to help a child or young person in their own right, they will be able to proceed to do so as with any other client.

Person with parental responsibility

Where there is a parent, carer or guardian, they are the person likely to have 'parental responsibility'. This gives the adult the legal responsibility of looking after the welfare of the child. This is a 'duty' rather than a 'right' over the welfare of the child. The duty will extend to ensuring that they make decisions which are in the interests of the child or young person in terms of where they live, what religion they follow, which school they attend and whether they should receive medical treatment.

Given this role of the person with parental responsibility, the adviser may be approached by them for advice and assistance in relation to matters which affect the child's welfare. If the adult indicates that they wish to make decisions about the young person, for example in relation to where they live, it will be good practice to ask them if the young person agrees to that form of action. In this context the concern is to ensure that the young person feels safe and consulted.

Depending on the nature of the problem, and whether or not it is one on which both child and parent or guardian are united in terms of the outcome they are seeking, it may be more useful to meet the young person together with their parent or guardian as being the best way forward to resolve their problem. An example of this is challenging a school's decision to exclude a child or not to give the child a school place which both parent and child are united in resolving.

Advising the child or young person on their own

There are various rules about when legal decisions or consent can be given by young people in different contexts. There are certain legal decisions that a young person can take; eg under the age of sixteen they will generally be able to make decisions about their health care.[6] There are also guidelines given in the context of family proceedings, such as divorce, and linked arrangements for the welfare of children, which will involve consulting with the child and, where considered appropriate, ensuring that they have separate legal representation.

If you are approached by a young person or child alone, who says they want you to give them legal advice, you should establish if there is a person in their life with parental responsibility. If there is, you may need to establish if the child or young person is telling you that they want to make certain decisions on their own. They may want your advice on challenging a decision being made about their lives by the person who has parental responsibility for them or by a statutory service, such as social services. If you are not sure as to a young person's rights to challenge decisions which affect their legal rights, help and advice can be obtained from an organisation such as the Children's Legal Centre.[7]

6   This is usually referred to as 'Gillick competent' after a case of that name.
7   See appendix A for contact details.

Where a child or young person says there is no person in their lives (or in this country if they are from abroad) or they are unwilling to be seen with that person, the adviser will see the young person alone and will ensure that the child or young person is able to give instructions and understand advice and act upon it. The adviser may find that what they are being told by their child client (for example, the reasons they have missed school or left home) may conflict with what a parent or guardian has said about the child or young person, and the adviser will need to focus on not only what the child client's wishes are but also what is in the best interests of the child or young person and discuss that with them. Care should be taken where a child raises any question of abuse or criminal behaviour being perpetrated against them by an adult or carer in their lives and advice will need to be sought as to the duty to report certain information to the relevant authorities. It may be that a new adviser will exercise some caution before they see a child or young person alone and will seek guidance from supervisors or external agencies that specialise in matters relating to children's legal rights.

4.5 Clients using a different language

There will often be circumstances in which it is clear that your client is going to be communicating with you in their second language or for whom language forms a communication barrier.

In addition, where a client is deaf and their first language is English they may need to communicate with an adviser using British Sign Language. It may be that a client who does not share the language of the adviser will communicate in their own sign language and this will need to be interpreted into your language: a two-stage process. For example, a client may sign in Spanish to a Spanish-speaking signer. A Spanish-to-English interpreter will then need to be told by that person what the client said in order to relay this to you in English. A third situation which may arise is that the client will need to communicate through the medium of an interpreter due to the nature of a medical condition (such as Cerebral Palsy), which can sometimes impair speech.

It should never be assumed that the client can communicate effectively in the language which you will use to conduct the client interviews, or alternatively that they are comfortable in communicating in that language. Clients will often indicate that they are able to do so in order to avoid 'making a fuss' or because they may be forced to do so in other areas of life. In addition, they may not initially realise that they will need to give their adviser often detailed information and understand advice which can at times be somewhat technical.

If you have any concerns about your ability to understand your client or for them to understand you and give you instructions you should always ask such a client if they would find it helpful to have the service of an interpreter or someone who can communicate using sign language.

Using an interpreter or translator: costs

Interpreters are usually privately self-employed individuals (although some local authorities retain interpreters in sign language as a low-cost service) who need to be paid for their services. Sources of funding should therefore be checked to see if the organisation is funded to pay for an interpreter or translator.

Where cases go to a court or tribunal, the court and tribunal system will usually pay an interpreter to assist a witness in giving evidence. This will be at a fixed rate, often linked to public funding of a case. The adviser will need to discuss with the interpreter if they are willing to go to the court or tribunal with the client and accept the fixed rate of pay, which will nearly always be lower than the interpreter's own private rates.

Using an interpreter: procedure

There are some golden rules about using an interpreter to assist in communicating with a client. Guidance can be obtained in the key skills from the National Occupational Standard LA30. These are:

- Look directly at the client, not the interpreter when you speak to them.
- Encourage your client to look at you when speaking back to you – their interview is with you and not the interpreter.
- Tell the interpreter that it is important that he or she interprets what your client is saying and does not *explain* what he or she is saying. It is your role to analyse and process the information your client gives you and to advise based on what they say.
- Look for signals from the client's expression to try to gauge that they are taking an active part in the process, ie that they understand what you are saying and feel that what they say has been clearly relayed back to you.

- Regularly check with the interpreter that they have clarified the stage the interview is at with the client, including summarised progress so far.
- Try to allow as much time as possible. As a guide, you should double the time you would take when both adviser and client are communicating in the same language.
- Build in rest periods or suggest having interviews in more than one segment at different times.

4.6   Strategies for dealing with clients' differences

In summary, the aim of the adviser is to be able to communicate effectively and efficiently with a client in order to progress their case and to keep the client on board throughout the process of giving advice and progressing the client's case.

Because clients present with different needs it is important to identify those needs and to work with them in progressing the case.

A chart summarising the strategies for dealing with clients' differences as outlined in this chapter is set out overleaf.

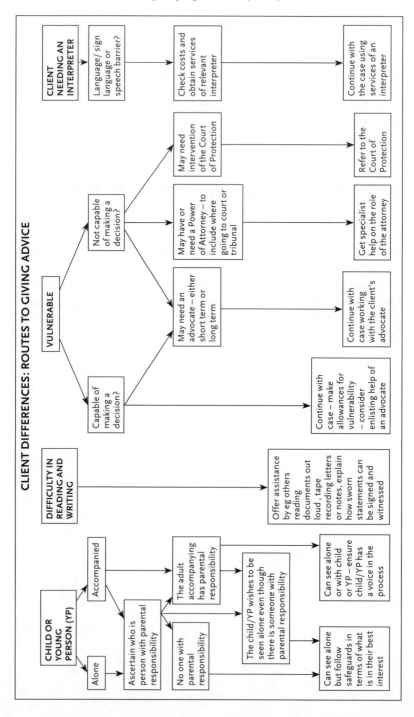

CLIENT DIFFERENCES: ROUTES TO GIVING ADVICE

CLIENT NEEDING AN INTERPRETER
→ Language/ sign language or speech barrier?
→ Check costs and obtain services of relevant interpreter
→ Continue with the case using services of an interpreter

VULNERABLE

Not capable of making a decision?
→ May need intervention of the Court of Protection → Refer to the Court of Protection
→ May have or need a Power of Attorney – to include where going to court or tribunal → Get specialist help on the role of the attorney

May need an advocate – either short term or long term → Continue with case working with the client's advocate

Capable of making a decision?
→ Continue with case – make allowances for vulnerability – consider enlisting help of an advocate

DIFFICULTY IN READING AND WRITING
→ Offer assistance by eg others reading documents out loud, tape recording letters or notes, explain how sworn statements can be signed and witnessed

CHILD OR YOUNG PERSON (YP)

Accompanied → The adult accompanying has parental responsibility
Alone → Ascertain who is person with parental responsibility

No one with parental responsibility

The child/YP wishes to be seen alone even though there is someone with parental responsibility

Can see alone or with child or YP – ensure child/YP has a voice in the process

Can see alone but follow safeguards in terms of what is in their best interest

CHAPTER 5

Taking instructions, identifying needs and outcomes

5.1   Introducing the client to the organisation

In chapter 3 we looked at the expectations which a client will bring to an adviser when seeking a solution to their problem. These included the overall expectation that the adviser will share the burden of the client's problem and use their skills and knowledge to resolve it.

There are several preliminary stages for the adviser to go through with their client prior to reaching the point at which they begin to resolve their client's problem. All these stages are part of the building blocks which are necessary in order to have an effective adviser/client relationship. They will be relevant whether the adviser takes on the bulk of the task of resolving the case for their client or whether the adviser's role will be limited to advising without taking steps on behalf of the client.

The first stage is to ensure that the client is fully familiar with your organisation, how it functions, what service it provides and how and when they can gain access to it.

Services provided

You may be able to give a new client information leaflets about the organisation. You should in any event check to see that they know what service you will be able to provide for them. This will include how they will be able to use the service, including opening hours and physical access. Some of the services the organisation may offer, such as providing an interpreter or doing home visits, may not be immediately obvious from the organisation's information sheets and these aspects of the service should be made known.

Complaints procedure

The client should be told at the outset how the organisation's complaints procedure operates and the name of the person who will deal with the complaint including any appeal processes. Firms of Solicitors are obliged by their professional Code of Conduct to provide this information and most other advice organisations will have a complaints system in place, often as a condition of funding. In any event a transparent complaints procedure shows that you are always willing to listen to clients' concerns and that you have a structure in place which is systematic and fair to all concerned.

Funding

It will help to explain to the client if the work for clients is driven by external funding. Many clients who use a free advice service may not appreciate that even though they are not required to pay their adviser, the resources of the organisation and the adviser will often be limited by the requirements of an external funder.

It may be that the adviser can only allocate a certain number of hours to that client or that the adviser needs to demonstrate to a manager, management committee or external funder that they believe that the client's case has a reasonable prospect of success before taking it further for the client.

Explaining funding arrangements to a client will help them to understand any possible limitations in relation to time or resources available which the adviser may have in offering to assist a client. This information may help the client to appreciate more fully why an adviser may be unable to take certain steps in the case.

5.2 Introducing the client to an adviser: roles and relationship

The adviser will need to explain to the client exactly what the function of the adviser is, what they can achieve for that client and how the adviser and client will work together. An example of how the adviser will explain this process might be:

- the adviser and the client will meet at intervals in person to discuss progress, to review documents or letters sent and received, to allow the adviser to continue to advise the client and to plan next steps;
- the adviser will in any event keep the client informed of all developments in relation to the client's case, for example, letters received or sent or offers to resolve or settle the client's case (for more on resolution see chapter 16);
- in particular, the adviser will not only record the advice they give in writing at regular intervals but will keep the client informed in writing of any risks which exist or which might arise as the case develops; for example, a risk of the client losing their home or their job (depending on the facts of the particular case);
- the client will keep the adviser informed of any developments which might have a bearing on their case, such as a change in family or financial circumstances; and

- the adviser will keep all the client's affairs confidential but at the same time will expect the client to be open with the adviser about matters which are relevant to the client's case.

Style of communication

The adviser and client should early on establish how they will address each other. In this day and age of relative informality, many advisers will be quite happy for clients to address them by their first names. The adviser should discuss with the client how they would like to address the adviser and how they would like to be addressed. Some clients, perhaps for cultural reasons, or where they are part of an older age group, may prefer to keep the mode of address on a more formal, family or last name basis. The adviser should ensure that the relationship starts as a professional one and one in which the adviser is a professional and not a friend or mere 'listening post'.

5.3   Identifying the client's needs

The first step the adviser will take in seeking information from the client will be to identify the client's needs in relation to the service as well as in relation to the matter they have come to see the adviser about.

Needs relating to the services on offer

By this stage the adviser will have explained to the client how the service operates and how they will be able to work with the client as their adviser. The adviser will address the client's needs in relation to the service. For example, if the service offers to refer the client to debt counselling, or has a money adviser who can assist as a result of a client's unforeseen reduction in income, the client may wish to take advantage of that aspect of the service.

Needs relating to a resolution of the client's problem

A client may attempt to 'lead' the adviser: 'this is my problem and this is how I want you to resolve it for me'. The resolution which should be agreed will include addressing the client's needs and taking into account the proposals which the client is making in relation to how the problem should be resolved. The agreed resolution will also include consideration of how, in the adviser's experience, matters like this are usually resolved, as well as external factors which will have a bearing on how far the adviser can fully address the client's stated needs, one of which is likely to be how the law operates in this sort of area.

For example, if a client has lost their job and wants the adviser to help in getting it back, the adviser will have to explain that either this is a process which can only be negotiated between the ex-employee and their previous employer and agreed, or alternatively what legal powers an employment tribunal has to order an employer to reinstate or re-engage an ex-employee.

Clients' needs in relation to resolving their problem are likely to be far-reaching and they may include:

- wanting to change a fundamental aspect of their lives – their immigration status, employment relations or housing circumstances;
- wanting to recover money they believe they are owed or be awarded money by a court or tribunal;
- wanting to obtain money (eg, a welfare benefit);
- wanting justice – a sense of the wrong they feel being recognised by a third party and recompense made to them as a result.

All these needs should be noted and addressed by the adviser. When the adviser comes to advise the client about how they will manage the problem for the client, they will deal with each one of these expressed needs and explain how and whether they will be able to address them in the process of trying to reach a resolution for the client.

5.4 Taking instructions

Initial instructions

The process of taking instructions has two meanings. The first meaning is related to the adviser's requirements to listen to the client's story, and the second to ensuring that the adviser acts in accordance with the client's wishes.

We will look in more detail at the process of interviewing clients and advising them in chapters 8 and 9. However, it will be important for an adviser taking initial instructions to be able to guide the client through their story and to give the adviser details which are relevant to the client's problem.

This is a process which requires some finesse as the client will not always be able to identify what is and what is not relevant and will not always tell their story in a logical sequence. The adviser may need to seek additional information from the client following initial instructions and/or filter out essential information from the client's instructions so that the adviser can take the client's matter forward.

An example of this would be a client who comes to an adviser with a rent arrears problem. The client may tell the adviser:

- that they have some letters from their landlord demanding payment;
- that they have financial problems and cannot make rent payments regularly;
- something about how this is affecting them and their family.

The adviser will need to know:

- the kind of tenancy they have;
- the exact contents of any document from the landlord;
- the exact arrears figure if known;
- the exact details of any payments made recently; and
- any particular circumstances, such as family illness, which have made it particularly difficult for the client to make payments of rent.

An integral part of taking instructions therefore will be for the adviser to ask questions about all these aspects of the client's problem in order to clarify the essential information required to formulate the nature of the client's problem and to begin to gather information which the adviser needs in order to begin to resolve it. Some advisers will write to their clients in advance of an important interview and outline for them the information they are going to require from that client at the interview. This helps the client to prepare.

Instructions to the adviser

At a later stage of taking instructions the adviser will have heard the client's story, given the client some advice about appropriate ways of resolving their problem and will then ask the client to tell the adviser what they would like the adviser to do next.

An example of this would be an adviser taking instructions about a loss of luggage on holiday, then advising that the client has a good claim against an insurance company for the value of the lost luggage (see scenario set out in the letter in chapter 3, pages 42–44). The client may then request that their adviser writes a letter to the insurance company on their behalf or they may ask the adviser to assist the client in writing that letter. They may ask the adviser to commence a claim in the small claims court if the adviser has advised that this would be an appropriate option All these actions are examples of a client giving instructions to their adviser.

5.5 Identifying and agreeing outcomes for the client

An important stage in the initial process of adviser/client relationship is for the adviser to work with the client on identifying suitable outcomes and to reach agreement on the best way to reach those outcomes. An outcome for the client is a result which has been achieved by virtue of the adviser's intervention in the client's problem. The outcome may take various forms. It may mean:

- the client obtains money, eg, a benefit;
- the client has a successful court or tribunal hearing;
- the client recovers compensation;
- the client is able to change something fundamental in their lives, such as where they live or how much money they owe or what their immigration status is.

It should not be assumed that because the client approaches the adviser with a legal problem, the solution to which is one with which the adviser is very familiar, that this is the only or indeed the appropriate outcome for the client. The client may state an outcome which they would like to achieve which differs from the accepted outcome or possible legal options for that type of problem.

Dealing with clients' stated outcomes

Where the client's stated outcomes do differ from the adviser's recommended outcomes, the adviser will need to balance what is the most likely or usual outcome to this type of problem with the outcome the client wants to see achieved. Examples of this apparent tension between the two approaches might be as follows:

- **Employment**. The client may tell the adviser that they have suffered discrimination at work. The adviser can advise that they have a good case to obtain compensation for that discrimination but the client's preferred outcome is just to leave the job and have no further contact with the employer. The adviser will have to balance this desired outcome with that of the client's expression of their sense of injustice and their wish to see their employer take responsibility for that treatment.

- **Debt**. The client may tell the adviser that they owe money to a number of different companies but some of their accounts are in joint names and they do not wish their violent partner to be aware of their level of debt. The adviser will then have to balance the efficacy of entering into an arrangement with these creditors as against the client's wish for confidentiality.

- **Housing**. The client may say that they want their landlord to repair their rented property but do not wish the adviser to contact the landlord as they fear repercussions. The adviser will need to balance this genuine concern with the client's legal right to require the landlord to keep the premises in repair.

In these situations the adviser will have to explain to the client that they may need to make a choice about the way in which they and their adviser reach their desired outcome. It may mean that the adviser cannot take all the steps that would usually be taken in order to achieve the most effective outcome for the client or one which addresses all their needs. The adviser will need to agree with the client how their preferred outcome can be reached as well as explaining that there are options for achieving a farther-reaching outcome.

What the adviser cannot do, however, is to go beyond what the client wants. The adviser cannot take steps which differ from their client's instructions or which exceed those instructions. If, for example, the client states that they do not want letters to be written threatening legal action, the adviser will be bound by their instructions on that respect, however frustrating that might be for the adviser.

5.6   Agreeing the process of taking a case forward

The adviser will often be required to mould their tried and tested methods of resolving a common problem to that particular client's circumstances.

Once the adviser has taken initial instructions ('heard the client's story') and identified with the client what their needs and desired outcomes are, the adviser will have to link the facts of the client's case, their knowledge of the law or regulatory procedures relevant to the client's problem, and the capacity of the adviser or the service within which the adviser operates in order to reach an appropriate resolution for the client.

The adviser should have in mind a checklist to help them decide on the most appropriate way of taking the client's case forward and reconciling the client's stated needs with an appropriate outcome.

Adviser checklist: achieving an appropriate outcome for the client
- What is my client telling me about what happened to them?
- What type of problem is this?
- Is this a problem which I have the resources and expertise to address?
- What is the most efficient way to reach a resolution in this case?
- Does my client understand the process and have I explained it sufficiently clearly?
- Is this the resolution which my client wishes to achieve?
- Is the client happy with my advice on how to achieve that resolution?
- Is that route going to cause my client difficulties given what they have told me about their preferred outcomes?
- Is there any alternative way of resolving the case which matches the client's desired outcome?
- Can this be effected?

The adviser then needs to reconcile these possible conflicts and agree with the client on the way in which they are going to take the client's case forward for them.

The adviser will then need to give the client the following information:

Information to agree with client before taking case forward
- Summary of the facts of the client's case
- The facts the adviser will find most helpful or relevant as a way of resolving the client's case
- The way in which the case is likely to be resolved (eg writing letters, making telephone calls, going to a court or tribunal)
- How that procedure works
- A suggested way forward, using an appropriate procedure

The adviser then needs to confirm that the client has understood this information and that the adviser has understood what the client's preferred method is of taking the case forward.

What follows then will be the adviser's advice (for more details of which see chapter 9) on the client's prospects of reaching a favourable resolution given these variables.

Once the adviser is happy that the client has understood and accepted the advice as being the most appropriate for them, the adviser and the client can begin to agree the way to progress the client's case.

The adviser should give the client the following information at the outset of their case and continue to agree it with the client at each stage of advising or conducting their case.

Key information for the client

- Facts and overview of the case
- Advice on how to reach a resolution for that client
- Steps to be taken by the adviser to reach that resolution
- Steps to be taken by the client to reach that resolution
- How long it will take to reach the resolution as now agreed between adviser and client
- Any risks inherent in attempting to reach the resolution
- Any factors which might cause delays or set-backs in reaching the agreed resolution
- Summary of the desired outcome and likely outcome

Recording the information: client care letters

The above information should be recorded in a letter to the client (a client care letter). That initial letter will also include the following information:

- any relevant information about how the client's case will be funded;
- any financial risk to the client of proceeding;
- the organisation's complaints procedure.

These initial letters are usually referred to as client care letters as they not only provide the client with preliminary advice about reaching the client's preferred resolution but they also provide the client with an overview of the route to be taken to resolve their problem, the time this will take and the risks involved, if any. The letter will also give the client more information about the service offered by the organisation, how and when the adviser can be contacted and the organisation's complaints procedure.

The letter in chapter 3 (pages 43–44) is a simple example of a client care letter, as it contains most of these elements. More detail is likely to be included where the facts or legal or procedural issues are more complex.

5.7 Explaining the process of reviewing actions on a case

It may be that the adviser can agree to embark only on a preliminary stage and then agree to review progress at that stage before any further steps are taken. Where, for example, the first agreed step is that the client or the adviser will write a letter to a landlord, employer, or shop, once that step has been carried out it is more than likely that the adviser and client will need to review the initial agreed action plan if a reply is received to that letter. It is very often the case that new facts or allegations are put into the arena as cases progress, which will mean that advice and action plans need to be flexible and subject to review at all stages.

This information must also be given to the client at the outset: in other words the client will need to understand that an initial agreed plan of how to take the client's case forward must be flexible and must have a built-in proviso that this agreed action will always be subject to review as the case progresses.

Clients will need to be supported by their adviser in this process of review and update of action plan. They will need to be reassured that it is commonplace to find that information which they gave to their adviser as being clear and accurate may be subject to challenge or change and that this is a necessary part of the process of resolving clients' problems.

Review process: how it arises

An example of this occurring might arise out of the sample initial client care letter set out in chapter 3 (pages 43–44). That letter indicates that the client's holiday insurance covers her in all instances of lost or stolen luggage, as that was the client's recollection. On that basis her adviser stated that it would be appropriate to make a claim against her insurance company. The letter also makes it clear that the adviser has not seen the client's insurance policy and that once it has been seen by the adviser her advice may need to be reviewed.

If we assume that the client did forward to her adviser her holiday insurance policy after that first meeting, a number of factors could lead to a change of direction. The insurance policy could state any of the following:

- no claims can be met unless the policy holder informs the local police of any loss within 48 hours of loss;

- no claims can be met where any item is unsecured (has no lock on it);
- only claims up to a certain value can be met;
- any claims will be subject to an excess (a reduction off the sum paid out).

These clauses are not uncommon in insurance policies and any advice that a client will be able to recover from her insurance company the full value of her lost luggage will therefore need to be reviewed and revised should any clauses like this appear in the policy entered into by the client.

Thus if the adviser offers advice which will have the effect of the client being able to fully recover his or her losses, that advice will always need to be tempered by the possibility that this advice may need to be reviewed in the light of certain developments in the progress of the case. Typically, where the client is working on his or her recollection of what a document says, the adviser will always offer advice based on the client's present recollection indicating that this advice may vary once the adviser has themselves seen the document. This is part of the organic process in which advisers and clients will need to work together to reach a helpful resolution to the client's case.

CHAPTER 6

External influences on the adviser/client relationship

6.1   Introduction

For a client, the adviser is the sole person they have to advise and assist them in resolving their case. They will place the adviser at the centre of the case and will expect the adviser to be available for them and to deliver on the commitment they have made to initiate and/or assist in the process of resolving that case. A client may introduce into the arena a number of external influences on the case which in reality have no bearing on it but which will have an influence on their relationship with their adviser.

On the other hand the adviser will have various additional demands on their ability to process the client's case and they will need to be aware that they should have a clear direction for each of their clients. They should also ensure that they build into each relationship the external factors which will influence that relationship, and take a realistic approach to how they can best conduct the case for each client.

It is important for the adviser or would-be adviser to take on board the busy environment in which advice work is conducted and the pressure on them to deal with a number of competing demands on their time and to ensure a fair balance of time and resources is expended on each client. We will look later at good practice in relation to case management (see chapter 13) which gives the adviser a structure in which to manage advice work and cases for a number of different clients. However, the adviser should be forewarned of the factors outside the adviser/client relationship which are most likely to impact on their ability to manage each client's case efficiently. The adviser should take on board external factors which the client brings to bear on the case and deal with them appropriately in the context of advising or conducting a case for that client.

6.2   The adviser's other clients and tasks: systems for time management

For the adviser, one of the most problematic aspects of giving advice is how they efficiently manage their time. The adviser will have the following competing elements to deal with:

- calls on their time from other clients or other client-based tasks;
- calls on their time from the organisation they work in;
- rescheduled priorities as a result of developments in clients' cases; and
- necessity to demonstrate value for money to funders.

Other clients

An adviser should always be realistic about how many cases they are able to handle at any given time. Some advisers will say that this is something that they have no choice about but are given targets by reference to numbers of cases being conducted or time spent on casework at any given time which is set either by the organisation or by their funders or both.

Where an adviser is fortunate enough to have the freedom to choose how many cases they conduct, they should look at new cases in a realistic light. Many client enquiries which appear to be simple at first sight can gather in complexity as more information is received and it is often a question of educated guesswork as to how long a case will in reality take to conclude or how many hours might be spent on each case.

Nevertheless, all advisers will be advising a number of clients and will need to ensure that they manage their time so that each client receives the same level of service. Sometimes advisers can be drawn into spending more time with clients who contact them on a regular basis than with those who do not, although the latter may well be equally as deserving of the adviser's time. One way to ensure consistency is to draw up a case plan for each client. This means the adviser has not only planned the likely progress of the case with each client but can refer to each case plan to ensure that progress is being made on all their cases.

Case plans

A case plan is a document which an adviser can develop themselves on each matter in a format which suits them or their type of client or organisation. There is rarely a requirement to have case plans in legal matters. Where a legal case is publicly funded it will sometimes be necessary to draw up a detailed case plan which outlines the complex structure of the case and underpins the high level of public funding which will be allocated to the solicitor conducting the case. Otherwise using case plans is a matter of good practice and a way of ordering progress on each client's case.

An example of a simple case plan concerning a housing association tenant who has rent arrears might be as follows. Detailed knowledge of the law relating to this type of problem would not be necessary to see the pattern of steps the adviser will plan to follow.

Case of Ms X: Rent arrears and claim for possession of property

Case plan

- Take initial instructions on whether arrears admitted and any reason given as to how and why they have arisen.
- Obtain client's documents from client and put into logical and sequential order – discuss significant documents with client.
- Obtain copies of landlord's documents, and take client's instructions on these.
- Note and diarise any court appearances.
- Ensure steps taken comply with any court deadlines.
- Take witness statements from client and any supporting witnesses.
- Discuss with client the significance of any witness statements provided by landlord and advise accordingly.
- Advise client on next steps and merits of case.
- Attend court with client.
- Review case following any court appearances.
- Take any further follow up action with client, including further advice on client's next steps.

The contents of this case plan may and probably should be reflected in an initial advice letter to the client but the sort of summary set out above which appears on the file or on the computerised case plan system will help the adviser to keep on track for each client.

Organisation-based tasks

An adviser will not be spending all their time working on clients' cases. They will have a number of competing demands on their time and resources and these should be realistically addressed. They will need to deal with some or all of the following tasks:

- attending meetings;
- telephone advice sessions;
- carrying out administrative tasks such as filing, typing;
- covering for other staff off sick, on visits or at courts or tribunals;
- attending training;
- writing reports or papers for funders or management bodies.

The other vital competing activity is that of e-mails. The way in which advisers allocate their time and tasks can often be driven by e-mails. Just like post, e-mails must take their place as part of the information coming in to the organisation or the adviser. The adviser will need to ensure that they have planned for how and when they deal with their incoming e-mails.

Using a diary to manage time

An adviser should give consideration to, and be able to estimate, how much of their time they spend on organisation-based activities and how much time is given to client-based work. They should, as far as possible, be able to arrange their time in a structured way so that they feel that they have achieved tasks they set themselves. Some advisers set up their computers to provide reminders of tasks they have put into their electronic diary. Others will use a handwritten diary but will check it regularly for tasks to do and tasks done.

Either way the diary should be structured. Some advisers will split their week up so that there are days or blocks of time devoted to various tasks. There may, for example, be days when they try not to see clients to allow for other tasks to be done. Others will ensure that they manage the day so that administration and client-based work each gets its fair share.

This approach to time management should in any event dovetail with the vital task of time management on a client's case. A client's case is likely to have deadlines which arise from time to time. Because of this and of the need to juggle a number of cases each with their own deadlines and priorities, it will be important for the adviser generally to manage their time across all the activities which will have demands on their time and which will compete with each other.

Rescheduling priorities: the need for flexibility

Even the best time management system can go awry if there are unforeseen developments on a client's case. However, when these developments arise, which they surely will, the adviser needs to be able to cope with them and still ensure all their clients receive a satisfactory service.

Even where there are few support services in an organisation, the adviser should be able to deal with emergencies or unforeseen developments, often by dint of re-arranging less urgent tasks around that new development. A typical example is a client calling in with details of a court hearing they have to attend or a meeting they need to prepare for which they have not told their adviser about perhaps due to stress, misunderstanding or confusion about what a letter said or meant. The adviser will need to assure the client that they can accommodate this development if indeed it is one which is pertinent to the client's case or one which the adviser had envisaged could arise during the conduct of the case.

This means that the adviser must have an open and flexible approach to their diary and to the case plans they develop for each client's case. They must be prepared to reschedule and to revisit tasks. One of the learning stages for an adviser is to observe a more experienced adviser who is capable of being interrupted from a task in hand to deal with a more pressing matter, and then to reschedule so that other matters also get dealt with.

Funders' requirements

Advice work in the voluntary (not-for-profit), charity and statutory sectors will always be driven by external funding and this will inevitably have an impact on how individuals in an organisation work. See chapter 1.

Funding underpins how advice services are provided and which groups in the community will be targeted for advice. In the context of how much time can be allotted to an individual client by an adviser, this question will often be answered by understanding a funder's requirements in this respect or how advisers are required to record their time or the sort of work they are able to do for each client. In addition, the adviser will always be required to use their case management system to demonstrate to the funder what work is being done and what outcomes have been achieved.

An adviser will therefore usually see the requirements of funders as an integral part of how they conduct their casework. They should be building in to the time they spend on cases not only their client contact time but any additional time in preparation, contact with other parties, relevant research or training as part of justifying funding being received for the provision of the service.

6.3 Clients' additional advice needs

A client will come to an adviser with a set of expectations about what they hope their adviser to achieve for them.

Even though these will be agreed as targets between the adviser and their client at the outset, the adviser will often find that the client may also bring into the equation other needs which the adviser has not agreed to address or cannot address. For example a client who has rent arrears may need a debt counsellor or a client who is an asylum-seeker may have social services needs.

An adviser will plan to ensure that the client is made aware of exactly what needs their adviser can address but will do their best to try to address their client's other needs even if this involves signposting or referring the client to other sources of advice.

Forging links with other agencies

The adviser should be wary of 'compartmentalising' their client's problems too rigidly. The examples given above are very common ones of overlapping needs and problems and it may also be that the adviser needs to liaise with other advisers also assisting their client in order to reach a helpful solution to the client's problem which they are addressing.

For example, if they are assisting with a rent arrears problem and they know that the client has been helped by another adviser to obtain a benefit then, subject to their client giving them permission to do so, the adviser can make representations to a landlord that their client will be able to pay off their rent arrears in a way they could not before as they have a new source of income.

6.4 Client involving others in the advice process

It will often be the case that a client will come to see an adviser accompanied by friends or family, in order to help them to recall what they need to tell the adviser or to give them some confidence. Sometimes another individual may ring the adviser and speak to them on behalf of a client or the adviser will speak to another person when they telephone the client.

Maintaining client confidentiality

At a first interview, if a client comes along with someone else the adviser will tell the client that they will expect a full and frank exchange of information to take place between them but that they, the adviser, will respect the client's confidentiality. The adviser should ask the client in the light of that to confirm that they have no objection to the person accompanying them being a party to the discussion which is about to take place and to hear the advice which the adviser will be offering to their client at the conclusion of that meeting.

This gives the client the opportunity to invite the other person to withdraw if the client realises that they would prefer the discussion to remain confidential between themselves and their adviser. If they do not ask the person to withdraw then the adviser should make a note of who was present at the discussion. Confidentiality in the adviser/ client relationship is also discussed in chapter 10.

As part of this duty of confidentiality the adviser will need to remind their client of their obligation to communicate at all times directly with the client. It will sometimes be inconvenient to ring a client and find they are not available. It may be that an urgent message needs to be given to the client and there is a willing family member who offers to take that message. No matter how tempting that might seem, an adviser should not discuss the details of their client's case with anyone else, even their closest relative. Even if a client tells an adviser that they consent to the adviser giving information about their case to close family members the adviser can never be sure which information should be given out in this way.

More importantly, the adviser can never be sure that there is not a conflict of needs or interest between the client and a close relative, partner or friend, for example in relation to money, housing or property rights. The adviser can never be sure that the client has not been placed under any pressure to divulge confidential information to close family members which may be used against that client's interests.

If a client does indicate to their adviser that they do not mind the adviser leaving messages for them or speaking to others to give or receive information to others or in front of others, the following guidelines will assist.

Guidelines for speaking to a client's associates and for leaving messages

- If a client does authorise an adviser to communicate with another person, this should be confirmed in writing by the adviser.
- Although the adviser can never be sure that there is no conflict of needs, clients sometimes choose to be accompanied to interviews and appear satisfied that others can speak to the adviser about the client's case. This is the client's right and all the adviser can do is to check each time that the client is happy for that person to be in attendance.

- Particular care should be taken not to leave a client a message on their landline telephone as the adviser can never be sure who will hear the message. This will extend to a message to call the adviser back as the adviser will be identifying themselves and possibly also leaving contact details. The client should always specifically authorise their adviser to leave messages for them in their absence.

6.5 Tribunal or court procedures

If a client comes to an adviser with a request to assist them in relation to a problem which has put them or will put them into a tribunal or court system, the adviser will need to explain to the client that the processes of that tribunal or court must be carefully followed. There are many penalties associated with a failure to comply with the rules of a tribunal or court and these include not being able to pursue a claim or case, having a defence to a claim or case struck out, or facing an order to pay the legal costs of an opposing party.

Unforeseen hearings or events

It will quite often be the case that planned hearings will be postponed or that hearings will come up at short notice as a result of the court or tribunal's decision to list them or where an opposing party has been in touch with the tribunal or court to ask for a hearing. (See chapter 18 for an overview of the legal system.) At this stage the emphasis is on the adviser and the client being aware of the impact that the tribunal or court timetable will have on their agreed timetable and the need to accommodate their actions around that timetable. Clients are often thrown into confusion and distress by a requirement that they attend a court or tribunal and will find the process unfamiliar and stressful. The adviser therefore needs to counsel their client about this process but also make it clear that the client will need to comply with these externally-driven deadlines in order to maximise their chances of a successful resolution to a case. See chapter 11 for more on counselling as part of advice work.

Diarising and double-diary system

The adviser should diarise all court deadlines and dates of hearings and where they have offered to represent or accompany a client they should ensure that they can meet that commitment. These events will need to take priority in an adviser's diary for a client involved in tribunal or court cases and any subsequent adjustment of other tasks will need to give way to this.

Many advisers will also operate a double-diary system by warning themselves some days or weeks ahead in a diary of a hearing or date by which action needs to be taken so that they give themselves sufficient time to prepare for that event.

6.6   Funding limitations

Funding for the adviser's work

As well as the adviser knowing that funders' requirements are likely to dictate how they much time they spend on the case and how they record their casework activities, the adviser may also find that funding is limited to doing advice work in certain specific areas. The organisation may not, for example, have any funding to provide advice in debt, but is funded to give housing advice.

This might mean that an adviser, no matter how experienced they might be in that area of advice, will have to refer the query elsewhere. This can have the effect of fragmenting a client's case and can be time consuming and frustrating for a client who would naturally prefer all their linked problems to be dealt with under one roof. It may also mean that an adviser will have to allow extra time for referrals and/or to liaise with other organisations dealing with linked aspects of the client's case.

Funding to achieve outcomes

In addition a source of funding may be short-term or provided to achieve a specific goal in terms of advice services. For example, funding may be provided as part of a regional or national drive to increase awareness among individuals in consumer rights, or to target certain sections of the community, or to reduce debt. Advisers sometimes therefore need to balance their requirement to work in the context of the client's best interests with a requirement to demonstrate that a particular outcome has been achieved as a result of contact with that client.

Client satisfaction surveys

Many organisations will need to report regularly to funders and will devise client satisfaction surveys which include in them questions to the client about named outcomes being achieved. The process of doing this will add to the tasks surrounding advice work. The surveys might ask a client to say if they have received advice which has resulted in any change to their lifestyle and if so what that change was. Information received from the surveys will help the organisation and the individual adviser to show that the necessary outcomes linked to the funding are being met while that source of funding is in place. The survey will also assist in the process of ensuring that the service on offer to their clients is regularly monitored and reviewed for any improvements or additions to the service.

CHAPTER 7

Advocating for your client

7.1   The meaning of advocacy

Many people who see the word advocacy will associate it with a barrister or solicitor who appears in court and presents a court case for their client. While this word does describe this function it is important to know that advocacy means more than that and that the adviser is likely as part of the client relationship to be advocating for their client. They will therefore need to understand what advocacy is and how it operates in the adviser/client relationship.

The dictionary meaning of this word is 'one who pleads for another and who speaks on behalf of that other'.

Being a champion for the client

In the context of advice-giving, advocacy will function in two different ways. The first meaning relates to the idea of the adviser being a champion for their client and in this sense all advisers will engage in a form of advocacy for those that they are advising.

The client and the adviser will agree that in a range of situations the adviser will speak on behalf of the client by taking steps such as making telephone calls or writing letters and in doing so will represent what the client wants to say to others.

Furthermore, the adviser will argue for, or advocate, any changes in the client's status which might be affected by an outside body or organisation. This is the aspect of advocacy which not only means the adviser acts as the client's voice but is also advocating for a client in the sense of putting the case for someone. In almost all advice work situations the adviser will be acting as a voice as well as putting the case and so will be acting as the client's advocate as part of the advice work role.

An example is a client who tells their adviser that they have been wrongly accused at work of failing to carry out an important procedure. The client has been invited to write to their employer to explain themselves in order to avoid a disciplinary hearing taking place. The client will ask the adviser to write to the employer telling the employer the facts as they see them. For example the client will tell the adviser that they were specifically told on that day by a manager not to carry out that procedure for health and safety reasons. The client therefore wants the adviser to:

- tell the employer the client's view of the fact;
- put across any disparity between the client's version of events and the employer's version;

- explain why they failed to carry out the procedure;
- explain that they do not believe they are at fault for failing to do so as they were following orders;
- invite the employer to agree that there was no fault on the part of the client; and
- invite the employer not to regard this as a potentially disciplinary matter.

In this sequence of events the adviser has gone beyond speaking on behalf of the client and has moved into 'pleading' with the employer in order for the adviser to achieve, on behalf of the client, the client's desired outcome, ie no disciplinary hearing taking place.

There are skills associated with this process of 'pleading' which will be looked at below. However, an adviser should be aware that there are a range of situations in which advocacy will be employed as part of advice-giving and these also will need to be examined.

Pleading in a formal setting

The second and more skilled meaning of advocacy is where a professional advocate will plead their client's case in a formal court setting.

In most settings the court will expect the advocate to be formally qualified as a lawyer before they can address the court on behalf of their client. This is what is known in legal parlance as having a 'right of audience'. Legally qualified personnel will have undertaken training in the skills of advocacy and will have studied the laws of evidence. The idea of appearing in a formal setting for a client can be very daunting even for a trained advocate. For someone who has no training it can be even more so.

There are, however, a number of other formal situations where advisers who may or may not have any advocacy training or experience will go and advocate for their clients. Examples are case conferences in a social service setting, school exclusions appeal panels and employers' disciplinary hearings. There is also a range of tribunals where advocacy will be employed either by lawyers or advisers on behalf of their clients. These can be relatively formal and will often be making significant decisions about a person's future. Each forum, panel or tribunal will have specific rules and procedures but will not expect anyone who represents a client to use any formal advocacy tactics. They do not require those appearing before them, and advocating on behalf of their clients, to have a right of audience.

Some advisers will never have the opportunity to advocate in this or any formal setting but, for those who do or who wish to do so at some point in the future, an outline of the advocate's key skills is set out below as well as some encouragement to take part in the process if the opportunity should arise.

7.2　The skills of advocacy

In whatever context the adviser is working, in order to plead their client's case, there are key skills they will need to employ in order to advocate effectively for that client. The skills set out below are based in some respects on the more formal rules of advocacy but there is no reason why those rules cannot be employed and the skills practised in a variety of settings, some more formal than others. The key skills are discussed in more detail opposite.

Rules and procedures

Before an adviser embarks on putting a case for a client or arguing for a specific outcome they will need to familiarise themselves fully with the organisation they are dealing with. This may be an organisation their client is in dispute with such as an employer or a school, or it may be a panel or tribunal (such as an employer's appeal panel) which has been set up to hear evidence and make decisions. The adviser will not only need to know how that organisation works and what its powers are but also how it expects people to conduct themselves when they approach the organisation and seek to ask it to do, or stop doing, something. An employers' appeal panel will usually have a set of rules and procedures. These will set out what will happen at any appeal, eg against dismissal. The panel will be required to hear from those who appear before it in a set pattern. Its rules and procedures will state in what order people will speak, whether questions can be asked, and to whom these questions can be put.

A panel or other decision-making body will also have written down what its powers are and what decisions it can or cannot make. Some will be able to reach a different decision from the original hearing and will be able to review all the evidence they have seen including that which was before the original panel. Others will only be able to decide whether or not they agree with the original panel's decision. If they do not agree with the original decision they will often expect the original panel to hear the case again and take on board any criticism of their decision or the process they used which has been made by an appeal panel.

Thus it will be vital for the adviser to know what they are able to achieve. If a panel cannot substitute its decision for that of another decision-making panel on appeal then there is little point in the advocate asking for that outcome.

Summary of skills of advocacy

Understand the rules and procedures
Know the rules of the environment you are operating in. Familiarise yourself with the procedures of the organisation you engage with in order to plead your client's case.

Know your client's case
Know your client's case well. Ensure you have read all his or her documents and are familiar with them as well as knowing what it is you and your client have agreed you will say on their behalf.

Know the opposition case
Find out as much as you can about any points or arguments likely to be put to you in order to defeat your client's case or prevent them reaching the outcome they want to reach.

Be prepared
Prepare in advance all you want to say on behalf of your client, any questions you might want to ask of another person or witness and any arguments you wish to present to support your client reaching his or her desired outcome.

Get organised
Organise in a logical way any documents you may wish to refer to and any documents you may wish others to refer to so that the sense of them is immediately apparent. Ensure that documents you refer to are relevant to the case you are pleading.

Be flexible
Be prepared to be flexible in how you plead a client's case. Allow for new situations developing which might influence how you present the case or what outcome the client can realistically expect to achieve.

Your client's case

An adviser needs to know their own client's case to advocate effectively on behalf of that client. The adviser needs not only to know what the client has told him or her about their case but also to ensure that they have explored all additional angles, including the awkward corners, and anticipate what the other party may say to counter the client's claims. It may be that a client will be accused of not acting properly, or of not being truthful, in a particular situation. The advocate should be prepared to present evidence to ensure that what their client wants to say will be accepted, and that they are prepared to counter with helpful evidence any allegations that this is not the case.

For example, in the workplace situation outlined above, the adviser may find that they are asked to advocate for that client in a disciplinary meeting. At the meeting the manager may deny that they instructed the client not to follow the necessary procedure. They may produce a written note they made of the client refusing to carry out a reasonable request. This may not come out until the disciplinary hearing itself.

In advance of that meeting however, and as part of their preparation for it, the advocate will have checked with the client the exact words the manager used or whether there was anything written down at the time. The adviser will seek to establish with the client if they were ever shown any written notes or whether there were any witnesses to this conversation with their manager. This additional probing will help the adviser to resist an accusation that the client is wrong, mistaken or, worse still, untruthful, by pointing to any other possible evidence available to show that the client is telling the truth.

Adversarial: two opposing parties

An adversarial situation will arise where there are two opposing parties with two different view points and a panel or court will be required to decide in favour of one party. So if an employer has disciplined an employee and the employee is arguing that they want that decision to be overturned, the panel will be deciding if the employer was correct to discipline or if the employee is correct in saying that the decision to discipline was wrong.

The advocate will be pleading on behalf of their client to achieve a specific outcome and will need to be clear what obstacles they need to overcome in order to do so. This will usually mean knowing what these obstacles are and what challenges lie in the way of achieving them. Sometimes it will be a question of knowing what evidence a panel has before it in order to reach a decision one way or the other or what evidence it considered in order to reach the decision which the client is now challenging as being wrong or adverse to them.

The advocate will need to have possession of all the evidence. If they do not have it, they will need to request it from the relevant organisation or panel as being required as part of following that organisation or panel's procedures in the matter in dispute. The advocate will therefore need to obtain any written rules and procedures as referred to above and all the documents or statements they have in their possession in relation to this matter. In addition, the adviser will need to obtain copies of documents or statements which their adversary has and will be relying on to support their case (as well as providing them with copies of their own documents).

Preparation

It is vital to prepare for meetings at which you will be pleading a case for a client. This preparation not only includes knowing all the matters outlined above but also preparing to present or plead the case. Most advocates suffer from nerves and so in order to allow for this they will ensure that they are fully prepared. They will ensure that they are familiar with the documents and that they have rehearsed their arguments in advance. The double-diary system of recording key dates well in advance, as discussed in the previous chapter, will allow the adviser time to prepare for a meeting or hearing at which they need to make a case for a client.

Preparation is necessary to clear the mind to deal with any issues which might come up in a meeting or panel which the advocate/ adviser will need to deal with in order to achieve the best result for their client. For example, a document may be presented at a hearing which the adviser has not seen before but which needs to be dealt with as it goes to the heart of what their client is trying to prove happened. The document may be a memo sent by a manager to an employee reminding them that they must carry out a certain procedure at work. The adviser will need to balance this evidence against their client saying that they were verbally told not to carry out that procedure. The adviser will need to ask themselves when the document was written, or whether the client is going to say they have not seen it before. The adviser then needs to decide if it is genuine and relevant.

See checklist overleaf. As part of preparation, the use of highlighter pens, page dividers and post-it notes can all contribute to a well-prepared pack to refer to at the meeting or panel.

Adviser's preparation checklist

- A document outlining the facts, eg a statement by the client.
- A document listing key events and dates in relation to the matter under scrutiny.
- A set (sometimes called a 'bundle') of relevant documents in date order, eg letters, memos, and a note as to why they are relevant (post-it notes can be helpful in this process).
- A list of questions to ask any adversary (or their witnesses or employees) or a panel.
- A summary of the points to be made in favour of the client achieving their desired outcome which refer to all of the above and how it helps the client's case.

Organisation

As indicated above, the key to being able to refer quickly to a document which has been prepared for a meeting or panel is to have a logical system which allows for easy access.

Alternatively, some panels will prepare a set of documents which they have been given in advance by various individuals. This may include documents to and from the adviser's client. The panel will expect everyone who appears at the meeting to have these documents in the same order. This possible requirement should therefore be checked in advance by the adviser so that they have their documents in the required order. It is usually the case that the more formal proceedings get the more likely it is that panels or tribunals will dictate how representatives prepare their documents ready for a hearing.

Either way the adviser should be familiar with the exact way in which the documents are set out and ensure that they have an organised set of documents.

Flexibility

An advocate who is over-prepared may lack the necessary requirement to be flexible in pleading a case for a client. A key feature of advocacy is being prepared to deal with the unexpected. It will inevitably be the case that what you have been told by your client and what evidence is put forward by others will conflict and the advocate will need to decide how to deal with that when it happens. If the client insists in sticking to their story no matter how high the cards are stacked against them their adviser will need to explore with the client any possible reason for the disparity. Has the client failed to recall key events or lost letters they were sent? Is there a legitimate reason for this? For example, have they been unwell?

Making concessions

If it seems that certain aspects of a client's case are not going well then it will often be better to make concessions but still make a case for other aspects. For example, if your client says they were told by the manager not to carry out an important procedure but then admits that they did receive a memo reminding them to do it at a later date, the client may not have a good reason for failing to carry out the procedure at all. They may be able to argue that the memo was difficult to understand or was sent late and so they have a good argument still for not being disciplined for failing to carry out the procedure.

Looking for opportunities

Where an opportunity arises to strengthen the case which the advocate has not foreseen, they should be prepared to grasp it. For example, if the employer admits in a disciplinary hearing that they failed to alert an employee to a change in procedures then it should be suggested that the employee could have no way of knowing that they needed to follow a changed procedure. That may determine whether an employee should be disciplined or not. Once a helpful point is made it will be best to move on and come back to it at the end of the meeting or panel hearing and refer to it as part of the case in favour of the client's desired outcome.

Accepting outcomes

Flexibility can also mean that both the adviser and the client should be prepared for the possibility that the case may not go according to plan. This is not necessarily going to be due to anyone's fault. Even where a case is very well prepared and argued it can be possible against all the odds for the outcome to be different from what was predicted or hoped for. Clients can often become quite involved in the personalities they encounter at formal meetings or hearings, not least because the outcomes are so personally important. They can become involved in a way that the professional adviser will not be able to, since the professional adviser needs to keep their distance in order to act in the client's best interests. Part of the adviser's role is to advise on whether the outcome achieved can be taken further and equally important when it cannot. This may involve challenging unfair conduct of a hearing, asking a panel to review their decision or seeking to appeal the decision at a higher level. In addition, the adviser's will advise and counsel on whether the client is able to accept the outcome which has arisen. This will be looked at in more detail in chapter 11.

7.3   Advocating in courts and tribunals: an introduction

Even where it is unlikely that the adviser will represent their client at court or in tribunals it will be useful to have an overview of the procedures and protocols. See chapter 18 for more detailed guidance. The guidance in this section is aimed to give a new or untrained advocate confidence when they go to a court or tribunal.

Where the client needs to attend a court or tribunal it may be the case that the agency offering advice will not have the resources, skills or funding to represent that client at court. It is still the case that court and tribunal hearings are often conducted by barristers who are trained intensively in the laws of evidence and the skills of advocacy and an adviser who finds that they are on the opposite side of a case to a trained advocate may feel disadvantaged.

Where an adviser who is not legally trained does have the opportunity or ability to represent clients in the formal setting of a court or tribunal they should be able to take heart from the fact that it is part of a professional advocate's duty to extend courtesy to an untrained or lay opponent. By the same token a judge or tribunal chair should extend courtesy to such an individual and should ensure that they are familiar with the procedures they are now a part of by attending that court or tribunal.

Jargon busting

For those new to the experience of being in the court or tribunal system, there are formalities which advocates need to be familiar with and ensure that these are understood and accessible to both the adviser and their client.

In addition there will be language or jargon used in the formal court setting which it is worth familiarising oneself with. It is still often the case that professional advocates will use jargon which describes everyday things in different ways. Some do this more than others and often do it quite unwittingly.

Jargon	Everyday meaning
1. What do I call you?	
My opponent	The person who represents the other party (the employer, the landlord, Home Office etc)
My friend	The same person as above
My learned friend	The same person as above but that person like me is a barrister
Your honour	A Circuit Judge in the county court
Sir/Madam	A District Judge in the county court or the magistrates' court
Chairman or Madam Chairman	The person in the centre of a tribunal panel of three who is running the tribunal

2. What is the judge or tribunal chair saying?

Appearing before me, or appearing	Stating that you are the person in the proceedings who is representing a particular client
Opening your case	This is asking you to go first and present your case by calling witnesses
Not to lead a witness	Asking you not to give the witness the answer you want as part of your question (eg 'You didn't take the money did you?')
Inviting you to cross examine or saying 'this is now your witness'	Inviting you to ask questions of another party's witness which are designed to help your client's case (eg 'Do you agree that someone may have been confused by a memo which appeared to contradict your original instruction?')
Asking you to sum up or present your submissions	At the end of the hearing or meeting asking you to summarise what you believe has happened and the points which you think have been established in your client's favour

3. What are people calling the documents?

A statement of truth	A sworn statement at the foot of a statement of case or a witness statement that indicates the truth of the contents of that statement

continued

Jargon	Everyday meaning
A bundle	A set of documents which everyone has copies of and which the court or tribunal will be asked to read or refer to and which a witness will also be asked to refer to
A paginated and/or indexed bundle	A set of documents with page numbers and an index referring to what each document is called and what date it was produced

Getting familiar with formal proceedings

There are, and may be, opportunities for advisers to represent in court, perhaps in a small claim or a possession action, or in a social security, immigration or employment tribunal and they should not feel such an activity is beyond them. It will always be useful to sit in on these hearings even where they do not have responsibility for them. Familiarity with how things work will provide confidence in the system. In addition, it means that the adviser can tell their client what is likely to happen when the client goes to court even where the adviser themselves will not be representing the client at court.

As we shall see in chapter 18 they will also be able to unravel for the client some of the mysteries of what is taking place in court and who the various personnel are.

Finally if the adviser does decide to engage in the formal court process for their client they should be able to function there as long as they follow the guidelines set out above which are the benchmarks of good advocacy. There will rarely be a good excuse for not being prepared or not knowing what are the procedures of the system you are dealing with and so once you have the confidence to engage in the process the rest is usually just a case of hard work and careful preparation.

Advice skills

Interviewing

8.1   Setting the scene

Planning

The process of effectively interviewing a client is a core skill deployed in advice work. The interview will be seen as the primary vehicle for building on the adviser/client relationship, for ensuring that the adviser is aware of all the relevant aspects of the client's problem, and as a mechanism of agreeing action to be taken to take the matter forward. Advice and counselling, which will be examined in more detail in chapters 9 and 11 respectively, is also offered to the client as part of the interview process.

Prior to embarking on an interview with a new client the adviser should be planning how they will conduct the interview. The steps set out below may not be necessary on every occasion, but it will be useful to have a standard 'pre-interview checklist' which helps the adviser prepare before seeing the client and to focus on the key issues to be addressed.

Pre-interview checklist

- Put together a summary of facts already known about the client's problem, as a result of initial telephone conversations or letters received from the client.
- Compile a note of gaps in knowledge of facts or events which need to be filled by further questioning.
- Produce an outline of what the problem appears to be about.
- Outline the advice which might be offered, including a note of any preliminary research the adviser has made relating to the client's problem.
- Suggest lines of enquiry or development which might arise out of the first interview.
- Organise any particular arrangements which need to be made for the first meeting (eg arrange for an interpreter).
- Make a note of how much time the adviser has planned to allocate for the first interview.

The interview environment

Another preliminary step will be to ensure that the environment in which an interview takes place is appropriate. Many advice agencies operate in very limited spaces and cannot always offer their clients an environment for seeing them which is entirely suitable. In an ideal world the interviewing environment should be

- confidential;
- comfortable;
- child-friendly (if the client is accompanied by children); and
- safe and hazard-free for both adviser and client

Confidentiality

Confidentiality will be looked at in more detail in chapter 10. If possible the interview should be conducted in a separate interview room where other clients or advisers cannot overhear what is being said. If this is not possible, and there are other advisers nearby, the adviser should make a note to assure the client at the outset of the interview that the organisation as a whole is committed to each client's confidentiality and will not breach that confidence.

Comfort

The client should be made as comfortable as possible and their needs for drinks and comfort breaks should be borne in mind by an adviser when preparing to interview. If the client needs to smoke during a long interview, a break should be arranged for them to go to an area where this will be possible.

Child-friendliness

Many clients will need to bring small children to advice sessions and this should be accommodated within the resources of the advice agency. Some agencies collect toys donated by their own staff or their friends or relatives so that children can play while the adult is seeing their adviser. It may be that the agency has volunteers who can spend time with small children in an area where they can still be seen by the adult. If children do accompany parents, guardians or carers to interviews, the adviser may need to be realistic about how long an interview is likely to last and may need to plan for a split interview. Some clients may even bring a pet dog to an interview and the adviser needs to be aware if there is any safety policy which applies to such an arrangement.

Risk assessment: health and safety

Many of these factors so far discussed in planning for the first interview involve a health and safety dimension. The adviser should in any event ensure that a risk assessment is made in relation to client interviews.

There is likely to be a general policy of risk assessment procedures relevant to seeing clients which the agency will have in place. The adviser should be familiar with it. The risk assessment policy should contain a number of safeguards for the adviser as well as the client. In addition to making a check of the appropriate procedures in relation to seeing clients in an enclosed interview area, or offering toys or other resources to clients' children, the procedure should allow for the adviser's safety should a client become distressed, ill or angry.

In particular, where an adviser has arranged to go and see a client in their home, there should be clear safeguards in place for the adviser who is working off-site. This is likely to include a full note being left in the diary as to where the adviser is, including a note that they have taken a mobile telephone with them and how long they expect to be away. If the adviser exceeds their expected time away the agency should have procedures in place to check on the adviser's safety.

8.2   Mapping the interview process

Sometimes an adviser will only need to see a client once for an interview in order to provide helpful advice and to offer a resolution to the client's problem. If the adviser is going to be involved in following a number of stages through in order to reach a resolution of the client's problem there are likely to be milestone interviews arranged. The following is a possible pattern of what each interview is likely to be able to achieve.

Interview stage	purpose
First interview	• Sets the scene; • adviser/client relationship is formed; • client gives initial instructions about the facts or what their problem entails and seeks help in resolving it; • initial advice is offered to the client; • next steps and review process are agreed.
Second interview	• Discussion and advice offered on any replies to initial letters written or any steps taken by the adviser to attempt to resolve the client's problem; • further tactics for resolution discussed.

Third interview	• Preparation for any court or tribunal hearings or any meetings or panels with the client; • evidence which will need to be gathered, preparation of any witness statements or documents.
Fourth interview	• Discussion of any final stage reached in the client's case (which may or may not involve a resolution); • final advice on the outcome of the case and on any steps to be taken by the client hereafter and/or by the adviser to bring their file to a close.

Where, for example, there may be meetings, panels or hearings to prepare for, there may be a number of preparatory interviews between the adviser and the client.

In addition, where no external hearings or meetings form a part of the client's case, there are likely to be instead repetitions of the second stage interview as further steps are made towards a resolution of the client's problem.

8.3   Key elements of an adviser/client interview

Once the adviser embarks on the interview process, they will be using a number of skills and approaches to ensure that they are in full possession of the relevant facts, can advise their client effectively and can use the interview process to progress towards a resolution of the client's problem.

Key elements of the interview are:

- outlining the process
- questioning
- noting and interpreting client's answers
- summarising
- reviewing and reflecting
- advising
- making decisions
- agreeing next steps

Outlining the process

Before embarking on an interview with the client the adviser should outline what form it will take and what outcome they should both expect to achieve at the end of the interview. In the first interview the adviser will explain that they need to ensure that they know all the relevant facts and are given sufficient information to be able to advise the client on a suitable course of action.

The adviser should say that he or she will begin by asking the client questions after which he or she will be in a position to advise the client on how well their chances are of achieving their desired outcome. The adviser will at the outset assure themselves that they understand what the client's desired outcome is by checking this with the client. They will explain that they will offer advice to the client and that by the end of the interview they hope to be able to agree with the client on a suitable plan of action to take the client's problem forward which is likely to involve both the adviser and the client in taking next steps.

The adviser will tell the client that following on from each meeting the adviser will write to the client to summarise what the client told them, and to record in writing their advice, and the agreed plan of action arising out of the interview. This will help to allay any fears the client might have that they must remember all that takes place in the interview as they will be given the information in writing following on from the interview.

Questioning

At the outset the adviser will need to obtain from their client all the facts which are in the client's possession (a process usually referred to as taking the client's instructions) as well as taking from them their instructions on how they wish to go forward in the light of the adviser's input. This second stage of taking instructions will come towards the end of the interview. Furthermore the adviser will need to question the client for any comments they may have on the adverse aspects of their case, and/or on a conflicting set of facts which may have been put forward by others.

When seeking to obtain the facts the adviser should begin by asking open questions ('what happened?' and 'what happened next?') but should then be ' funnelling' those questions, or making them more focused in order to get as much detail as possible. So if a client says they went to a meeting with a housing officer in which rent arrears were discussed the adviser needs to find out what figures were agreed, if any, if the housing officer threatened any legal action, and what arrangement, if any, was made to pay off the arrears.

The questioning should be detailed. If anything is overlooked it may well be to the client's disadvantage. Worse still, it may be brought out for the first time in a meeting or hearing by the client's opponent and thus affect the ability of the adviser to use it in any way which is helpful to the client because they have not had the opportunity to prepare to deal with it.

The adviser should also be asking questions which are designed to test out what the client is saying and to ensure that it can be held up for scrutiny or that it cannot be challenged. If for example there is a letter from a landlord stating the amount of rent owed, and the client denies that they owe this much, the client must be asked why they think the landlord has come up with that figure, if the client has made recent payments of rent, and if there are receipts for that payment or a note of them made in a rent account.

In questioning a client the adviser should be non-judgmental. If the client discloses that they have behaved in a manner which the adviser themselves believes to be unwise or even reprehensible, it will not be for the adviser to comment on that behaviour. Instead their role will be to advise as to how that behaviour might affect any desired outcome on the part of the client.

Noting and interpreting client's answers

The adviser needs to record what their client tells them. This will be looked at in more detail in the next chapter but it should be noted that a key element of advice work is to make full notes of what is said and what action is agreed during client interviews. This may be done longhand or on a computer. Notes should be taking during the interview which may stand as the final record of what took place or which may then be written up later. With experience it should be possible to write or type good notes during the course of an interview which will stand as the final record of content and agreed outcomes. At the same time the adviser will need to ensure that they remain engaged with their client as well as recording what happens in an interview.

As a matter of courtesy the adviser should inform their client at the beginning of an interview that they will need to record what is discussed but that they will nevertheless be able to give the client their full attention. Sometimes clients will find an adviser who gazes fixedly at a screen as they record an interview gives the appearance of not listening or not engaging. The adviser will need to think carefully about how they combine their personal interview skills with a need to record that process.

As well as faithfully keeping a record of discussions with their client, the adviser will need to decide how answers they record will flow into the issues they are exploring. For example, in planning the interview the adviser may have made a note to establish if what the client tells them about the rent arrears differs from the figure given in a letter which has already been copied to the adviser. The adviser will have perhaps noted that once they have that information it will impact on advice they give to their client. Thus they need to flag that up as they record it with a note (eg 'NB this figure differs from the figure given by the landlord in their letter to the client of 20 May – check with client/advise'). The adviser should not pepper their notes with comments (eg, 'client's figures are wrong') but should be interpreting what they hear or read ('client's figures differ from those set out in landlord's letter – check this with client – write if necessary to landlord?').

Summarising

As part of the questioning process the adviser should be regularly summarising what the client has told them. This gives the client an opportunity to reflect on what they have said and if necessary to correct it until they are quite satisfied that what they have said is what they wanted to say. The adviser should summarise any advice they give as well, as sometimes they will need to give advice which is dependent on other things happening, such as the client agreeing to pay off more rent arrears or, alternatively, failing to continue to pay their rent.

Reviewing and reflecting

This aspect of the interview involves the adviser taking stock at various points in order to reflect on the stage reached so far. This will be particularly relevant where the adviser has begun to advise the client that their prospects of achieving their desired outcome are more limited than perhaps at first envisaged by both the adviser and the client due to external developments and/or further information being received by the adviser from the client.

The adviser will be reflecting with the client on what the implications are for the client if, for example, the adviser has advised that the client has little prospect of paying off their rent arrears. If the client's desired outcome is to keep their home then the adviser may need to review how that will stand up to the advice that the level of arrears is likely to lead the landlord to consider taking steps to repossess the client's home.

Advising

The skills and the process of advising both in an interview and in letters or on the telephone will be looked at in chapter 9. Advice is something which clients will rightly seek to obtain as it lies at the heart of the adviser/client relationship and there are a number of skills to be acquired and tips to be assimilated in order to advise effectively.

Making decisions

It should always be the case that decisions which are made which affect the client, and which affect the way in which they will resolve the problem, should be made jointly. The adviser should not take ownership to the extent of telling the client that they have no option but to pursue a course of action or that the adviser will pursue a particular course of action for the client. Indeed, it is likely to be at this stage of the interview, once the facts are known and advice offered to the client, that the adviser will take the client's further instructions and will ask the client, in the light of any advice or new advice, what course of action the client now wishes to take. This will be a part of the process of making a decision about how the case will go forward.

There can often be a process of negotiation between the adviser and client leading to decisions which affect the conduct of the case but, even where the decision is not one which the client came into the process expecting to reach or agree to, it should be arrived at jointly.

Agreeing next steps

Following on from the joint process of making decisions, the aim at the conclusion of each interview should be to agree what next steps need to be taken. These may involve both the adviser and the client. The adviser may offer to write a letter or make a telephone call and/ or to make certain enquiries on behalf of the client. The client may agree to start to outline a statement to bring to the next interview or to locate documents they believe they have in their possession and bring them to show the adviser. The adviser should be able to give the client an estimate of how long it will take to conclude the matter and to reach a resolution to the client's problem.

8.4   Skills employed by the adviser in interviewing a client

Listening

The adviser should at all times listen to their client. Some clients will have greater difficulty in communicating than others, and part of the questioning process involves a non-judgmental approach to what a client tells you. It is also important to listen for hidden messages. A client may find it hard to say something to their adviser for reasons of embarrassment or distress. They may want to talk about discrimination against them but find it difficult to express that as such. They may be in debt or rent arrears due to an unruly child or a violent partner who has taken money from them or been dishonest with them about finances, a matter which they may find very difficult to discuss with an outsider.

The adviser may need to probe gently to see if the client wants to tell the adviser anything which can help the adviser to explain why the arrears arose or why the client was treated in the way that they were. The adviser can always invite a reluctant client to come back on a subsequent occasion if they have anything extra to add or to write the adviser a note explaining something they found hard to put into words. If the adviser comes across to the client as a good, non-judgmental listener then they will hopefully have a strong chance of finding out from the client all they need to know to solve the client's problem.

Sensitivity to client's needs

Being sensitive to a client's needs is an essential part of establishing trust with a client. The adviser should not only be conscious of the clients' physical needs, for breaks or rests during a long or stressful interview, but also be aware of their need to be understood, offered sympathy which is nevertheless constructive and professional, and a need to be believed and their problem recognised and not trivialised. Many clients are doing battle with large organisations on a daily basis which involves being treated as a small cog and if their needs are taken seriously by their adviser it will make a substantial difference to their self esteem and their ability to manage any obstacles or setbacks in the conduct of their case.

Understanding specific nature of the client's case

It can be easy for an adviser to get side-tracked or to run away with a client's case. Advisers may say that they have seen these cases many times before and that they are aware of how best to resolve them. Even if this is true, they should ensure that they solve the problem with that particular client in mind and for their benefit.

An adviser should also beware of misreading signals from the client. An apparent reluctance to co-operate in the process of resolving the case may in truth be a fear of disclosing something which the client believes to be harmful to their case or embarrassing. So the adviser should be regularly checking with the client in order to understand what the client is saying about their problem and what it is they want the adviser to achieve for them.

Keeping control of the interview process

Although much of what should happen in an interview should involve joint decisions, the adviser should nevertheless ensure that they maintain overall control of the interview process and not allow the structure of the interview to fall apart. This can happen when the client wishes to intercept, make comments or offer information in a random order or once that stage in the interview has been passed.

Although the adviser will need to be flexible to a certain extent as to the order in which they conduct the interview, they should keep a firm hand on the structure and if, for example, the client seeks advice right at the outset, the adviser should remind the client that they will offer advice once they have established the full facts and agreed with the client on the main issues to be decided upon to reach a satisfactory conclusion for the client.

This is another reason for the adviser to reflect and review on a regular basis throughout the interview, to allow the client to see the structure which is being followed and the various stages reached.

Time management

Finally it will be up to the adviser to manage the time spent interviewing. They may be driven by funding in terms of how much time they can spend. They may also have to fit the interview in with other work commitments.

The client may have limited time and may, for example, have to contend with tiredness where an interpreter is involved, or with the competing demands of a small accompanying child. The adviser should therefore set the time parameters of the interview at the outset and regularly check to see if the interview is going to reach its agreed outcome in the time allotted. If it is not, then this must be addressed sooner rather than later so that the adviser and the client can plan when to meet again and for how long and what they can hope to achieve that day and on the next occasion they plan to meet. If there is any urgent action to be addressed then that aspect of the case should be highlighted and dealt with in the time remaining.

8.5   Problems which may be encountered during interviews

Time

Even the best planned interview can encounter unforeseen problems in reaching a satisfactory conclusion or one which the client hoped for or the adviser planned for. Advisers should be on the look out for problems which can jeopardise the interview process and be ready to deal with them.

The first one is that time begins to run out and the adviser has not achieved what they hoped to achieve. The solution to the problem of running against the clock is to reschedule. There is little point in sitting for three hours with a client who is becoming tired or distracted as they will not be able to contribute effectively to the interview.

When arranging the interview with the client, the adviser should agree with the client how long the adviser thinks the interview will last and ensure that the client is available for that period. If the client cannot commit to that length of time then the adviser needs to explain to the client the priority actions which need to be dealt with in that interview, such as preparation for a court hearing. The adviser will need to arrange an interview which deals with that priority and will then need to arrange a further interview dealing with other essential aspects.

Time can be saved in interviews by sending out a preliminary questionnaire to a client who is able to complete such a document. This may cover essential personal information about the client, their finances and names and addresses of individuals who have an impact on their problem and whom they may ask their adviser to contact for further information. Furthermore some clients will have access to a computer and will be willing to begin to draft a preliminary statement about what happened to them. The adviser may also set the interview in motion in advance by sending out a list of questions they would like the client to address in their statement. Time in the interview can be saved by going over the answers rather than by raising the questions and then going over the answers.

Conflict of interest

Every advice organisation should have in place a system which checks whether they already advise someone who is likely to be in opposition to the client in relation to particular case. A simple example of this is where the agency is advising both the landlord and the tenant on a dispute relating to a tenancy. If this is the case, the agency will be regarded as having a conflict of interest; they cannot act impartially for both parties. The solicitor's professional code of conduct requires the adviser to explain the problem to the second of the clients to be instructed and to withdraw from that client's case.

It can happen that a conflict is not immediately apparent. In immigration cases, for example, it can be the case that both parties to a marriage are seeking advice on the wife's immigration status with the Home Office. Careful checks may need to be made that the husband is truly acting in the best interests of the wife in what he says about the state of their marriage. Where any likely conflict arises between two clients, the agency should not continue to advise the second client. The adviser needs to ensure that they present a picture of genuine impartiality.

Problems taking instructions

There may be a number of problems in taking clear instructions from a client during an interview. Apart from the practical difficulties that may arise with a client who has genuine problems in communicating (see chapter 4) an adviser may get a sense that the client is deliberately withholding relevant information or is becoming unreasonably defensive or angry with their adviser. Where there is any question of the adviser's safety being at risk, the adviser must be fully familiar with the agency's health and safety procedures and should use them to bring the interview to a close.

Otherwise where the adviser is unable to elicit from the client any coherent or consistent information, they will need to point this out to the client in a calm manner. The adviser will need to explain to the client what information they require in order to assist the client and invite the client to decide whether they can offer this information on this occasion or would like to meet on another occasion having reflected on what the adviser is asking them to do. If they still cannot offer any information then the adviser will be bound to offer advice based on what instructions they have received. They will need to explain to the client that their capacity to take matters forward will be limited to what the client has told them and that this may limit the client's chances of success.

Unless the client appears to be deliberately failing to co-operate with their adviser for no apparent reason, the adviser should not be judgmental about a lack of willingness to discuss certain matters or face certain issues. The adviser can only point out the limits on what they can achieve for their client.

If, however, it does appear to the adviser that there is a break-down in the adviser/client relationship the adviser will point this out and may need to withdraw. This is discussed in further detail in chapter 10.

Case does not go to plan

Finally it may be the case that information is given to the adviser in the course of the interview, either by the client or through documents which they both see, that will lead the adviser to revise completely the advice they initially gave to the client. They may be required to change advice from that of a positive outcome for the client to advice which informs the client that they have no prospect of achieving their desired outcome in spite of any efforts the adviser can make on their behalf.

In these circumstances, the adviser may not be able to continue to assist this client. This will depend on the policy of the organisation they work for, but many organisations will not be able to put resources into cases which have no prospect of success.

Where the course of the case is radically altered, either for the worst or otherwise, the adviser will need to discuss with the client at the interview how that will affect the way in which they can continue to assist. If the client is unwilling to agree to this course of action the adviser may need to indicate that all they can do is assist in the manner now indicated and that they will record that situation in writing for the client so that the client can consider it and decide if they will accept it. A client who is unwilling to work with their adviser will not be able to demonstrate that they have the necessary trust and confidence in them for the adviser to continue to act as an adviser. It may be that this point will need to be made to a client for them to consider. In any event it will not be possible to continue if the adviser and the client are pulling in opposite directions and the relationship will need to be carefully reviewed if that appears likely.

CHAPTER 9

Advising and recording

9.1   Researching the client's problem and solutions

Giving advice is at the heart of the advice worker's environment. As we shall see later it can take many forms, from the practical to the complex legal. It needs to be accurate, helpful and relevant to the client's situation and above all it needs to be clearly understood by the client so that they can act on it. It can be offered in a number of situations and it should be offered as part of the interview process outlined in chapter 8.

Even before an adviser has met their client they may be in a position to know enough about the client's situation to begin to do some preliminary research which will assist them in advising the client. They may have received a note of a telephone conversation from a receptionist which might indicate that the client has rent arrears or unpaid wages or has bought a defective toy for their child. Even with this amount of information the adviser will be able to begin research as to what this situation might mean, for example in legal terms, and the sort of remedies available for individuals in these situations. This will help the adviser to make further enquiries of their client as to the facts of their particular case and how, if at all, it might fit into the pattern of similar situations and their solutions. A note should be made of any preliminary research so that it can be added to once the client's story unfolds.

Once that story unfolds it is likely that further research will need to be done to supplement the preliminary outline. The adviser will therefore need to be aware of their particular resources for researching their client's problems. The adviser will need to have some expertise in researching their client's problems in order to offer them helpful and relevant advice. If they are using textbooks or handbooks these will need to be up to date and/or be the latest editions: advice based on law or procedures which are out of date will be of little practical use. They may use reference works which are looseleaf and which are updated by the publisher who provides relevant pages providing changes to previous editions. The job of updating these volumes should not be left to chance. They may use on-line reference systems or internal intranet information systems. The latter tend to be more up-to-date but this should be checked. We will look later in chapter 19 at basic legal research.

In this and further chapters that look at the adviser's skills and how the adviser progresses the case, a case study (see opposite) is used as a means of demonstrating some of these skills and steps. The outline of the case study is relatively simple but strands will emerge which will demonstrate some of the challenges advisers may meet in resolving a client's problem.

Cathy's case

Cathy Clark comes to see her adviser Ada Adams. She raises two problems which she wants to ask Ada to help her with. She is a 22-year-old single woman and lives in a one-bedroom housing association flat. She has an 'assured tenancy agreement'. She has fallen behind with her rent.

Cathy also recently left her job as a nursery nurse. She worked as a part-time nursery assistant at a private nursery called Kidglove for a period of approximately three months. A week before leaving she took some days' paid holiday. On the day before she was due to return to work from her holiday she received a telephone call from the owner who said she wouldn't be able to keep Cathy on as there were not enough children enrolled at the nursery.

Cathy says she is owed a week's pay as her first week was unpaid and she was told she would be paid for it when she left the job. She wasn't given any notice to leave.

Cathy wants help in dealing with her rent payments so she can keep her home. She also wants to know how she can claim her unpaid wages from the Kidglove nursery.

Ada's preliminary research

Prior to seeing Cathy, Ada will have researched the following possible aspects of her case:

- The legal action a housing association may take when a tenant is in arrears of rent.
- Whether the housing association landlord has any policy about dealing with rent arrears. Ada may find that this is written down and she can obtain it from the housing association.
- Whether that policy includes the threat of legal action and at what stage that threat is likely to arise.
- Whether Ada can refer Cathy elsewhere for any assistance in money advice and if so where (see chapter 14 on signposting and referrals).
- How Cathy can best recover her unpaid wages. What possible legal action she can threaten or take.
- What other monies might be owed by the nursery to Cathy such as notice pay and how Cathy can go about recovering these sums.
- What possible legal action she can threaten or take.

The case study has elements of housing, employment and debt problems in it. Knowledge of how the law works in those areas is not essential in order to understand the way in which the case study unfolds. In any event in part 6 of this book an introduction will be given to social welfare law with introductory chapters on housing law and employment law which will assist in following the key areas covered in the case study.

9.2   Advising on success and outcomes

It is often the case that a client will want to know from the outset how they will fare; will they win the case, recover the money, obtain immigration status, or get out of debt. These are all vital to a client with a problem relevant to these desired outcomes. For a new adviser it can be daunting to be faced with such a request as the adviser will have the twin concerns of wanting to tell the client what they want to hear and wanting to ensure that the advice they give is accurate. One thing is clear: advice must be given and it cannot be avoided by repeating the facts of the case and agreeing the next steps. The client needs to know why the next steps are to be taken and why they are appropriate in the circumstances.

Advice on outcomes

It will rarely be possible to offer advice at the outset of an interview with a new client. It will of course be possible to agree with the client on a desired outcome but the adviser will need to explain to their client that although their problem has the hallmarks of many similar problems, advice can only be given once the facts of the client's own particular case are established and then matched to the usual remedies available in similar cases.

For example, a client with rent arrears can hopefully look at outcomes which may range from reaching an agreement with their landlord to pay off the rent arrears at an affordable level, or negotiating with a landlord in order that court proceedings are avoided or, where the case has reached court, asking the court to make what is known as a 'postponed' possession order, whereby they can remain in their home as long as they continue to pay off their rent arrears at a set rate. Nevertheless, the adviser needs to look at this client's history in order to be able to advise if any of these outcomes are likely or possible.

Advice on prospects of success

Furthermore, the adviser should be able to predict with some accuracy what the client's prospects of success are likely to be.

Merits and quantum

The advice given on prospects of success is referred to by lawyers as advice on the merits of the case. In addition to advising on prospects of success, where there is the possibility of the client recovering or being awarded money, the advice will be on 'quantum', meaning the likely amount the client may obtain. Put very simply, the advice will take two forms:

- will the client succeed; and if so, where relevant,
- how much money are they likely to recover or obtain.

The adviser will rarely, if ever, be able to tell the client that they have no prospects at all of succeeding or, conversely, that they are definitely going to succeed. Such categorical advice on total failure or total success is rare due to a number of as yet unknown factors which are likely to affect the client's prospects of success. These will include:

- more information to be provided by the client;
- more documents to be disclosed by an organisation (eg, a school appeals panel) the client is seeking redress from;
- more documents which might be disclosed by any adversary (eg, a landlord or an employer);
- other steps which the adviser and/or client could take to move towards a favourable resolution;
- things which a client or any other witness might say in advance of, or at, a meeting or hearing which will affect the outcome of that meeting or hearing; and
- the way in which a panel or hearing may choose to interpret information it is given in spite of any pleas to interpret it in a manner favourable to a client.

Sometimes the advice on prospects of success will be expressed by the adviser on a percentage basis (eg there is a 60 per cent chance the client will succeed in achieving their desired outcome) and for some funders of advice a requirement to be able to advise on a more than 50 per cent likelihood of success may be a requirement of funding that client's case. The above factors will have a bearing on the weighting of the percentage in favour of the client succeeding. The adviser will in any event constantly review the advice, based on how the problem unfolds and develops.

Cathy's case: advice on outcomes and prospects of success

Adding to the client's story

In the course of her first interview with Cathy, Ada has obtained the following additional information:

- Cathy has received a letter from her housing association landlord inviting her to come in and talk to the housing officer about her rent arrears;
- Cathy's boyfriend Ben is working and he has offered to lend Cathy some money to help out with her rent arrears until she gets back on her feet;
- Cathy has already written a letter to Kidglove nursery asking for her back pay and the letter has been returned by the Royal Mail marked 'gone away';
- Cathy has a new job in the local supermarket starting next Monday; and
- Cathy tells Ada she is not very good with money and she owes on some loans she has taken out.

Advice on outcomes

After receiving this information and explaining to Cathy what the possible options are for avoiding a possession action by her landlord and recovering the money she is owed by her ex-employer, Ada will advise Cathy as follows in relation to possible outcomes:

- If Cathy meets her housing association landlord as offered in their letter to her she may be able to come to an arrangement to pay off her rent arrears. This may be achieved by Ben lending her money or by her negotiating with them that she will pay off the arrears over a period of time out of her supermarket wages.
- There is a 'protocol' setting out the steps a housing association should follow before starting a claim for possession in court. This includes trying to agree affordable repayment of the arrears by the tenant.
- There is the possibility that the housing association may at some stage start legal action against her to recover her property if Cathy fails to reach an agreement or breaches any agreement.
- If Cathy or Ada can contact the owner of Kidglove nursery Cathy will be entitled to claim from them a week's back pay and a week's notice pay.
- If this money is not paid voluntarily Cathy can start legal action to recover it.
- If Cathy finds it hard to manage her money she may have continued difficulty in keeping up her rent payments.

Ada will also advise on the prospects of Cathy being able to achieve these outcomes.

Advice on prospects of success

- Ada will advise Cathy that if the rent arrears are not too substantial and she goes to meet her housing officer she should be able to succeed in coming to an arrangement to pay off her arrears and avoid legal action being taken by them to recover her flat.
- Ada will advise Cathy that in order to keep to that arrangement Cathy may need help and advice on managing her money as well as using the money Ben loans her and her supermarket wages towards paying off the arrears.
- Ada will advise Cathy that if legal action is threatened by the housing association it should be possible to use the information in court which Cathy has told Ada about her finances to avoid Cathy losing her home outright.
- Ada will advise Cathy that she can start legal action to recover the money she is owed by the Kidglove nursery and she should succeed. However, the prospects of recovering the money ordered by a court or employment tribunal may be slight if Kidglove can no longer be located.
- Ada will advise Cathy that there is a difference between obtaining a tribunal or court order for someone to pay over money and actually receiving the money. It can often be the case that monies are never actually paid over, even though courts have powers to enforce unpaid court orders or 'judgment debts' as they are usually called.

At this stage Ada may advise Cathy that there is a 75 per cent chance of her being able to keep her flat but only a 25 per cent chance of being able to recover any money from Kidglove nursery.

9.3　Effective advice-giving

Confidence

A new adviser often lacks confidence. They can be unsure of the legal or practical background to their client's problem or they can be concerned that the advice is not reliable and the client will have placed great reliance on it or acted in reliance on it. This is quite understandable and as the adviser progresses they will gain confidence in their ability to offer advice.

There are two aspects to this concept of advising confidently. One is that an adviser should be able to assure their client that they know their subject area and are experienced in dealing with similar situations.

The second is having the confidence to know their limitations.

In other words if a client presses an adviser for advice but the adviser needs to consider the matter further or pursue some further research, the adviser should have the confidence to be able to decline to advise in detail until they are in a position to do so. It is more beneficial to indicate to a client that there are areas to explore prior to offering advice than to feel obliged to advise on a matter outside the adviser's areas of knowledge and/or to offer incomplete or inadequate advice which will not be of benefit to the client.

The adviser should, however, always be prepared to advise and not to avoid doing so, which might be the case with someone relatively new to advice work. There would be no harm in discussing advice you wish to offer to your client with a supervisor or a colleague and/or drafting it out to be checked by you and them prior to sending it to or discussing it with a client.

Plain language

Given that advice will be so important to the client it will be necessary to ensure that it is communicated in a way in which the client can understand it. In particular, if the advice includes explaining how a court case or a legal claim may develop, any legal jargon should be avoided at all costs and, if written, the advice should be broken up into sections. It is perfectly possible to offer advice to a client which involves law in a way in which they can understand. Two examples are offered below as to how Ada might advise Cathy on her unpaid wages problem. Clearly the second example will be more accessible to the client.

> 1) The Employment Rights Act 1996 requires that claims to the employment tribunal must be made within the relevant statutory time period (which is three months from the date of the deduction) failing which the tribunal will have no jurisdiction to hear the claim unless there are extenuating circumstances.
>
> 2) Employment law requires you to send in a claim for unpaid wages no later than three months after your employer failed to make you this payment. An employment tribunal will normally not be allowed to consider a claim made after this time but they can do so if they are given a good reason for the lateness of the claim

Professional attitude

The client will expect their adviser to adopt a professional attitude when giving advice. They will expect the adviser to put advice, favourable or unfavourable, in neutral terms and not to comment on advice they offer. If, for example, the client feels they have been badly treated by a third party and the adviser agrees with that, and advises that they can take action, the adviser should not take too much of a partisan approach in relation to that third party.

The adviser must tread a fine line between adopting a sympathetic stance and an empathetic one. The client does not require the adviser to step into the client's shoes, emotionally or practically, and will expect the adviser to offer a positive way out of their problem which may well include the client being able to obtain a just victory over an abusive or unpleasant opponent.

In addition, if the client finds it hard to be objective about other individuals in the case, such as their opponent's adviser or a housing officer, the adviser may feel exactly the same but must not reveal this to the client. Instead the adviser will sympathise with how the client feels but the approach he or she should take is to assure the client that they will take steps to deal with that person's actions on behalf of the client and thus remove from them the stress of dealing directly with that person. The adviser must also adopt a non-judgmental approach to their own client, for example by not expressing a view about their apparent inability to keep up their rent payments.

It may be that the adviser can do nothing to change other peoples' behaviour and they may need to explain to their client that a person's attitude may well be defensive if they are themselves angry or upset about being involved in the client's problem. This is an aspect of the adviser taking from the client part of the burden of their problem. Part of the adviser's role is to take an objective stance to aspects of the client's case, such as other personalities, which the client finds is adding to their distress.

9.4   Contexts in which advice is given

Different contexts in which advice will be given

It should be noted that advice is not always given to a client in formal setting or indeed in the same way. The most common contexts in which advice will be sought and given will be during a telephone call, either to an existing client or as part of a telephone advice session or as part of the interviewing process.

There may also be more informal contact with clients where they will be seeking advice. This will include travelling with clients to accompany them to meetings or court hearings, waiting with clients for meetings or hearings to start and possible chance encounters with them, for example when they call into the adviser's organisation to leave messages, collect information or leave documents or letters for their adviser.

It is important therefore to be aware of this range of advice-giving contexts and also whether it matters that some contexts are more formal than others and whether that affects the way in which advice is given and the type of advice which is given.

The general rule is that any advice given to a client, no matter in what context, will count as advice. Just because it takes place in an informal setting will not change the fact that it is advice and it is likely to be regarded by a client as being of equal importance with advice given in a more formal setting.

Levels and style of advice

Comprehensive advice

The level and style of advice will vary according to the context in which advice is being given. As part of an interview, or in a letter or during a telephone advice session, a client should be offered comprehensive advice on the likely outcomes and prospects of success taking into account the facts and issues relevant to their case. This comprehensive advice needs to relate to all these matters and will be offered as the main service to a client or, when there is further contact, at the outset of their case and as it develops. This advice should not be offered in an informal setting as it is too important a feature of how the adviser relates to their client.

Supplementary advice

At various stages there will be the opportunity or the requirement to offer a client advice in much smaller segments which relates back to the overall picture the adviser has painted in their comprehensive advice or which develops the advice already given. Even where this is given in an informal setting it should be recorded by the adviser (see section 9.5 below). See opposite for examples.

Cathy Clark, after receiving comprehensive advice from Ada on her outcomes and prospects of success, may have a number of supplementary issues she might raise with Ada. She might raise them arising out of Ada's comprehensive advice or as part of a further milestone towards the resolution of the case. In the former situation her questions might be hypothetical. She might ask:

- What are my chances of keeping my flat if my boyfriend Ben doesn't loan me any money after all?
- What if the housing officer refuses my offers to pay off my rent arrears?
- What if my ex-employer denies that I am owed any wages?

Ada will need to clarify any advice she has given in relation to the possibility of Cathy facing court proceedings from her landlord for rent arrears where no agreement can be reached. She will also clarify with Cathy the fact that if she starts a case against her employer for unpaid wages she will need to prove her loss and deal with any denial that money is owed. She will need to find any documents which might help to prove her claim.

After she has seen her housing officer Cathy may tell Ada that the offer she has made to pay off her rent arrears has been accepted as long as she starts payments straight away. She might then ask Ada:

- How I can I start to make payments off the arrears straightaway if I am paid a week in hand at my new job?
- What if I don't make all the required payments and there is a shortfall?

Again Ada will need to clarify advice about the possibility of court proceedings being commenced against her for rent arrears and the view the court might take of her landlord for refusing to agree to an offer to pay off the arrears.

Practical advice

At all stages of the adviser/client relationship the adviser will also be offering practical advice to their clients. Clients will need to know for example:

- how to prepare for a meeting or court appearances – what to bring and what to wear;
- how long interviews or meetings are likely to last;
- whether they can take friends to meetings or court hearings;

- who will help them in an emergency if the adviser is off sick or the advice agency is closed.

All these and a range of other issues will be part and parcel of advice-giving and should be recorded internally but not always externally to a client.

9.5   Recording advice

As indicated throughout this chapter the recording of advice is an essential part of the adviser's skills. It is important for a number of reasons.

Why record advice?

- the adviser needs to have a clear record of their advice to refer back to;
- the client also needs a clear record and will want to be able to refer back to advice given by their adviser to see how it fits in with the chain of events;
- the adviser is likely to need to record advice in order to maintain a source of funding for that advice service;
- the adviser needs to demonstrate to their supervisor that their advice is relevant and helpful;
- the adviser may be absent or taken ill and the organisation will need to see the record of their advice in case another adviser has to step in;
- the organisation will have insurance in place in relation to the possibility of negligent (wrong, inappropriate or inaccurate) advice being given to clients, and insurers will need to see the record of advice given where there is a complaint or claim raised against the adviser and/or the organisation for the advice given.

What to record

There are two aspects of recording. The first is to maintain a clear record of all contact with the client that is legible (if handwritten), faithful to what was said and agreed, and records events and contact with the client in a logical sequence.

The second aspect is to record in writing advice given by the adviser to the client. This not only means the advice that the adviser would normally also record in a letter to the client but all aspects of advice, including supplementary or later stages of advice to match the progression towards resolution, as well as in some cases practical advice.

Where advice is not followed up in writing to a client, for example because it was brief supplementary advice clarifying how court cases work, it should nevertheless be recorded.

How to record

The way in which the adviser will record their client contact and advice is likely to partly depend on how a funder may require recording to take place. An adviser will need to be aware of what these requirements might be. It will also depend on what systems the organisation has in place for recording. Many advice organisations now have on-line case management systems for recording certain aspects of the adviser's work (see chapter 13) as well as files or folders for each individual client.

In spite of these varied approaches to recording client work and advice there are still some general guidelines which can be followed to ensure that the recording process is consistent and comprehensive.

In this chapter and chapter 3 we have looked at the information which goes out from an adviser to their client, what it should cover and how that should look. Later, in chapter 13 (Case management) we shall see what Ada's own file or folder or on-line system is likely to have in it and how it should be organised. Before reaching that point, the next chapters will continue to outline and analyse the adviser's skills.

Recording client work and advice checklist

Method of recording
- Are you recording by handwritten notes or on a computer?
- Is it a combination of both? Decide what information needs to go into a computerised case management system and what hand written notes or letters need to go on the client's file.
- Does the computer record show what other classes of information can be found on the file?
- Does the file or folder cross refer to computerised recording where used?

Timing of recording
- Are you recording as you interview clients?
- If so, are you still able to engage with the client?
- Are you recording later?
- If so, have you diarised when you need to record these actions or advice? (If possible this should be on the same day as the client work was done)

Style of recording
- Are you writing in a clear accessible way? Could another adviser understand your records?
- Are you using jargon-free language?
- Is your style of recording free from commentary or personal opinion?
- Do you use the same style for all clients? If not is there a good reason for this?
- Do you have a hierarchy of detail? In other words providing full details of everything your client tells you about their problem and less detail of your explanation to them of a well known piece of information, eg where to find a tribunal office or what forms to use to make court claims?
- Are you thinking of your client reading your advice letters as well as what your funders or organisation requires you to put into letters?
- Are those letters easy to follow and logical?
- Is it clear in your letters at which point you are offering advice or is it hidden in 'next steps' or 'your instructions to me'?

CHAPTER 10

Impartiality, independence and confidentiality

10.1   Impartiality

Definitions and frameworks

The adviser who acts fairly and freely for their client will need to ensure that they have no personal involvement in a case or with a client which will prevent them from acting in an objective manner. In addition impartiality carries with it the wider definition of ensuring that choices about who an adviser helps and how they offer their services are free from considerations which might be discriminatory and embrace an inclusive approach to serving the local or wider community.

Equality and equal access to services

Any organisation which is regarded as being in the public sector and which helps and advises its local community will need to be mindful of its obligations under anti-discrimination laws. There are now duties on what are described as 'public authorities'[1] to promote equality in relation to the provision of public services in respect of race, gender, disability, and most aspects of religion. There is also a requirement in law not to discriminate on the grounds of race, religion, gender disability, age and sexual orientation in relation to the provision of goods and services. An advice agency will be providing goods and services and voluntary sector advice agencies are also likely to come within the definition of an organisation providing a public service.

Advice-giving organisations will adopt equal opportunities policies and procedures which ensure that they do not discriminate on the basis of any of the prohibited grounds in terms of who they offer their services to and how they provide those services. Reasonable adjustments will need to be planned for disabled users of premises and services to enable them to access these on equal terms.

Furthermore, the organisation's equal opportunities policy is likely to embrace a consideration not only of who makes up the local community, ensuring that all sections of that community obtain equal access to the organisation's services, but also ensuring that 'hidden' members of the community have equal access. These individuals may include the housebound, deaf or hard of hearing or those who represent a small minority ethnic group unlikely to be able to communicate in English or with a limited access to interpreting services due to the minority nature of the language they communicate in.

---

1   As defined in the Equality Act 2006.

The adviser's stance

An adviser will need to be aware of their organisation's policies and of equal opportunities principles. They may also require training in delivering an advice service in a diverse manner. This training may include awareness of differences in client groups and the support which some clients may need to access the service.

Part of the principle of providing equality of opportunity involves the concept of all clients receiving an appropriate service and one which is offered equally. As we saw in chapter 4, clients will present themselves to advisers in different ways and some can be more demanding of an adviser's time and patience. In order to maintain impartiality, the adviser needs to find the right approach to a client who, due to their limitations, is more demanding of their adviser's resources. The adviser may also find that clients will from time to time border on the obstructive or express irritation or even anger with their adviser or their opponent, owing to the stress associated in dealing with the difficulties inherent in their case. The adviser needs to be prepared to assist in shouldering the burden of stress arising from dealing with a difficult problem or opponent.

From the adviser's standpoint, the adviser should at all times maintain impartiality towards each and every client they offer to help. The adviser will undoubtedly feel a stronger affinity with some clients than others due perhaps to the nature of the client's problem or the way the client communicates with their adviser. Such partisanship, however, should not be overtly demonstrated in the way the adviser deals with that client as this is likely to conflict with the adviser's duty to act impartially for all clients.

Impartiality threatened

When it comes to the client expressing themselves forcefully, perhaps due to stress, nerves or anxiety, the adviser will need to decide first that they are able to continue to act or advise. They will be able to do so where the client does continue to cooperate with their adviser. Where the problem is instead more substantial and may involve the client being abusive or expressing prejudicial attitudes, the adviser may need to explore this with the client to assist in the continuance of impartiality. Although it would not be necessary to do this in all cases, where there are problems which arise with good client communication the adviser will be able to outline to the client the following principles:

- The adviser is impartial. They do not have any personal interest in the case or the client.
- The adviser nevertheless will do all in their power to relieve stress and anxiety for the client by helping to shoulder the burden of the client's case.
- The adviser and the client will need to communicate freely and this process will be helped by agreeing appropriate language.
- The ethos of the organisation is to treat all clients and service users equally and that this includes a commitment to equal opportunities and a use of language which reflects a tolerant approach to diversity in the wider community.

Where there are such communication difficulties with an individual client, it may assist for the adviser to write a letter to that client in which these principles are outlined and to invite the client to comment on them and to agree a helpful way of communicating.

It will sometimes be hard for an adviser to maintain their impartiality in the face of a client who appears to be acting discourteously or expressing views which are different from the adviser's views. However, an adviser should never assume that they can automatically withdraw from a case as soon as such behaviour occurs. They should be asking themselves why this behaviour has occurred, if it is going to the root of the adviser/client relationship and destroying it so that the adviser has no choice but to withdraw.

If it falls short of such damaging behaviour the adviser will give the client the opportunity to consider with their adviser planning ways in which they can freely and constructively communicate with each other and clearing up any misunderstandings which might have occurred.

To illustrate this are two examples of statements which might be made to an adviser by a client:

> 'I'm fed up with you telling me that my court case is going to have to be put back – why don't you change the record?'
>
> 'I've been coming here so that you can sort this case out for me and so far you have done nothing – you're useless!'

The first statement is in reality a complaint about a situation which the adviser may not have any control over. Court cases are often adjourned against the wishes of one or both parties involved in the case and for various reasons. It appears that the client is involved in a court case which they want to see progress and they have expressed clear annoyance that progress is being halted. The client does not appear to be blaming the adviser for this state of affairs; they are saying how angry they are that this is the situation they are in. It is a case of 'shooting the messenger' – berating the bearer of bad news. The adviser should explain why the case is being put back and what if anything the adviser can do about it.

In this case, the client may not wish to see an end to the relationship but they have been rude and blunt in how they have expressed their frustration. The adviser will attempt to set down some ground rules for a courteous approach to communications between the adviser and their client but at this stage is unlikely to form the assumption that the client has lost confidence in their adviser.

In the second statement a clearer message is coming across. The client is indicating that the adviser has not followed instructions or taken any steps on behalf of the client. They are also demonstrating a lack of confidence in their adviser by referring to them as 'useless'. This may leave the adviser with no option but to withdraw from the case. If this is a 'one-off remark' the adviser may, depending on the circumstances at the time, be prepared to give the client the benefit of the doubt and assume it was said in the heat of the moment. The adviser will point out the potentially serious consequences of it to the client. If it is not a 'heat of the moment' remark or is part of a series of actions or remarks which point to the client displaying a lack of confidence in their adviser the adviser will be entitled to withdraw from the case. They may write a letter as set out overleaf.

Hopefully the need for writing such letters will arise rarely if at all but they may need to be written if the adviser cannot continue to act for this client with any degree of impartiality due to a lack of confidence being displayed by the client in the adviser's ability to advise or assist them at all.

Two clients with conflicting interests

Another allied but slightly different angle to the question of what might impact on an adviser's impartiality arises in relation to what is known as a conflict of interest. This has already been referred to in chapter 8 (at section 8.5), explaining circumstances where the adviser may be placed in a position of not being able to assist two separate clients because of their close links with one another or their opposing interests in a case.

Dear Client,

Re: Your case

I refer to our meeting at court on 30 September in which you raised your voice and stated to me that I had done nothing to progress your case and was 'useless'. Both I and my colleague Jack Carter heard you make this statement.

Unfortunately this is not the first time that this has happened and I refer to our last interview in my office on 28 September when you told me that you thought you should have a more 'experienced adviser'.

I have formed the view that these remarks indicate that you do not have confidence in me to continue to act as your adviser in this case and am therefore writing to withdraw as your adviser. I have discussed what appears to be a request for another adviser with my supervisor, Jack Carter, and he has confirmed that I have the sufficient experience to deal with your case and that there is no other adviser in our organisation whom it would be appropriate for you to see.

I referred you to our complaints service in my introductory letter of 10 July.

I will keep all copies of all correspondence and documents on your file and will be happy to forward those to any new adviser you decide to instruct upon receiving your written authorisation for me to do so.[2]

Yours sincerely,

Ada Adams
Adviser

An example of this might be where a local advice organisation provides legal advice and support to another community organisation. The advice agency is approached by the wife of one of the members of that community organisation with claims of domestic violence. In this example there are two possible clients. One is the community group that the advice agency already advises from time to time, and one is the individual coming for help with a domestic violence problem.

If the agency does start to offer her some help or advice they may have a potential conflict of interest as between her and her husband. They are both potential clients of the advice organisation. In this situation the agency will speak to the second potential client, the wife

2   See chapter 14 for the procedure in referring a client to another organisation.

with the domestic violence issue, and tell her of their relationship with the community group. It will be explained to her that the advice organisation cannot assist her and can refer her to another agency for help with their problem. No matter where the adviser's sympathy's may lie they must retain their impartiality in relation to the client who came to them first.

10.2 Independence

An adviser, or the organisation they work for, should be free to act independently for their clients. This means that they must be free from any outside influence which seeks to affect the way in which the service is offered and/or to whom it is offered.

There can be areas in which this independence can be threatened and advisers will need to be aware of these situations and understand how to deal with them.

1) *An organisation which is funded by another organisation or statutory body*
Clients come to the advice organisation for help in taking action against the funding body.

> **Example**: a local advice agency receives funding from its local authority. The local authority is also a large local landlord. The advice agency will advise and assist the employees of the local authority in employment disputes against the authority as an employer.

2) *An advice organisation governed by a board of trustees or a management committee.*
Clients come to that organisation for help in taking action against other organisations in which members of the advice organisation's governing bodies are also involved.

> **Example**: The advice agency has a claim against a local community organisation as an employer for unfair dismissal of one it its employees. A senior manager of that organisation also sits on the management committee of the advice agency.

Although the independence of the advice agency may be queried as well as their freedom to help the client in these situations, the adviser will be free to continue to assist the client in each of the above examples. There is no conflict of interest in that there are no other clients involved. The only challenge is that the other body or individual may seek to influence either the adviser or the client themselves by indicating that the adviser should not assist the client due to the organisation's links with that body or individual. This of itself is not sufficient reason for an adviser to withdraw from the client.

10.3 Confidentiality

Defining client confidentiality

The principle of keeping confidential a client's affairs is central to the adviser/client relationship. Any information which is given to the adviser by the client should not be disclosed by the adviser without the client's permission.

Levels of information

There are different levels of information which will be exchanged between a client and their adviser. Initially the adviser and the client will agree from each level what information is appropriate for the adviser to disclose to an outsider or they will agree on information which neither party in any circumstances will disclose to another. The different levels are:

1. Facts of the client's case: what happened to them?
2. How the client may have suffered loss or hurt as a result of what a third party has done or failed to do and what the loss or hurt entails for that client.
3. Personal information about the client, their medical, financial or family details.
4. Information the client gives the adviser regarding what others say to the adviser about the client's situation.
5. The advice which the adviser gives to the client (see chapter 9).
6. The client's further instructions to the adviser: what steps the client wishes the adviser to take based on the advice given to the client by the adviser.

Advice and client privilege

The adviser has no obligation to disclose to any third party the advice they give to their client, or the discussions surrounding that advice-giving (see level 5 above). The adviser should not only explain this to their client but also let the client know that the client has no obligation to tell anyone what their adviser advised them or what discussions took place around the adviser giving the client advice. This is known in legal circles as client privilege or privileged information and for a lawyer it means they have no obligation to tell anyone (including a court of law) what passed between them and their client as part of the process of offering advice.

There are, however, often debates about which information is truly privileged and there are occasions when a summary of the advice given to a client may usefully be offered to an outsider (with the client's permission). It is in this context that more of an examination should be made of these different levels.

How confidentiality operates

The notion of what is confidential can be agreed from time to time between the adviser and the client. This might operate as follows:

Facts

The adviser may be authorised by their client to disclose facts to an outsider as relayed to them by their client in order to clarify with that party what exactly happened or what their client is saying happened to them. This often happens where there is a dispute as to what the true facts of a situation are.

Losses

The adviser will in all probability need to relay to an opponent what their client's losses are or how they felt about what happened to them where the client is making a claim for losses or compensation.

Personal information about the client

On the face of it this information is highly sensitive. However, there may be circumstances where it would be appropriate, with the client's consent, for an adviser to disclose it to a third party. This might be for the purposes of giving substance to a claim for an injury (medical information) or to support a claim for benefits or an offer to pay off rent arrears.

Commentary

If the client's comments regarding what others say about the client, their problem or case are necessary to show a difference in opinion as to what happened or what the client did, they may, with the client's consent, be relayed to a third party as part of the client's instructions to the adviser. This is likely to happen in an attempt to encourage an open debate on the issues which the client is seeking to resolve.

Advice to the client

The discussions surrounding advice-giving need never be relayed outside the adviser/client relationship. Often however, with the client's consent, the adviser will offer a summary of the advice offered to clarify the client's stance or what action the adviser or client mean to take to resolve the client's problem.

Further instructions to the adviser

As indicated above, these are likely to arise out of the advice relayed to the client. The client's further instructions can in appropriate instances and with the client's consent, be relayed elsewhere. If for example the adviser says that a client has a good chance of recovering money, and a sum is discussed, that sum can be relayed to a third party in the context of the client's instructions to their adviser to accept that sum or near that amount.

Checking on instructions and maintaining confidentiality

Because client confidentiality is so important, advisers should if at all possible send drafts of letters to their clients which their clients have asked them to send to their opponent or an organisation the adviser is dealing with on their behalf. Where time does not allow for this, the client will authorise the adviser to send the letter in the terms agreed between them and receive a copy of the letter sent. By checking letters and e-mails which the adviser intends to send on the client's behalf the client is able to satisfy themselves that the adviser is not only following their instructions but is also keeping confidential the matters which they have agreed will remain confidential. By the same token if a phone call is to be made it should be discussed between the adviser and client before the adviser makes the call.

It will not be necessary for an adviser to clear all external communications with their client before sending them out. For example, if the adviser and the client agree on a schedule (or description) of the client's incomes or losses and the adviser is then going to send it on to a third party as agreed between them, the client is likely to authorise the adviser to do this in advance. Another example would be where the adviser is sending off copies of documents which the client has agreed need to be shown to a third party. The rule of thumb is that the closer the communication is to the heart of the issue or case, and the more it requires the adviser to summarise the client's instructions or their advice to the client, the more likely it is that it should be approved by the client before it leaves the advice organisation.

Case study: letters which deal with levels of information

To illustrate how these levels of information are used in the context of confidentiality, letters are set out overleaf from our case study which pass between Ada Adams, the adviser, and Cathy Clark's housing association landlord regarding the question of Cathy's rent arrears.

Letter from landlord to Cathy

The following letter has been sent to Cathy from the housing association and she has brought it to Ada for advice and assistance in replying:

Ms C Clark
1 Railway Street
West Side
Middleton

20 July

Dear Ms Clark

Re: Your rent arrears

Further to your meeting yesterday with Mr Green, your housing officer, we write to formally respond to your offer to pay off your rent arrears.

The arrears stand at £500 and you have offered to pay off £5 a week on top of your weekly rent of £45. Unfortunately we cannot accept that as being a reasonable offer as it would take too long to discharge the arrears. We are also concerned that you stopped paying rent for a period last year for no reason, which gives you an unreliable payment record.

You told us that your boyfriend would lend you money and that you were starting a new job in the near future and also that you were considering taking your ex-employer to court for money they owed you.

We do not accept these to be sufficiently stable arrangements. In addition it has come to our attention that you own a car which indicates a lifestyle which should support a much higher level of repayments.

We are willing to accept an additional sum of £20 a week to pay off the arrears failing which we are prepared to commence court proceedings.

We look forward to your response.

Yours faithfully

Westside Housing Association
4 The High Street
West Side
Middleton

Ada's advice

After discussing the letter with Cathy, Ada's advice to Cathy is summarised as follows:

- The figure of £20 proposed by the landlord is too high for Cathy to afford due to the uncertainty of her income and her other debts.
- The court would in any event be unlikely to find it a reasonable basis on which to make a court order requiring Cathy to pay off her arrears once it is made aware of all Cathy's circumstances.
- Nevertheless the court could make an order in those terms, which is a risk.
- In any event Cathy risks being taken to court if she fails to agree to pay off the arrears at £20 a week as proposed by the landlord.
- In trying to negotiate a figure for paying off her rent arrears, Cathy should not make promises that a third party (her boyfriend) will be able to assist in paying them as in reality she does not have full control over his actions.
- Furthermore she has no guarantee at this stage that she will recover any money from her ex-employer for the unpaid wages.

Cathy's instructions

Cathy's further instructions to Ada are:

- Cathy still would like to offer less than £20 a week and suggests £10.
- Cathy suffered from a depressive illness last year but at this stage does not want her landlord to be told about this. This was why she stopped paying the rent for a period. This had never happened before or since.
- The car is her mother's which she occasionally uses to drive her father to hospital appointments. She thinks this should be relayed to her landlord as otherwise they will get the wrong idea about her disposable income.
- She does not want to tell them that she has other debts at this stage although she accepts this might have to come out to avoid the court case.
- She can get a letter from the supermarket to confirm that she starts the job next week and what her wages will be.

Reply from Ada Adams to Cathy's landlord

The following letter is the reply which Ada sent to Cathy's landlord housing association on her instructions once it had been checked and read over by Cathy.

Compass Advice Centre
6 East Avenue
West Side
Middleton

28 July

Dear Sirs

Re Cathy Clark: rent arrears

I am instructed to reply to your letter to Ms Clark dated 20 July.

My client accepts that there was a period last year when her rent payments ceased. This was due to matters beyond her control. You will note in any event that this was the only time during her tenancy that payments were missed. We have therefore advised her that this does not disclose an unreliable payment record.

You should be aware that Ms Clark does not own a car but occasionally has use of her mother's car when she takes her father to hospital for appointments.

She notes what you say about the stability of the financial arrangement she offers. For this reason she believes a reasonable sum should be agreed. She would be able to pay £10 a week from her wages as from the end of the month. She is willing to forward to you her employer's letter of offer and start date and details of salary and is offering to pay the arrears off out of her wages.

We have advised Ms Clark that this is a reasonable offer and that your proposal would not be looked upon favourably by a court.

Yours faithfully

Ada Adams
Compass Advice Agency

In this letter it can be seen that some of the advice is reflected in instructions relayed on behalf of Cathy and that information from most of the levels above is passed on. It can also be seen that information which is truly confidential is not passed on.

CHAPTER 11

Counselling in the context of giving advice

11.1   Counselling in the context of advice work

It may seem odd that the subject of counselling is dealt with in the context of the skills of an adviser whose role is to offer advice and not to counsel. Counselling is a specialised field of expertise and there is no assumption made in dealing with this topic that an individual engaged in advice work has or should have the necessary skills of a trained counsellor.

Nevertheless it will be inevitable that the adviser will be required to counsel their clients in the context of advice work. Their clients will often be under great stress and may have problems (other than the problem that they bring to their adviser) which they are likely to mention or even to ask for help with.

Additionally, the very act of advising or taking action for a client is going to involve the adviser's client in more stress, not least because they have to keep facing the problem they want to resolve. They may continue to be thrown up against an opponent whom they feel to be unsympathetic to them. Advisers are likely to counsel their clients in a range of situations. They will be counselling their clients not only in terms of supporting practical solutions or ways forward for the client but also supporting the client through the problem which they bring to their adviser. The adviser therefore needs to know not only the contexts in which they will be counselling their client but also what skills they will bring to this process which differ from the skills of a trained counsellor.

11.2   When counselling will take place

Talking about the problem

Many clients will find it hard to talk about the problem that they bring to the adviser. They may be surprised to find that their adviser will require them to talk about it in considerable detail. Their assumption may have been that the adviser would be able to carry out whatever researches are necessary and take the matter forward. While that may be true, it will also be the case that their adviser will need to know every detail of the client's problem and surrounding circumstances and will need to come back to the client on a regular basis to check out facts and events especially if these are challenged by others.

The adviser needs to explain this to the client and offer the client the support they will need to provide all the details of their problem which the adviser needs to know, which for the client can often be a painful process.

Other underlying features of the client's problem

There will also be other aspects of the client's life which may under-lie the problem which they have come to see their adviser about and which will come out as part of the advice process. It may be that the problem has resulted in negative effects on the client's health or well-being. The adviser needs to know how to deal with this aspect of advice-giving.

Money worries

Money worries often underlie the problem which a client talks to their adviser about and can be hard to face up to and deal with. Debt advisers and counsellors will be able to tackle these for a client but an adviser who is dealing with another aspect of the client's life will find that they will need to adopt a sensitive and supportive approach to this aspect of their client's life and will need to ensure that their client has confidence to talk to them about these matters.

This may be necessary in order for the adviser to deal more effect-ively with the problem that is brought to them by ensuring that it is taken account of in the advice given. It may also be necessary for the client to get expert help in relation to money worries in order to assist in the process their adviser is being asked to resolve.

Discrimination claims

In some areas, such as employment problems or complaints about goods or services, clients may feel that they have suffered discrimi-nation. They may find this difficult to talk about and the adviser will need to devise strategies for gaining the client's confidence so that they are able to face talking about the situation and how it has affected them. Clients may find it hard to face up to the place of work or the shop and write letters or talk to people there if that is a suggested way forward.

Fear of persecution

For an asylum-seeker the key issue is their well-founded fear of per-secution that forced them to leave their home country. Many asylum-seekers will have experienced or witnessed extreme poverty, hardship and torture. As well as knowing the support systems that clients can be referred to for the effects of these experiences, the adviser will need to create the right environment for that client to be able to tell their adviser what they need to know in order to pursue the asylum claim, eg their housing problem or their health and welfare concerns.

Homelessness

The fact of a client's homelessness may be the problem they need help with or it may be that they are a homeless client who has other problems they need advice on. In addition, a client may be faced with losing their home perhaps due to domestic problems or debt. The need for shelter is one of the basic human needs and the stress and anxiety of having nowhere to live have a significant impact on how an individual can cope with their day-to-day lives. Advisers will need to be sensitive to that consideration when dealing with either that issue or another aspect of that client's problems.

Illness and stress

A client may be suffering from a medical condition, including one which is stress-related, that has no particular impact on the case or problem. Alternatively, clients will often report stress symptoms as a result of the particular problem arising from, or as a result of, working with their adviser to get it resolved. Symptoms such as irritability, sleeplessness and anxiety or lack of ability to concentrate are common for those suffering stress. In the context of advice, such symptoms will often be raised by a client or noticed by an adviser. The adviser should be able to take an active part in minimising the effect of those symptoms by the supportive approach they take to the client.

When advising at the outcome of the client's problem

The adviser will reach a point with their client when they are not only telling the client what steps they have taken for their client to resolve a problem or case, but what decisions have been made by others in relation to the client's case or problem. This may include tribunal or court orders where the outcome has been reached. The adviser will need to explain, in layperson's terms, what a meeting, court or tribunal has decided in relation to a client's case.

At this point the adviser themselves may only have just reached the conclusion of the case or only just themselves been told of a decision. They may find the outcome is different from what they had advised their client might happen. It may be better or it may be worse. If worse, the adviser may themselves be upset or exasperated at what they see to be a wrong or unjust decision. These feelings will need to be put aside in relaying that outcome to the client. The adviser must be prepared to counsel the client on this outcome and its implications for the client. The adviser will discuss with their client what this means to the client in terms of their future life or livelihood.

11.3 Skills of counselling as an adviser

As indicated at the start of this chapter, the adviser has no need to take on the mantle of the trained counsellor; their primary role is to advise the client and assist them in reaching a helpful resolution of their case.

Nevertheless, in the contexts which have been outlined above, the adviser will need to:

- engage in listening skills;
- be prepared to identify hidden problems;
- show sensitivity to the client's needs;
- be aware of when the client may need expert assistance; and
- offer the client appropriate support in the context of the advice being given.

Listening skills

As we have seen in chapter 8, listening skills are an inherent part of how the adviser interviews and advises their clients when interviewing. Part of the adviser's skill will be not only to seek out the facts of the client's situation but to be aware of other influences which the client brings into the adviser/client relationship and to be able to counsel the client in the context of these influences having an impact on the process which the adviser is dealing with for the client.

Hidden problems

It may be that the client has something underlying the problem that they have come to talk to their adviser about. If the adviser shows themselves to be patient and to allow the client to volunteer information they will be able to find these hidden problems and offer the client appropriate support.

As long as the client trusts the adviser and realises that these hidden problems may be relevant he or she should have the confidence to tell his or her adviser what they are.

Hidden messages

In the example opposite, the hidden problem has a direct impact on the conduct of the case Ada is helping with. There are other situations where the client will be burdened by something which does not have a bearing on their case but which is affecting them.

Examples may be illness or being unhappy due to a recent life event such as bereavement. If a client is finding it difficult to communicate or to concentrate, the adviser should consider tuning in to the possibility that the client has something else important happening in their lives. One or more of the following strategies may assist:

- An adviser may indicate that they are aware that the client does not appear to be able to cope at this particular time. The adviser will say that they do not necessarily need to know the reason for this but may invite their client to return on another date to meet the adviser if they are finding this interview hard to deal with at this particular time.
- A client may then want to tell their adviser what the other problem is and the adviser should express sympathy and again suggest that the client (if timetables allow) may want to see their adviser when they are feeling better.
- If the client asks for help with another problem which falls outside the adviser's remit, the adviser may be able to indicate that they will do all they can to refer the client elsewhere for help with that problem.
- If the client tells the adviser what the problem is but wants to continue with an interview the adviser must be sensitive to the client's needs.

Showing sensitivity to the client's needs

If a client is struggling to function in dealing with their adviser for any of the above reasons, the adviser will need to be sensitive to what their client's particular needs are. This is a part of their counselling role and part of the process of showing the client that they can trust their adviser to be supportive as well as to resolve their problem.

Case study: example of identifying hidden problems

- In the case study about Cathy Clark we need to ask how it was that Ada was able to identify Cathy's other debt problems. How did she come to tell Ada that 'she was not very good with money'?
- As it turns out this information is helpful to the advice Ada will be giving to Cathy about how much she should be offering her landlord to pay off the arrears. The line of questioning which Ada will have pursued will involve her giving Cathy the opportunity to tell Ada anything else which she believes will help Ada to resolve her problem.
- Ada may have put the question to Cathy in one of the following ways:
  - If we offer the housing association £10 a week to pay off your arrears is there anything I need to know which might make that hard for you in the future?
  - If we look at your finances to see if you can afford to pay off the arrears at the rate of £10 a week where should we be looking for problems or gaps in your finances?
  - Is there anything you might want to tell me about your finances to help us agree a sum to put to the landlord that you can afford?
  - Is there anything else you think I should know about to help you in deciding if you can afford this sum each week?

All these are in essence a version of the same question – what more can you tell me that is relevant to what we are discussing but which might be hidden from sight at present?

The client's needs may be

- *physical* – a question of comfort and ability to sit or stand for periods of time;
- *emotional* – a question of how the client reacts to information or expresses their feelings;
- *mental* – a question of what stress symptoms the client shows, such as anxiety or inability to concentrate.

In each of these situations the adviser shows awareness of the client's needs by a range of strategies. These will include:

- In the interview situation offering the client breaks and refreshments.
- Where a client becomes visibly distressed, offering the client a quiet time alone and a drink of tea or water and suggesting that the interview is re-convened when the client has recovered.
- Where a client shows anxiety symptoms or appears to be finding it

hard to concentrate, offering the client the opportunity to discuss or explain in so far as this will give their adviser the opportunity to advise and support in the best way possible.

- Offering the client the opportunity to have shorter interviews.
- Offering to send letters or questionnaires out in advance of any subsequent meeting or interview which will help the client to prepare in advance.

Being aware of when the client may need expert assistance

An adviser will not always be able to deal with the other problems which a client has and which they need assistance with.

For this reason the adviser should know when that problem needs expert help. If it is clear that the client has chronic debt problems or is suffering from psychological trauma as a refugee or someone suffering from discrimination, the adviser should be able to suggest other avenues the client can explore to resolve those problems.

How far the adviser can go with a referral will of course depend on the geographical area they are operating in. In rural areas it will be harder to find referral sources.

Many advisers build up good links with other local organisations which allow for referrals and if the adviser can demonstrate to the client that they have these links it will give the client confidence to see if they can approach their various problems 'in the round'.

This holistic approach to advice work means not only that the client has the opportunity to resolve more than one problem but it also allows for advisers, with their clients' consent, to liaise over the best way each can resolve the aspect they are advising on.

Offering the client appropriate support in the context of advice-giving

This concept is at the heart of a positive and supportive approach to giving advice. A client may look to their adviser for some support in how they feel about the problem they are discussing with that adviser. While the adviser needs to be impartial and professional they will often indicate their support for how the client feels about or is coping with a problem. At the outcome of the case the adviser may be asked to offer encouragement to a client who may be looking to use a positive resolution of their case to enhance their lifestyle or choices.

One problem solved may solve another

A client may decide that they are going to face another problem as a result of the adviser resolving one of their problems. They may decide that if they can remain in their home then they will be able, for example, to seek work or look for ways to ensure they can pay rent. These issues are often discussed in the context of a strong adviser/client relationship and it is often the case that the client will be able to say that the help they have received on the problem they came to their adviser with gave them the encouragement to tackle other problem areas in their life.

Avoiding undue influence over a client

The adviser must take care, however, to avoid their professional status influencing a client in an inappropriate manner. If, for example, advice can result in recovering money, the adviser may be asked to suggest ways in which their client might best want to use that sum. This is not a question the adviser should answer and they should make it clear that they would not wish to influence the client in any way. However, if the client him or herself suggests that the money could be used to buy children's clothes or toys or to pay off debts, the adviser as part of their counselling role may be able to encourage and support options which will enhance the client's lifestyle or reduce their indebtedness.

Counselling clients on outcomes

Once an outcome is achieved on a client's case, the adviser/client relationship is likely to terminate.

Nevertheless, many clients will not only seek to know the exact meaning of an outcome or a decision but what it means for them as an individual in their future lives. Many clients come for advice because they want to see justice done as well as obtaining an outcome that is beneficial for them. So their interest is not only in what effect an outcome has on them but what it will mean for others who have been involved in their problem or case.

They may ask their adviser to predict how an outcome will affect their future lives, financially or practically. The adviser must be careful to give only a general picture. The adviser will, for example, be able to indicate that a person who wins a homelessness appeal will be offered accommodation but will not be able to predict with any great accuracy what type and location and how re-housing may affect their quality of life. Such an expectation on the part of the client should be put into context by the adviser indicating that their role is limited to resolving the client's problem or case. It will be important to 'draw the line' and agree when the adviser will no longer be involved with their client, although they will offer encouragement and support to their clients for their future plans and actions.

In relation to others involved in the problem, the adviser will not be able to predict with any particular accuracy if justice and a helpful outcome for the client will change the behaviour of an opponent. They should, however, be able to discuss and agree with their client aspects of the process they have gone through and aspects of the outcome achieved which have positive as well as negative elements. This will involve encouraging the client to take a positive and realistic view of how this process has changed them and may be able to change others.

CHAPTER 12

Supervising and being supervised

12.1   Functions of supervision in advice work

There are a number of reasons why advice work requires supervision. An effective system of supervising advice work means a whole range of essential organisational goals are being met, not least of which is best practice in the provision of advice.

The way in which supervision works will vary from one organisation to another but there are general principles which will apply and which should be followed. Note that supervision is a two-way process and that an adviser who is being supervised needs to fully engage in that process, and to understand that its purpose is not only to give them structures and support but also to continue to develop organisational goals which the adviser is a part of.

The key functions of supervision in an advice organisation, which will be examined below, are:

- to support advice workers in their advice work;
- to offer ways of developing the advice worker as an individual;
- to ensure that the organisation's internal and external targets are met and complied with;
- to demonstrate compliant systems of operation to external funders or potential funders and to managing bodies;
- to develop an organisation's capacity, including looking for best practice and developing it.

Supporting advice workers

A supervisor's primary responsibility, like that of an advice worker, is to provide an appropriate and helpful service to the organisation's clients. A supervisor in any event is likely to be a senior case worker or a manager who is themselves familiar with the process of giving advice.

In addition, the supervisor supports the adviser to provide a quality service and to develop their own capacity to the full. The supervisor's role is to identify strong and weak areas of functioning as an adviser, to challenge deficiencies where necessary and to support and encourage compliance with the organisation's agreed goals. For this reason the supervisor and the adviser should have a positive and constructive relationship as they are both working towards these common goals.

The supervisor should be fully familiar with the organisation's requirements in relation to case management and client care and any specific recording requirements, some of which may have been dictated by external funders or by the organisation's managing body. They will use this knowledge to support and develop a new advice worker or to ensure that existing advice workers are comfortably within the frame.

The supervisor will not require each adviser they supervise to work in exactly the same way as they will need to make allowances for differences. Some advisers will have strengths in the way they communicate in writing, others perhaps in face to face client contact. Some will be more confident at negotiating resolutions (see chapter 16) and others at counselling distressed clients. All these strengths and skills will be built on by the supervisor as part of supporting the adviser they are supervising.

Offering ways of developing the advice worker

The supervisor is not only concerned with the advice worker in the context of the organisation's goals but will also look for opportunities to develop an advice worker's strengths as an individual both within an organisation and more specifically as an advice worker. The supervisor is not just looking to 'tick boxes' for good practice compliance but also to develop an organisation's capacity. This is also achieved by having advice workers who are confident in what they do and who are engaging in the process of advice-giving, seeing achievement goals for themselves within an organisation.

If, for example, the supervisor finds that an adviser wishes to develop skills, perhaps in relation to tribunal representation, they may see if those skills can be developed by that individual within the organisation.

Complying with targets

External

It will always be the case that the organisation will have targets to meet that are both internally and externally driven. External targets are likely to include demonstrating to the funders that goals are being met in relation to:

- time spent on individual cases;
- the range of advice work offered;
- sectors of the local community the organisation services; and
- demonstration of outcomes achieved for clients.

These will be borne in mind as part of the supervision of the service. In any event it is usually a requirement of funding for an organisation to demonstrate that supervision procedures are in place.

Internal

There will be internal targets which an advice-giving organisation will have set. They should include:

- meeting stated aims of reaching out to the community served by the organisation;
- meeting the requirements of the organisation's equal opportunities policy in how the work is carried out;
- ensuring that health and safety risk assessment procedures are complied with and acted upon;
- generating policy documents or reports arising out of the organisation's work

Demonstrating compliant systems

A key feature of advice supervision is accountability. The supervisor will be able to show to those that manage or fund organisations that the systems it has developed for smooth running are working well and are being followed by all the relevant personnel.

The supervisor does this by working with case workers or advisers on a regular basis to ensure that there is a smooth flow in work and that the work maintains the same standards throughout. Even if advisers deliver their services in varying ways and with different clients (such as doing off-site advice sessions for a particular sector of the local community), how they work should be capable of being incorporated into an organisation-wide system.

The systems worked with must be the same across the organisation. For example, the ways in which advisers record their work and the supervisor monitors that work should be the same.

Developing capacity and best practice models

Supervision does not just encompass the notion of checks and balances on existing procedures. It is also about developing a service or an organisation by being able to draw out good models of working and expanding the capacity of an organisation.

The supervisor will be part of a chain and will be aware that above them in the chain the management of their organisation will have an obligation to maintain standards and ensure that the organisation is sensitive to the needs of the local community and can adapt to those needs.

For example if a supervisor notices that housing advisers are regularly encountering clients in debt on a particular housing estate where rents have recently been increased, a number of approaches might be made by that supervisor:

- advisers may be offered more training on dealing with debt as part of housing advice;
- referral systems to advice on that topic which the advisers are currently using will be tested for effectiveness;
- management may be invited to consider the policy aspects of the rent increase with the social landlord concerned as a joint initiative to reduce homelessness and indebtedness.

By the same token, an adviser who has been able to raise the link between debt and arrears with the social landlord may have begun a best practice initiative to work on reducing the link which the adviser's supervisor can encourage and take forward within the organisation.

12.2 Key elements of supervision

A supervisor should not only be familiar with the organisation's systems for advice-giving but should themselves have had or continue to have experience of using those systems and in the process of advice-giving.

Even though there will be different systems in each organisation there are still key elements to effective supervision which will apply to all advice-giving organisations.

Familiarity with systems

The supervisor should demonstrate that they are familiar with the organisation's systems and knows how they operate. In this way the supervisor is testing procedures out both as an adviser and as a supervisor. This demonstration of experience will help build rapport between the adviser and supervisor.

People skills

A supervisor should have the necessary interpersonal skills to develop a rapport with those they supervise. This includes the requirement to be accessible and flexible not just during formal supervision sessions. They should be supportive to advisers, both in relation to how they work within the organisation and in relation to any work/life balance issues the adviser may have. Supervisors should be non-judgmental in recording observations. Neutral and non-critical language will be used in discussions and records, even where offering criticism or voicing concerns. For example, if an adviser is regularly failing to make written records of their client contact or interviews this will need to be stated as such with reasons why it must be done and a time-frame to review whether this omission has been corrected. This can all be stated without using phrases such as 'Ada knows she should be doing this' or 'Ada can't seem to understand that she should be doing this'. Supervisors should be aware that those they supervise will be shown file reviews or supervision records. The supervisor should have received specialist training on this and other aspects of supervisory skills.

Ability to monitor and review casework practice

This is the practical aspect which must be applied by the supervisor to the process of conducting advice work. Whether the organisation's systems are manual or computerised, or a combination of both, the supervisor should ensure that the process of conducting and recording advice work or casework is properly maintained by the adviser in accordance with the agreed procedures.

Discussion and appraisal processes

As part of ensuring that casework practice is properly maintained, the supervisor's skills will include discussing with advisers how their work is progressing, working with them to iron out problematic or unproductive ways of working and appraising their progress, both formally as instructed by the organisation and informally as part of encouraging the adviser's development. For more on appraisals, see section 12.5.

Mapping and recording objectives

The organisation should have in place an objective-setting and monitoring process that will enable the adviser to build on experience. These could be ways of dealing with practical obstacles to effective advice work, such as an adviser's apparent inability to record their work fully or to complete cases within agreed time-frames. They could be related to the adviser's overall development, such as an objective to develop a particular skill or line of advice work. While the first of these is more about keeping to the agreed systems, they are both relevant to the organisation's capacity-building as well as that of the individual adviser. It is part of the supervisor's role to agree objectives and targets for development or improvement with the adviser and to ensure that these are followed through.

Reviewing progress and processes

The supervisor will regularly be reviewing the adviser's progress in terms of how they are conducting their advice work. The supervisor should also be reviewing the process of supervision to ensure that it is working properly and that it highlights areas of good practice and any deficiencies in advice work. The supervisor will record this aspect as well as the day-to-day progress of file or case reviews. Part of the review process will be to monitor the adviser's progress in a developmental way and demonstrate a supportive approach to the adviser.

12.3 Being supervised

Understanding the procedures for supervision

The parameters of supervision should be clearly identified, ideally by way of an office manual or equivalent. This should answer the following questions:

- Is it supervision of file conduct alone?
- Does it include appraisals, meeting and setting objectives?
- Will it include goals for personal development?
- Is it linked to any performance pay or review systems?
- How often will it take place?

- Where will it take place?
- How much preparation will the adviser be required to do for supervision?

Building rapport

Ideally the adviser should get to know their supervisor at times other than those set aside for formal supervision. This will assist in the process of the adviser building up confidence in the process and to develop a good rapport with their supervisor. This will be especially helpful if the supervisor and adviser need to work informally together in that relationship, where the adviser can ask questions of, and seek support from, his or her supervisor as an integral part of doing advice work.

Where a good rapport is built up it is likely that the supervisor can work constructively with the adviser on his or her personal and professional development. Ideally the adviser should be able to regard their supervisor as a mentor and someone who can support them when they have problem areas in exercising their advice-giving skills which may arise or need resolving at times outside the formal supervision times. The rapport will also have the effect of ensuring that each client gets the best possible service.

Using clear recording systems

A supervisor will be looking to see that internal systems for conducting advice work are being complied with by the adviser. Whatever those systems are, it will be important for the adviser to ensure that their work is properly and promptly recorded at all times and not just when supervision is likely to happen. In this way they are demonstrating not only that they are ready to be supervised at short notice, but that their client's file (paper or otherwise) shows a clear trail of activities which would be understood by any other member of the organisation at any given time.

Even though an adviser may have set up his or her 'system' of working and it is one which appears to work well, there is always the possibility that another person has to step into that adviser's shoes at short notice or that external audits will be conducted. As well as the need to comply with an organisation's tried and tested ways of working these are additional reasons to be able to demonstrate to a supervisor that recording is consistent. The record should be understood easily by someone not familiar with the client or even with that area of advice work.

Knowing when to seek help and support

It is important for the adviser to understand the purpose and process of supervision. The supervision process is not there to act as a prop, or safety net. It may occasionally fulfil that function but the primary aim is to support and develop good practice in advice work.

The role of the supervisor is not to compensate for the adviser's lack of ability or to take on the work they have not done. The supervisor's role is to build the adviser up to full capacity to function within the organisation's framework for giving advice.

An adviser therefore needs to know that they can seek help and support when they are dealing with new or unfamiliar territory, such as unforeseen developments in a case or a difficult situation arising with a client. The supervisor can use their experience to attempt to resolve difficult issues. Once they have agreed general or specific objectives with an adviser they should expect the adviser to work independently towards these objectives.

Thus an important part of being supervised is to know what situations would be aided by intervention and which situations the adviser should be learning to manage as part of good practice. An adviser who is unsure when to seek help and support from their supervisor should be asking that question of their supervisor to help them understand the boundaries of responsibility in the supervisor/adviser relationship.

12.4 Core supervision activities

When supervising advice work the process will ensure that the adviser is compliant with all the strands of conducting advice work set out in the chart below. How this will function in practice will vary from one organisation to another; nevertheless, all these activities will be incorporated into the supervision process.

The activities referred to in the chart overleaf will also be reflected in an effective case management system which will be examined in part 4 of the book.

Chart of supervision activities

File reviews	Legal or good practice compliance	Organisation compliance	Client care	Adviser development
1. Evidence of file-opening and closing procedures being followed	Evidence that the adviser is aware of and complying with the relevant discrimination laws, health and safety regulations and data protection law	Evidence that the adviser is aware of and complying with organisation requirements, especially concerning equal opportunities policies and procedures, health and safety of staff and users, complaints procedures	Evidence that clients have been introduced to the service and are aware of their role in the adviser/client relationship	A system of reviewing adviser's work for each client and recording on the client's file the process and outcome of those reviews
2. Evidence that interviews, telephone calls and other contact is being recorded	Evidence of privacy checks being adhered to and that confidentiality rules are being observed	Evidence that organisations' recording systems, including time recording, are being complied with	Evidence that all advice, including oral advice is set out in writing to the client	A system for appraising the adviser's progress in terms of the processes of their advice work and any goals or objectives which the supervisor and the adviser may have agreed
3. Evidence of the adviser acting impartially, maintaining client confidentiality and a constructive client – care relationship	Evidence that the adviser is aware of good practice and/or professional rules in relation to conflicts of interest and interpersonal skills of advice-giving	Evidence that the adviser is complying with he organisation's guidance on checking for conflicts of interest and acting impartially	Evidence of an organisation-wide commitment to client-related skills	A system in the organisation for updating or training advisers in procedures in these areas and in client care skills

File reviews	Legal or good practice compliance	Organisation compliance	Client care	Adviser development
4. A system of keeping files which shows a clear order of advising and taking steps for a client	Evidence that the adviser is aware of the importance of file management in relation to being transparent and accountable about the process of giving good advice	Evidence that the system complies with organisation's set procedures	Evidence that the client is aware of any timetables or time limits and/or their part in meeting these	A system which encourages high standards of advice and record keeping and accountability for the processes of giving advice
5. A system of diarising dates and key deadlines, and informing clients of these	Evidence that the adviser is complying with legal or other requirements to keep to deadlines and is aware of the consequences of not doing so	Evidence that this system is linked to or part of a central system for recording key dates and deadlines	Evidence that clients are aware of key dates and deadlines and of any active steps to be taken by the adviser and/or themselves to comply with deadlines	A system for supporting advisers in relation to any pressing targets and any related time-management issues the adviser may have
6. Evidence of appropriate advice being given to the client	Evidence that the adviser is familiar with the area of law or advice being offered, by reference to research methods being referred to on the file	Evidence that the organisation is arranging for training and updates for advisers in their areas of advice	Evidence that advice is appropriate to the client's needs	A system for ensuring advisers are receiving training and development in their subject areas

12.5   Appraisals

Appraisals of individual staff in an organisation may take place as part of supervision or may, more usually, be carried out as a separate process, which will involve more input from the adviser being appraised than the process of supervision usually involves.

The appraisal process may in some organisations be linked to features such as performance ratings or pay reviews. In the advice context it is more likely to be used to evaluate progress and identify areas of strength or weakness or an individual's training and/or developmental needs or aspirations. The process will be looking at how that individual is regarded by the organisation in terms of their development and how they see themselves in terms of their progress and how they would like to develop within their role and the organisation as a whole.

Appraisals may only take place once or twice a year. The appraiser may be a supervisor or possibly a peer of the appraisee. The format will be set out in advance in that both the appraiser and the appraisee will be thinking about the same issues in advance of the appraisal. The appraisal will usually be non-judgmental and will involve open questioning about work-related goals and objectives met or planned for the person being appraised. Issues coming out of an appraisal meeting, such as a need for training or other work-related development will be agreed and signed off and a time-frame will be set for meeting the agreed goals and for reviewing them in another appraisal setting.

Case progression and resolution

Case management

13.1 Introduction

Good practice in relation to case management has been refined and developed over the years. In the advice sector the requirement to have a system in place for managing files is often partly dictated by external funders and the procedures they need to see operating within an organisation they fund. For example, solicitors firms or advice agencies who receive public funding from the Legal Services Commission are required to demonstrate that the organisation has in place systems for organising, monitoring and reviewing clients' cases and the files they work on for each client.

A case management system is evidence that the organisation has clear procedures in place for organising and running files and for managing enquiries, advice and casework. It should be consistent across the organisation and be the basis for good practice and compliance with legal requirements (see chapter 12). The case management system should be able to show, for example, that the organisation is aware of, and is complying with, its obligations in relation to how information is processed, so that the requirements of the Data Protection Act (DPA) 1998 are being complied with.[1]

Most advice organisations, no matter how small, will have what is generically described as a case management system, whether it is paper-based or a sophisticated software package. These will apply even where the adviser is not offering advice which is solely legal advice.

Case management focuses on a requirement for the adviser to demonstrate that certain steps and checks are taking place on each matter they handle for a client, that there is a file opened for each matter or case and that they have a system for managing all the files or cases which they are responsible for. The procedures necessary are:

- file-opening procedures;
- progressing a case; and
- file-closing procedures

---

1   Under the DPA 1998 the keeping of a filing system is likely to be regarded as 'processing data'. Certain rights arise out of that in relation to rights of access to information and privacy, for example. Guidance on the DPA 1998 can be obtained from the office of the Information Commissioner at www.ico.gov.uk.

13.2 File-opening procedures

There are a number of procedures which should be followed in embarking on a new case or file for a client. Even where the advice may only cover one interview or a telephone call, there will still be a requirement to record that contact and the outcome of it.

It may be that many of these procedures will be recorded on a computer-based system. Where this is the case, most advisers will also have a paper based file. It will be important to retain a paper-based file, not just to store papers or documents relating to the client's case, but more specifically as a back up to the computerised file. Copies of letters sent and received (usually referred to in recording activities as 'Letters In' and 'Letters Out'), memos of discussions, records of telephone calls and copies of e-mails will not only be stored onto a computerised system but also form part of a paper file. A number of aspects of ensuring that files opened comply with good practice are set out below.

Contact details

The full contact details of the client should be recorded on the file. These details should be accessible yet not externally visible in order to retain client confidentiality. The name and reference number of the person advising the client should also be easily accessible so that others in the organisation are aware of who is responsible for that case.

Check for conflict of interest

There is a difference between the notion of impartiality and independence and a potential conflict of interest which an adviser may have in offering to advise one client where they may already be advising someone close to that person, such as a spouse or an opponent. The adviser must be watchful for any potential conflicts and be aware of these from the outset. The possible conflict will not only arise from the adviser's own casework but in respect of all the clients currently being assisted by that organisation. The system for checking for any potential conflict should therefore be across the whole organisation. See further, chapters 8 and 10.

Funding and costs

Where the client's case is being funded, or is part of a project or group of cases being funded, by a funding body or perhaps under the Legal Services Commission's Legal Help Scheme, these details need to be recorded on the file and notified to the client. In addition, where the client may be involved in a court case they need to be informed of any possible implications for them in respect of paying legal costs, where it may be applicable. Costs in the context of court proceedings are referred to in chapter 18. They are not dealt with in any detail in this book but they may be relevant to how an adviser needs to conduct a case or exercise their case management skills, in which case the adviser will ensure they know the particular aspects of the rules regarding costs which will apply to a particular client's case. Organisations will have detailed procedures in place about funding including, where relevant, those required by the Legal Services Commission. The adviser's general requirement is to set out for the client at the start of the case any information the client needs to know about funding and costs to be incurred by the organisation and to update regularly as the case progresses. This information will usually be recorded on the file in the form of a letter. Initial and introductory letters to a client may combine funding and costs information with the other client care information required (see below), or there may be a separate letter sent out which only covers the question of funding and costs.

The organisation's procedures

As outlined in chapter 5, part of what the adviser will do when they first meet their client will be to introduce the client to the organisation. They will need to explain to them:

- what service the organisation offers;
- what service it can offer to that client;
- what the adviser's role is in the organisation;
- who the adviser is supervised by;
- what the adviser can hope to achieve for the client;
- how the client can access the service; and
- what the client can do if they are unhappy with the service or aspects of it.

This latter piece of information assumes that the organisation has in place a complaints procedure and that any user of the service can be informed about how to use the procedure.

It may be that all of the above is contained in one document, perhaps a leaflet or a standard letter, and it may also be that clients are required to sign and return these letters to signal their understanding of what service the organisation is offering to provide for them.

Key dates and milestones

The file must record in a distinct area of the file what the important dates are in respect of that particular matter. Even though this information will be communicated to the client in letters and in oral advice it will still need to be recorded in a separate place on the file. This is to ensure that the adviser looking after the file has a constant reminder of these dates and also it is to enable anyone else in the organisation, such as a supervisor, to check to see that key dates are noted and acted upon. Where someone else has to step in at short notice for an adviser, this information should be accessible for that person.

The file must cross-refer to a central record of key dates which the organisation should be maintaining. We have referred in chapter 6 to a 'double diary' system, where the adviser can set a reminder in advance of an important date so that they can do any necessary preparation for it. The idea of a central diarising system is to ensure that both the organisation and the individual adviser take responsibility for the important dates for each of its clients.

As well as key dates, which might be deadlines for providing information or court or tribunal hearing dates, the file should record any possible milestones. These may be dates when a child reaches their legal majority (ie 18), which might affect a housing application or a benefit calculation, or the date on which a divorce petition is made absolute by a court, or when an employee's notice runs out.

Statement of client confidentiality

Client confidentiality is an essential part of the adviser/client relationship. The adviser will have discussed with the client the fact that they will keep their client's details, and information they receive about or from their client, confidential and this should be recorded to the client, usually as part of the opening client care letter (see chapter 3).

Contents of the client care letter

The initial client care letter should contain the following information arising at the outset of the case:

- the organisation's procedures, including its complaints procedure (unless contained in a standard letter or leaflet);
- the adviser's name, availability and supervisor;
- statement of confidentiality;
- key dates and milestones; and
- funding and costs.

If the adviser has met the client with a view to advising or taking on the case, this letter will also contain the adviser's initial advice to the client.

In addition, the letter should set out what steps it has been agreed that the adviser and the client will each take to progress the matter toward the client's desired outcome.

An initial letter should restate to the client what the client's desired outcome is. In addition it will explain, as agreed between the adviser and the client, what steps the adviser will take in order to achieve that desired outcome for the client, and any alternative approaches which the client may have agreed to, such as pursuing a court claim if a letter fails to achieve the desired result. See the basic example of a client care letter set out in chapter 3 (pages 43–44).

13.3   Progressing the case

Once a client's file has been opened (which may include the above information being recorded onto a computerised case management system) there are a number of procedures on that file which will need to be transparent. Evidence of a number of activities should be shown.

Advice letters

Advice given to the client should be recorded in letters to the client. We saw in chapter 9 that even where advice is not given in the formal surroundings of an interview, it should nevertheless be recorded. Where a case is changing in its development, advice on the merits (prospects of success) and likely outcome should be updated in writing.

Documents in order

Any documents which are a part of the case should be kept in a separate section and should be kept in a logical order. Original documents should not be kept but copies taken and the originals returned to the client. If you are holding a client's original documents (such as a passport or a child's birth certificate) as part of their case, they should be kept in a secure place such as an office safe.

Details of experts used

If an expert such as a barrister, surveyor or medical consultant is approached for an opinion in order to assist in the resolution of a client's case, there should be a note of where they are drawn from and that this complies with the organisation's diversity policy in selecting appropriate outside experts. There should also be a record that the client has been consulted on the selection of an outside expert to assist with the case.

Prioritising activities

It should be clear from the file which activities are to be considered more important, either in terms of what they mean to the client or in terms of how quickly they need to be carried out. For example, if there is an urgent deadline for a court hearing this will be prioritised over the client's request for a referral to an organisation for advice on an unrelated matter. The file should ideally have a sheet of priority activities, with deadlines in ranking order of importance, which is regularly reviewed by the adviser. This is also part of the adviser's function in managing their time and their entire caseload.

Updates for the client

The file should show that the key dates and milestones which need to be recorded in a separate part of the file are being followed through as agreed. This is likely to be in the form of a file note attached to the correspondence section of the file or contained in the advice letters to the client. In addition, if costs are relevant to the client's case they should be referred to regularly and an update given to the client of the position on costs. Furthermore, if the adviser has drawn up a case plan (usually where the case is likely to be complicated and have a number of difficult matters to resolve) this should be regularly reviewed and referred to so that the client can see how the case plan is progressing.

File reviews and supervision activities

A supervisor will monitor and review an adviser's handling of a case. Whichever form this supervision takes it should be recorded on the file concerned as well as in a central record in the organisation. Forms can be devised which can cover both specific file review and general supervision of advice activities and these can be kept in both a file and a central place. Sometimes they will also be copied onto an adviser's personnel file.

13.4   File-closing procedures

For each individual client file or matter there should be evidence of an organisation-wide system of closing that file and taking certain steps to bring the matter to a conclusion.

It may be that once the client has achieved their desired outcome of recovering money, obtaining housing or compensation, there appears to be no more to be done. The adviser may at that stage be anxious to get on to seeing new clients and may be tempted to lay the file aside until they have time to close it properly.

The adviser must see the closing of a file as being part of the conduct of that case and properly reach the end of the process for the client. This will adhere to the organisation's requirement for proper case management and in some cases also to the requirements of external funders. It is often the case that, in closing a file, matters which have been overlooked, such as the repayment of money to a client or the return of documents to the client, are picked up and need to be acted on. If these matters are remedied sooner rather than later the adviser will be avoiding possible claims or complaints against them or their organisation.

A number of standard procedures should be followed in closing a client's file.

Recording the outcome

A letter should be written to the client which records the final outcome of the case and which then states that no further steps will need to be taken by the adviser. This not only gives the client the opportunity to have a written record of the outcome but it is also a way of confirming that both the adviser and the client are of the same mind, that it is indeed the case that there are no loose ends to be tied up and that there is nothing which the adviser has promised to do which may have been overlooked.

Dealing with compensation

Where the client has been paid any compensation by another party, the file-closing procedure and final outcome letter to the client must clarify the exact position and must make a 'clean break' in that there should be no money owing to, or owed by, the client when the file is closed.

Dealing with documents

Where the adviser has possession of any original documents belonging to a client for the purposes of conducting that client's case, these documents must be returned to the client and a note of that made in the final outcome letter to the client.

Archiving the file

Many organisations have a system of archiving a file at the end of the client's case. Legal practices will be required by the terms of their insurance cover as legal advisers to keep files for at least six years after the case is closed. This is because the legal limitation period for any claim against that legal adviser is normally six years. Advice organisations that do not have legally-qualified staff will also have in place insurance arrangements for the advice they give and their insurers may also require files to be kept for a six-year period after they are closed. The adviser will be told what the insurer's requirements are in their organisation and who will take the responsibility for archiving files which have been closed.

13.5 Managing a caseload within an organisation

As well as ensuring that individual files are run systematically, the adviser will also need to have a system which operates across all their files and cases to ensure that there is a proper balance of time and resources spent on each file and that they have a clear overview of how their caseload is operating at any given time. A number of approaches have already been suggested to assist in the management of a caseload. These include developing a system for time management, for dealing with competing priorities and for having a consistent approach to how files are run, including files which are properly organised and easily accessible.

Each individual will develop an ability to manage more files as they become more experienced. A new adviser is also often dealing with a new area of advice work and will naturally take longer to gather information and consider and research the advice they will offer. As time goes by, situations become more familiar, as do procedures. There are, however, a number of aspects of managing a caseload as part of an organisation-wide system. These will be discussed below.

13.6   Linking clients' matters

It will always be necessary to ensure that helping a client does not lead to conflict of interest where the organisation or the adviser may be helping someone linked to that client.

By the same token it will be necessary to ensure that if a client has more than one case or query with the organisation that any links can be made across that client's files which are necessary in order to provide a seamless service for that client. For example, if a client has a rent arrears problem being dealt with by the organisation's housing adviser and a housing benefit query being dealt with by the debt and welfare benefits adviser, then the links between these two matters across the organisation should be made, as the resolution of the housing benefit query will inevitably impact on the amount of rent arrears claimed by the landlord.

13.7   Operating within a centralised system of file management

The organisation will have a standard approach to how files should be run and managed by advisers and this will also be underlined by the supervision process. Each file should have key information such as key dates and deadlines kept in an accessible place on each file and the way in which the papers are organised in a file should be the same throughout the organisation.

A template for how paper advice files should look across an organisation would be as follows.

Documents

These will be kept in date order, starting with the earliest at the top of the pile and working down towards the latest. Where there are a lot of documents they should be kept in a separate file from the other information set out below. Some advisers will put their documents into a ring binder and will use dividers or markers to flag up the different types of documents they have in that file. These may be divided into copies of letters sent to the client by a third party, copy office memos, or e-mails, policy documents, rent statements, wages slips, etc.

The sooner the client's copy documents can be put into order the better, because it will help the adviser to find documents easily and also to prepare for any hearings or meetings or to send the client's copy documents out to another party, where required to, in an ordered and coherent form.

Court or tribunal correspondence and orders

If the client's case involves court or tribunal hearings, the correspondence they send to the client and/or the adviser and the orders or notices of hearings should be kept separately, on a tag or in a clear plastic folder above the documentation. In addition, a file may have on it copies of 'pleadings', the documents which include a client's statement of case or defence to a claim (see glossary in chapter 18 for a description of pleadings in the context of court proceedings).

Correspondence and file reviews

Letters passing between the adviser and anyone else on the adviser's file should be the first thing that the file has visible when it is opened. It usual for that pile of correspondence to be pinned together at the top left hand corner of the pile in a way that it can be added to (with the open end of the pin on top). Unlike the order in which documents are placed, the correspondence should be put on this pile in reverse strict date order, that is the most recent letter received or a copy of the most recent letter sent out on the top, with the earliest letter sent out or received at the bottom. Any reviews of the file and its progress, whether carried out by the adviser themselves or by a supervisor, will be in this section filed on the date they took place or these may be kept in a separate part of the file or in a file review folder.

Key dates

As already indicated, some information must be easily accessible on a file. One method will be to keep a pre-printed label on a file which will cover the following information by way of the adviser ticking and dating when the relevant steps have been complied with. The steps are:

- when key dates are and the dates on which they were complied with;
- dates when the client has been informed and updated with any costs information;
- the client's contact details (these should be accessible but not visible, for reasons of client confidentiality);
- when any file reviews or supervision sessions have taken place.

Centralised diaries as part of the system

There should always be a central record kept of each adviser's key dates and deadlines to allow for an overview of those essential steps to be taken on the client's files. This may be in the form of a handwritten or an electronic diary. Someone in the organisation will take responsibility for ensuring that it is up to date and accurate and that advisers inform that person of each client's key dates.

13.8   Strategies for managing the adviser's caseload

As well as being a part of a system of running files that feeds into and out of a centralised set of records, the adviser will also develop strategies for managing all their cases effectively. These will include:

Reviewing size of caseload

The adviser should regularly review how many enquiries matters or cases they are handling at one particular time. If there are targets in the organisation requiring so many cases to be taken on by each adviser these will need to be met within the resources that the adviser has and that the organisation can offer them by way of support and back-up. Alternatively, where the adviser is fortunate enough to be able to set their own goals and targets, they will be reviewing these to ensure that they have a sufficient caseload or one which is manageable for them, given his or her own resources and time. Where they have cases ready to be closed, these should be counted in as all the necessary closing procedures will need to be followed before the adviser can say that the file is no longer their responsibility.

Systems for prioritising work

The adviser will need to have a system which allows him or her to ensure that they can prioritise work which is urgent and at the same time ensure that all the steps needed are carried out as and when agreed. This system is one which needs to be an integral part of the adviser's working pattern and the adviser will need to be constantly reviewing and updating their priorities. How they set up the system will vary, but using a diary or an electronic diary with reminders is probably the most effective. A system which involves piling papers or files on the adviser's desk in some sort of priority can be unreliable and quickly lead to confusion.

Handling complaints

It is never pleasant to be on the receiving end of a client's complaint. An advice organisation's procedures will, however, always allow for complaints to be made and properly dealt with and each adviser or person who comes into contact with the public will be aware of that procedure and will communicate it to their clients. This procedure will be communicated to each client at the outset of the case by the adviser. Knowing the organisation's complaints procedures and ensuring clients are aware of them from the outset is part of keeping an overview of managing each client's case.

In addition, if a client expresses unhappiness or concern which falls short of a complaint, the adviser should have a strategy of openness and willingness to listen which they apply to all of their clients. So, if a client says that they have rung their adviser more than once before they speak to them or does not think they have understood what their adviser's advice letter really means, the adviser should be able and willing to remedy these shortfalls by listening to the client and explaining fully what the reason for any apparent delay or unavailability was, and reiterating advice given, ensuring that the client understands it.

Quite often, as soon as a client says that they want to raise something, an adviser thinks they should immediately refer the client to a complaints procedure. Common sense and good communication should, however, precede formality to ensure that a good adviser/client relationship is formed and maintained with all the adviser's clients.

CHAPTER 14

Signposting and referrals

14.1   The meaning of signposting

Identifying the client's problem

Many advice organisations operate in such a way that they have to offer a range of services to ensure that they can maximise the often limited resources they have. As well as offering advice and sometimes assisting with court or other hearings, they will offer a service enabling as many people as possible who approach them to find help and support within the local community. This will usually be known as signposting and the signposting service will usually either be done as part of a telephone advice session or as part of a reception service.

Many clients or potential clients who approach an organisation for help or advice are unable to label their problem or to identify it in such a way as to be able to seek the right course of help to get it resolved.

A signposting service will give the problem a name and context, such as 'a right to housing' or 'discrimination suffered in employment'. It will identify for that client the elements of the problem they come to the organisation with and will provide for the client a breakdown of what their problem is and the areas of expertise that they will need to access in order to resolve the problem.

The person who does the signposting therefore needs to be aware of the various types of problems which clients will present with and how these can be resolved. They will need to know if a specialist adviser will be able to resolve more than one problem for the client and whether referrals they make for that client will contain in them information about the other referrals to be made because of the links inherent in client's case which has more than one strand to it.

Offering a service which ensures that the client can seek a resolution to their problem

A signposting service does more than identify the client's problem for them. It also does more than to explain to a client that that particular organisation does not have the expertise to assist the client. The aim is to ensure that the client is not only given the benefit of understanding and labelling the problem they came to the advice service for but is also given the opportunity to resolve it.

The signposting organisation must therefore have in-depth information about the service offered by other advice and/or legal services in the area the organisation serves so that it can properly signpost a client in the direction of those services.

The ability to refer clients to a service

It will be necessary for an effective signposting service to be aware of the resources, skills and expertise of the organisations they signpost clients to so that the client is given a forward initiative to get their problem resolved. This means that information about those external resources and skills will need to be up to date and under regular review by the signposting organisation. The client will need to be assured that the information they are given is accurate and means that they have a real option to use other resources to resolve the problem they approach this organisation with.

14.2 Skills of signposting

Identifying the relevant issues

In order to offer a helpful signposting service, the person who is signposting needs to have training and expertise to identify the legal or advice issues which the client is presenting with. On page 186 we shall see how in our case study Cathy Clark's problems came to be referred to Ada for advice. The person Cathy was signposted by was able to understand from what she said that she had problems with debt, housing, and employment.

Given that clients can often be confused, may not speak the same language as the person they approach for help or assistance, or are embarrassed or worried about discussing a problem with someone in an advice agency, the person doing the signposting should be ensuring that they are asking the correct questions of the enquirer in order to identify properly all the issues that the client needs to resolve.

Where the signposting is done face to face, a proper amount of time should be allocated to it and if possible the discussions should take place away from a public arena such as a waiting room. The client will need to see that this is a service being offered and not a means of telling them that the organisation they have approached is unable to assist them.

The adviser will then be able to ask the client sufficient questions to enable them to identify all the issues which the client needs to have resolved. Some organisations will have a checklist of questions to ask callers for help and assistance which will enable the process of signposting to take place. This questioning process will also lead to irrelevant matters being screened out so that the signposting which then follows is accurate and helpful.

Identifying the correct source of help

Once the problem is identified, the signposting service then identi-
fies for and with the client the best resources available to resolve the
problem. The following factors will need to be borne in mind:

- How much information does the signposting organisation have
  about the service offered by the agencies or other organisations
  they are signposting towards?
- Is it known whether the agencies or other organisations have capacity to see new clients at that particular time?
- Will the client be required to pay for advice or assistance?
- How far can the client travel?
- Will the client need any disabled access, language support or other
  specific arrangements to gain access to a legal or advice resource?

In addition, the client will need to be signposted in the direction of an
organisation which does have the specialist skills to resolve the type
of problem the client presents with. Websites and leaflets of agencies
should be referred to by the signposting organisation and should be
up to date and kept under regular review.

Making a match

It is essential that the information which the signposting organisation has acquired from a client is sufficiently accurate to allow for the
signposting to be matched to the client's needs. Where the client has
a number of different but possibly linked problems, they may need to
be referred to more than one organisation and the client will need to
understand where to go with each aspect of their problem.

   It may be helpful for the client to be sent or given a form which not
only confirms the way in which they have identified their problem but
also provides information about the organisation which can deal with
that type of problem and the services that the organisation offers.
This latter piece of information may be taken from an organisation's
up-to-date website or information leaflet.

Providing a service

Given the various strands of, and skills associated with, signposting,
the organisation will label it as a service when dealing with callers or
recording their work. The hallmark of the signposting service is to
ensure that the client finds a route to resolving their problem. The

adviser and their organisation should therefore have ways of testing out whether the signposting service is effective.

As well as ensuring that information they provide about other organisations is accurate and relevant, the signposting service should be conducting client satisfaction surveys in conjunction with other organisations to test out the helpfulness of the signposting service. This will allow for amendments to the service where better signposting can be provided upon review.

14.3 Referrals: internal

There is a difference between signposting and referrals. Signposting is concerned with assisting the caller or client to identify their issues and to give them information about organisations which can assist them with those issues. Although follow up is often done by signposting organisations, it is usually for the purpose of ensuring that the service being provided is proper signposting and is giving the caller or client a valid onward route to resolving their problem.

A referral is a more personal process in that the client will be specifically referred to a person or an organisation and before the client approaches that organisation or person for assistance the latter will have signalled their agreement to see the client as they have accepted a referral of the client's problem from elsewhere.

It can sometimes be the case that once an adviser has seen a client they will find that the client has a specific problem which is different from the one they are assisting on and which the client also requires assistance with. It will often be the case that the adviser can refer the client to another adviser or case worker in that organisation to resolve the separate matter.

Where this happens, the referring adviser will need to provide a file note or memo to their colleague in which they provide as much information as possible about the matter being referred. The client will of course have sought that additional help and will be giving their consent to confidential information about them being passed on to a different adviser.

The referral should contain some or all of the following information:

- a brief overview of the adviser's role in assisting the client in order to provide a background;
- any financial circumstances which might be relevant to a new case being taken on (fees payable or legal help form to be completed);

Case study: Cathy Clark

In the case study example first raised in chapter 9 we have seen that Cathy Clark is receiving advice from Ada Adams. Cathy first of all rang the local council tenant welfare service. A form was completed by a signposting worker there to allow signposting to Ada's organisation, the Compass Advice Centre.

Middleton Council Tenant Welfare Service

Signposting form

Name and contact details of caller	Issues identified by caller	Issues to be resolved	Suitability of organisations offering assistance	Check that organisation contact and service details have been provided to client	Comments / client feedback
Ms Cathy Clark 1 Railway Street West Side Middleton Tel: 01178 444382 no mobile no e-mail	> Owes back rent and under pressure from landlord > Not good with money > Feels let down by last employer	> Advice and assistance in dealing with landlord's demands for unpaid rent. > Assistance to sort out finances. > Advice on whether she has a claim against previous employer for money owed	> Parsons Solicitors (NB will charge fees) do not do debt advice > Citizens Advice in Edgeton (NB free service) 15 miles to travel >Compass Advice Centre (NB free service) do not do debt advice	Yes Yes Yes	Client reported could not get an appointment for six weeks Client said travel would be too expensive Client reported was booked in to see Ada Adams the following week but still needed help with debt problems: AA will arrange referral

- a brief overview of the matter which the client has sought the referral on with any gaps in the referring adviser's knowledge to be made clear so that they can be filled in;
- the client's contact details and the best way to contact them and the most convenient times to arrange appointments for that client (or times or days to avoid); and
- a clear statement that the client has asked for the referral and is agreeable to it being to this named adviser.

Finally a note should be made on the referring adviser's file that they have discussed another matter with the client and have referred that client to a colleague in the organisation in relation to that matter. A copy of the referral memo should remain on the file.

Linked referrals

It may be the case that the overall outcome which the client wishes to achieve will be reached by more than one person in an organisation dealing with various aspects of the client's case.

For example, if Ada Adams has advised Cathy Clark that she should claim unpaid wages from her previous employer but does not have the specialist knowledge or skills to represent Cathy in her claims against her previous employer in either an employment tribunal or a county court, a colleague in the organisation may take on that aspect. If money is recovered for Cathy as a result of that action being taken, Ada's colleague will inform Ada, as well as Cathy, of the outcome (with Cathy's consent) as this will provide a possible source of funds for Cathy to pay off her rent arrears.

14.4 Referrals: external

There are a number of circumstances in which an advice agency will tend to make referrals of clients or potential clients to an outside organisation. These will include circumstances where the referring organisation carries out the same type of work as the organisation they wish to refer the client to. The four most common circumstances giving rise to a referral will be:

- referrals where a more comprehensive service is required;
- referrals where resources are limited in the referring organisation;
- referrals to a different specialism;
- client changes adviser.

In addition an adviser should also be aware of the information they require to *receive* a referral from elsewhere.

Referrals where a more comprehensive service is required

The majority of advice agencies provide what is sometimes called first tier advice. They will either deal with their client group by telephone and/or in person and they advise them as to the best course of action to take to resolve their problem. Part of giving this advice service will also involve taking some action for that client in order to resolve the problem. The sort of action taken will include making telephone calls or writing letters to an adversary or an organisation with some control over the client's affairs.

There will, however, be occasions when the limits of those organisations' services have been reached. At this point the service will refer the client to another organisation in order to finally resolve the problem.

The most common example of this will be when referring the client to an organisation such as a firm of solicitors or a Law Centre® who can represent the client in court on the matter involved. Where these referrals are made, the receiving organisation may require a great deal of information from the referring adviser. They will need to know 'the story so far' and will need all relevant documentation in order to continue with the case. This will be in addition to the practical information concerning contact details and when to arrange appointments referred to above in relation to internal referrals.

Referrals where resources are limited in the referring organisation

In this situation it is likely that the advice organisation has the skills and expertise to assist the client with the type of problem they bring to the organisation but at that particular time is not able to assist due to a shortage of resources. Where this occurs, advice organisations will often endeavour to ensure that the client is offered an arranged referral to another organisation carrying out the same work. This is to try to meet the client's expectations of the service being offered as being available to all. It also means that if strong referral links are established with other local organisations then the organisations can work together for the good of the local community and can work with inter-referrals to assist when resources are temporarily limited in one of those organisations.

The information provided for these types of referrals may be limited. It may be no more than contact and availability details for the client with a description of the nature of the problem being referred and a note of any deadlines for action to be taken. The receiving organisation then takes the client on from the beginning and the client is not required to explain their problem to more than one adviser.

Referrals to a different specialism

This model of referral is most like the internal referral outlined above. Here the adviser has been told of a problem by their client that the adviser would like to resolve but does not have the specialist skills to resolve it. The problem may be linked to the one which the adviser is handling or it may be a separate one. The adviser may offer, as a gesture of good will to the client and to another organisation, to refer that specific problem to the organisation. The information provided will be the same as for the internal referral model.

Client changes adviser

Sometimes a client will inform their adviser that they wish their case to be transferred to another adviser whom they have already identified and who is willing to take the case on. The reason for this may not be given to the original adviser who is not entitled to know the reason unless it is obvious or is offered to them. This is a different situation from when the adviser or the client has initiated the termination of the adviser/client relationship due to a breakdown in that relationship. When a client changes to a new adviser for a different, neutral reason, and when the adviser's papers are requested by another adviser, they need to ensure that the client has given written consent to the new adviser to request the papers. This is a safeguard for the client and both of the advisers. The referring adviser should copy their entire file and send it to the receiving adviser by recorded or guaranteed delivery to ensure its safe arrival. They will then follow the file-closing procedures set out in chapter 13.

Receiving a referral

An adviser who receives a referral in any one of the situations outlined above should ensure that the client is agreeable to seeing them and that there are no outstanding matters to be sorted out by the referring organisation. They should ask the client to sign a written authorisation requesting that papers are passed on to them from the referring organisation. Lawyers or other case workers who refer cases on to each other at the request of a client will also ensure that there are no outstanding questions of costs or fees. In legally aided cases the organisation receiving the referral will usually take over the public funding aspect of the case.

The receiving adviser will expect to see papers in good order and to be clearly informed of the matters they are asked to assist on and of any work done on those matters by the referring adviser.

14.5 Keeping records

In relation to both signposting and referrals, client records need to be retained. As we have seen with signposting, monitoring of that service will mean that it can be reviewed and checked for efficacy on a regular basis.

Records should be kept of referrals in case of any need for the receiving organisation to get back to the referring organisation. Where the case will be in a court or tribunal, it is particularly important that all records of the case are kept up to date by the referring organisation. The referring organisation should have a file on the client they refer as well as a full record of the referral made, to whom, what papers were sent and the referral date.

Monitoring of referrals made should also be conducted from time to time to ensure that clients are being offered a range of options and that the referral system complies with the referring organisation's equal opportunities policies.

Case study

In Cathy's case study, we saw that Cathy had a debt problem that Ada was unable to assist with. Ada advised Cathy that a resolution of that problem would in all likelihood assist Cathy with the housing problem which she had approached Ada with. Cathy wanted help not only in maximising her income but in dealing with her money so that she did not keep getting into debt. So after some discussion with Cathy, Ada identified a money advice service in Middleton and with Cathy's consent wrote them the following letter.

Money Advice Agency
6 East Avenue
West Side
Middleton

31 July

Dear Mr Perkins

Re: Cathy Clark

I refer to our telephone conversation today in which you kindly agreed to see Ms Clark on 3 August at 10 am concerning her financial affairs.

In particular Ms Clark has told me that she would like advice as to whether she qualifies for housing benefit. This would assist in her paying her rent of £45 a week.

She also has some debts including credit card debts. She has not given me the details of these but would like you to advise her on how she can best pay off her creditors and manage her finances.

If you do advise her to apply for housing benefit I should be grateful if you would inform me as Ms Clark would like me to ensure that this information is passed on to her housing association landlord.

She would also be happy for you to disclose to me any other information or advice you can give her which would have a beneficial impact on her rent arrears or rent payments.

Yours sincerely,

Ada Adams
Compass Advice Centre

CHAPTER 15

Identifying the case and putting the case

15.1   The meaning of a case in the context of advice work

So far we have referred to the client approaching an adviser with a problem and we have seen how the adviser will need to clarify for themselves and with the client the exact nature of the problem and the way in which they will approach resolving that problem. In chapter 3 there was a reference to the adviser 'taking on a case' for a client once they had formulated the problem and agreed to share the burden of it with the client.

In advice work, client's problems are resolved at many different levels ranging from a one-off telephone call to a lengthy or complex court case. Although the word 'case' is often associated with a court or tribunal hearing, it can have a variety of meanings in advice work. It can mean:

- A file which an adviser has on a client. Advisers will often refer to the cases they are conducting or will refer to their workload as their 'caseload'.
- A matter which is in a court or tribunal system. Courts and tribunals will allocate numbers to cases when they come in to their system and they are referred to as cases whether or not a hearing takes place.
- A statement regarding a client's position in relation to an issue or legal issue. For example, the client's case is that she did not leave the luggage unattended and therefore the loss is not her fault.
- The arguments, facts and evidence which are at the core of the client's problem are known as 'a person's case'. Their case might be that they need to resolve the threat of legal proceedings arising out of rent arrears or have unpaid wages they are seeking to recover.

It is this last area that will be addressed in more detail in this chapter. The role of the adviser is not simply to identify what is the problem in terms of their professional knowledge of such matters but to set about resolving it using a range of skills and tactics.

The adviser will explore with the client how they will conduct the case for that client as well as satisfying themselves that their methodology is correct and properly researched. How the case is to be resolved – by letters, telephone calls or at meetings or court hearings – will not necessarily vary the adviser's approach to the process of identifying and putting the case for a client. There will be the additional requirement in courts and tribunals to conduct the case in line with the required formalities and rules of that particular system. See chapter 7.

15.2 Identifying the case: facts and issues

Facts of the case

As we saw in chapter 5 part of the process of taking instructions is to obtain from the client the facts of the case. This means finding out from the client what their story is, or what loss or disadvantage they have suffered.

In order to understand the client's case fully, the adviser needs to ensure that they have all the facts of the case. This may not always be possible at the outset as a third party may have information in their possession which the adviser is unable to obtain. Such facts may emerge at a later date. Nevertheless, a clear outline of facts as known should be noted down by the adviser.

The facts will include any obstacles which are in the way of resolving the issue. For example, in our case study the obstacles will be a fact that Cathy Clark owes her landlord rent, and further the fact that the landlord has refused her offer to pay off arrears at a particular level of payments.

Noting the facts

The relevant facts should be noted down by the adviser in a logical and chronological order. In our case study, Ada has been told by Cathy that she is having problems in paying rent. The situation has now become critical and, as we shall see below, there are now a number of issues which Cathy will need to resolve with Ada's help. First, however, Ada will begin to list the facts of Cathy's case in a logical order and where possible in date order (see overleaf).

Procedural, policy and legal aspects of the case

Part of the process of establishing the case will be for the adviser to carefully research any necessary background to the problem raised by the client.

Researching a rent arrears problem

A problem with rent arrears will need research into:

- the *policy* of the landlord in dealing with tenants who have rent arrears;

Cathy's housing case: noting the facts

An example list of the facts Ada would need to establish are:

- when Cathy's tenancy began;
- the rent which is payable by Cathy;
- how many missed rent payments there have been;
- when the payments were missed;
- what the exact shortfall is;
- whether Cathy contacted her landlord or they contacted her about her missed payments at the time they were missed;
- the name of the person representing the landlord she had any contact with;
- what form that contact took (meetings, telephone calls or letters);
- what discussions or correspondence there was about the missed payments;
- whether Cathy gave her landlord any reason for the missed payments;
- whether the reason may have been noted by the landlord; and
- whether Cathy has made an effort to pay off her rent arrears and if so what payments were made and when.

- the *statutes* (Acts of Parliament) which give the landlord and the courts power to repossess properties from tenants who have rent arrears;
- any reported *court cases* about the circumstances in which repossession may not be ordered by the court;
- the *procedure* a landlord must follow if taking possession proceedings (found in the relevant statutes and court rules).

Researching how to claim unpaid wages and notice pay

A problem with unpaid wages and notice pay will need research into:

- whether in *law* the client is entitled to his or her week's pay in hand;
- whether in *law* the client should have been given notice to leave his or her job and if so how much notice;
- the correct *venue* for the client to put in his or her claims, ie in the employment tribunal or in the county court;
- what *differences* there are for starting claims in either of these two venues in relation to time limits for starting, costs or fees involved and how long the cases take to conclude; and
- whether the client can *enforce* a court judgment in his or her favour if the employer fails to pay and how this is done.

See chapter 19 for how to research law and statutes. Whether or not the adviser meets with a similar problem on a regular basis they should always be reviewing their knowledge of the relevant area of law or procedure to keep abreast of any recent changes or developments.

The issues

The issues in any case will be either the matters that need resolving by an adviser on behalf of a client, or the matters which are in dispute between two parties. In the former approach to defining the issues, they are likely to be set out by an adviser for their own and their client's benefit and will usually be expressed as a list of questions which need to be answered by the adviser as part of their advice and resolution of the client's case.

In the latter approach to defining the issues, there will be a list of questions or items which two opposing parties need to resolve, either between themselves or using the assistance of an outside agency, such as a court. They will be discussed between the parties and may be set out as part of preparing for a court case. The adviser is likely to move from their internal list of questions and matters to resolve, to a more formalised and public statement of how a court, or an organisation with powers to make decisions which will affect the client, will need to approach a resolution of a given case.

Time spent in thinking carefully about the issues and setting them down in writing will never be wasted. They do not have to be set out in a particular way but they do have to be logical and relate to the facts of the case. They must highlight what it is that needs to be resolved.

15.3 Building up the case

It will be necessary for the adviser to follow a tried and tested pattern in order to build up the client's case. As we have seen earlier, at the outset the adviser may not have all the necessary facts or information they need to bring a client's case to a satisfactory conclusion. The adviser will need to keep developing the progress and structure of the case by following a number of steps:

- ensuring that the adviser has all the relevant facts and documents and that they are regularly updated and the documents kept in good order;
- regularly meeting with the client to update on any developments on the case;

Case study: issues in Cathy's case

In chapter 9 we saw the brief facts of Cathy's case. We then saw in subsequent chapters how the case is developing. We know that Cathy's landlord will not at present accept Cathy's offer of payments to clear her rent arrears. There has been little progress on the claim to the recent employer as Cathy has told Ada she has no contact details for them. Ada has referred Cathy to Phil Perkins of the Money Advice Service for help with her debt problems.

We know that Ada has advised Cathy that the housing case could go to court if the fresh offer to pay off the arrears is not accepted by the landlord. Cathy also wants to recover her unpaid wages from her ex employer. What are the issues in these two cases?

Housing case

On the housing case Ada has set out a list of questions and matters she needs to resolve for Cathy. This will be for Cathy's benefit so that it is clear what Ada will need to focus on as a way forward for Cathy. The case is not in court and the issues are expressed in a relatively informal way.

Housing case: list of issues for Ada to resolve for Cathy

1. Whether the landlord is likely to apply to court in order to repossess Cathy's flat.

2. Whether Ada on behalf of Cathy can prevent this happening by agreeing with the landlord that Cathy will instead pay her rent arrears off in instalments.

3. If the landlord did insist on going to court, whether the landlord is likely to be successful in obtaining an outright possession order against Cathy's property as a result of her rent arrears.

4. Whether Cathy or Ada as her representative will be able to persuade the court to adjourn the case until she has applied for or received any benefits she might be entitled to.

5. Whether Cathy or Ada as her representative will be able to persuade the court not to make a possession order at all or alternatively to persuade the court to postpone the possession order so that Cathy can remain in her flat and continue to pay off the arrears that are owed.

Employment case

In terms of Cathy's employment case the list of issues which Ada will draw up in preparation to take the claim forward might look something like this:

Employment case: list of issues for Ada to resolve for Cathy

1. Whether Cathy can prove that her ex-employer owes her money and if so how she can prove this.
2. Whether Cathy can prove how much money her ex-employer owes her and if so how she can prove how much she is owed.
3. Whether Cathy has a legal claim against her ex-employer for monies owed.
4. Whether Cathy is likely to succeed in her claim, depending on how much evidence she has of the money owed to her.
5. Whether Cathy will have any prospect of recovering the money awarded to her by a court or claimed in a letter on her behalf by Ada from her ex-employer.

- maintaining contact with any organisation or opponent who has an influence on the outcome of the case (for example, a landlord or employer) and ensuring that all relevant information is received from them and exchanged with them;
- agreeing with that organisation or opponent what the issues are in the case and what are the differences and points of agreement;
- continuing to research any relevant background to the case, such as policy documents, statutes or regulations;
- regularly reviewing the case with the client and ensuring that they are happy with and understand how it is progressing;
- testing out with the client how their case is standing up to further developments which emerge along the way;
- making decisions with the client about the strengths and weaknesses of their case and about strengths of the case which should be better highlighted or weaknesses which should be discontinued; and
- being fully prepared for any meetings or hearings with the client or others involved in the client's case.

All these steps will be recorded on the client's file or reflected in the way that the file is being maintained by the adviser. The necessary activities in showing on a file the progress of a case have been examined in chapter 13. In addition the above activities are some of the building blocks which underpin the progression of a case. The adviser will at all times be thinking the case through and regularly returning to it in order to ensure it progresses. Some elements of an adviser's casework will be done in the adviser's mind as they think about what they have been told and how best to build up a case for a client. Part of this thinking will involve reflecting regularly on how they are conducting the case and, where appropriate, being prepared to change direction or take on board new developments or facts as they emerge either from the client's perspective or from any opponent.

15.4   Explaining the case to the client

It will be essential for the adviser to continue to keep a dialogue going with their client in which they are regularly updating their client with the process of running their case for them. Part of that will be to ensure that the client is aware of what their role and the adviser's role is in seeing the case to a conclusion.

Clearly setting out the case for the client

As part of an initial advice letter, the adviser will have set out to the client the facts known at that time and the agreed desired outcome as well as the preliminary advice on whether and how this outcome can be achieved. The adviser will need to ensure that the client clearly understands what their case is.

Different strands of a client's case

A client's case may have more than one dimension or strand and all aspects of it must be set out so that the client understands how it all fits together. For example, if a client says that her employer has deducted pay when she took holiday leave to look after a sick child, her case will be about getting the pay restored. The adviser will explain that this is the focus of the case and will then go on to explain the agreed strategies for getting the client's pay restored or recovered. It may also be about sex discrimination if the client is a female lone parent. When she came to see her adviser the client may not have understood this additional dimension of her case as easily as the simple fact of the loss of money. The adviser, having advised on how claims for discrimination can arise, will set out for the client that part of their case and the strategies agreed to remedy the effect of the discriminatory treatment. In this example, therefore, the client's case will be about her rights to pay in her employment contract and how the same facts might also give rise to a claim in discrimination law

Explaining the adviser's role in conducting the case

Having set out for the client what their case is, the adviser will go on to explain the role which will be taken by both the adviser and the client in moving towards a resolution of that case.

Acting as a focal contact point: conducting a case

The adviser will explain to the client what they as the adviser will be doing as part of reaching the desired outcome. The adviser will, for example, make telephone calls, write letters to and deal directly with other parties or organisations on the client's behalf, and read and interpret documents for the client. The adviser will make representations to others on behalf of the client about the client's case and will argue points in relation to the client's case on the client's behalf.

Where an adviser takes a case on for a client and takes a number of steps on behalf of the client they will often refer to themselves as having the 'conduct of the case'. As well as taking various steps to resolve the client's case, this means that they are authorised by the client to make contact with others on the client's behalf.

Sometimes clients are directly approached by their opponents and find this stressful. They will need to be assured that all contact should be made through their adviser who is taking over the necessary steps of actually running the case. The client's involvement will be different as we shall see below.

Using outside expertise

In addition, when outside expert help will be required, the adviser should offer to arrange that for the client as a way of building on or supporting a client's case or preparing for a hearing or other outcome. The adviser will be able to call on experts such as doctors, surveyors or barristers to assist in proving something for the client. Each of these individuals will be able to provide an expert opinion on a relevant aspect of a client's case. For example, medical evidence can assist in proving that a client may be vulnerable or is, or was, unable to function in certain ways or carry out certain activities.

The adviser's organisation will have a comprehensive list of experts they can call on. It will need to demonstrate that there is a fair equal opportunities process for selecting an expert to give an opinion or to give evidence. The organisation will ensure that their lists are drawn from a wide pool and are representative of the community served by the organisation. Where an expert is needed on a client's case, the adviser will discuss with the client who they propose to call on and ensure that the client is a part of the decision about who is chosen to assist.

Explaining how cases are put

The client will also need to understand how their case will be put by their adviser to the opponent or other organisation involved. It is likely to happen in a number of ways. The adviser may be setting out the client's case in letters or discussing the main points of the case on the telephone with an opponent. If the adviser needs to argue legal points they will explain to that client how the arguments will be set out. For example the additional aspect of discrimination involving a single parent with her holiday pay deducted will have legal arguments arising out of employment sex discrimination law.

The adviser will also explain to the client the resources they have used to build up the case, the policy documents they have relied on or interpreted and the law involved. The client should have any law relevant to their case explained to them in an accessible way using plain language, as well as how the adviser will use it to assist in the progress of the client's case.

Agreeing the client's role in conducting the case

Because the process of resolving a client's case is two-way, and involves the client as well as the adviser, it will be necessary to agree what the client's role will be. In addition to supplying information and documents, the client may have other functions to perform.

Supplying instructions

Throughout the conduct of their case the client will not only give the adviser information but tell them what they would like the adviser to do, especially in the light of any unforeseen or new developments in their case.

Preparing statements

It may be the case that the client will need to make a statement as part of conducting the case. The statement may be a written one. For example, it may be helpful for Cathy Clark to draw up a statement to present to her housing association landlord saying how her rent arrears arose, or what her finances are, as a background to offering to pay off her rent arrears. The adviser should be ensuring that all the relevant information is in the client's statement, but if the client appears willing and able to type up an initial statement themselves that will stand as a useful first draft for the adviser to hone and polish together with the client. Although the adviser will also draft parts of the statement and add to it in order to ensure that everything relevant goes into the statement it should, even when used in a court case, be in plain language and indeed written in the everyday language that the client would normally use.

Understanding how evidence is used

What a client says in a statement, what is said on their behalf by an adviser or what appears in documentation may count as evidence or proof of what the client's case is and may be used to persuade an opponent or court or tribunal to accept the client's case and to agree to the client's desired outcome. The client will need to understand therefore what counts as evidence and how that evidence can be used to persuade other people of the truth of what the client is saying.

There are rules of evidence which will be applied by trained court advocates in presenting their client's cases in accordance with those rules. Generally, however, evidence can be said to amount to what a person says or has written and, when it is used or referred to by advisers in letters or meetings as well as in court, it will need to:

- be consistent and not self contradictory;
- be persuasive of the issue the adviser is seeking to resolve in the client's favour; and above all
- give the appearance of truthfulness.

So for example, if Cathy Clark prepares a statement for her landlord about how the arrears arose and refers to an illness preventing her from paying rent she will need to give sufficient information about the illness, what it was and how long it lasted. She will need to show that the timing of the illness coincided with the non-payment of rent and she will need to show that an illness of that nature would have meant that she would not have been able to pay her rent for that given period.

In this way her evidence is not contradictory and the facts surrounding the illness will stand as a good reason for not paying rent as well as the detail she provides giving the appearance of truthfulness. This evidence will be persuasive of a good reason why she was unable to pay rent for a given period.

15.5   Putting the case for the client

Part of the adviser's role is to relay confidently and accurately to another party or organisation what their client's case is. It may be expressed somewhat more formally than when it is set out for the client, but essentially it will be the same.

A professional approach to putting the case

An adviser should put the case to the other party simply, accurately and concisely. As part of using their knowledge and skills as an adviser in putting the case, the adviser will adopt a professional stance. They will be courteous to their opponent or the organisation they are putting the case to. They will not hide information or use tactics designed to annoy or alienate the opponent. They will avoid delaying and will maintain a firm stance as to their belief in the correctness of their client's case without allowing themselves to argue with or hector their opponents. There are still individuals who adopt an aggressive or combative stance when faced with a claim or complaint but their style is best not copied. In addition a calm and professional approach will impress the client and make them realise that their adviser is truly impartial and free from any personal motives in the way in which they put their case.

Case study: putting the case

In chapter 9 we saw that Cathy Clark had written a letter to the nursery that she worked for and that it had been returned by Royal Mail. Cathy meets a friend who tells her that she knows the home address of the owner of the nursery, Brenda Brown. Cathy rings Ada and tells her the address and asks her to write to Mrs Brown and put her case to her in respect of her claim for her week's unpaid wages and her notice pay. She also asks Ada to seek the recovery of the money Ada has advised Cathy that she is owed by her ex-employer.

This is the letter Ada then writes:

Mrs B Brown
2 The Brents
North Side
Middleton

Ref: AA/Clark/112

28 July

Dear Mrs Brown

Ms Catherine Clark: nursery assistant, Kidglove Nursery

I should be grateful if you would note that I have been instructed by
your ex-employee Catherine Clark. Ms Clark has instructed me that
she was employed part time by the Kidglove Nursery at your premises
in South Side for a period of three months ending on 12 July.

When she first began to work for you she was told by you that she
would receive her first week's wages of £130 take home pay if and
when she left your employment. She received no pay at the end of that
first week.

She has instructed me that she took some days' holiday at the
beginning of July. On 12 July, the day before she was due to return to
work, you telephoned her to say that her employment was terminated
due to an apparent downturn in the number of children enrolling at
the nursery. You terminated her employment in that telephone call.

I have advised Ms Clark that she is entitled to be paid her first
week's wages in full as per the terms of her employment contract. She
is also entitled to receive a week's pay in lieu of notice as she was not
given the opportunity to work out her statutory notice period of one
week when you terminated her employment.

I should be grateful if you would forward the sum of £260 to me
at the address at the top of this letter within the next fourteen days,
failing which Ms Clark will have no option but to pursue claims for
breach of contract and wrongful dismissal against the nursery.

Yours faithfully

Ada Adams

Compass Advice Centre
6 East Avenue
West Side
Middleton

Knowing procedures in putting the case

We also saw in chapter 7 that the adviser who is advocating for a client will need to know the rules and procedures of the organisation or court or tribunal system they are operating in if that is where the case will be finally decided. Ada has not said in the letter to the nursery where any claim for the monies owed to Cathy would be made. She is likely to do this in further correspondence if the claim is resisted and Cathy still wants to go ahead and make a legal claim for the money she is owed. If she advises Cathy that she should claim in the small claims court and if she approaches her opponent to indicate that a claim will start in the county court she will show that she knows exactly how to begin the claim and in doing so will demonstrate to her opponent that she is confident in using that system.*

Keeping to instructions in putting the client's case

The adviser must never exceed or vary from their instructions in putting a client's case. If in arguing a point for a client it appears to the adviser that it would be better to put the point in a different way then the client would need to be consulted about that and their agreement reached.

Knowing the other person's case in putting the client's case

As well as knowing in detail what the clients' case is and all the facts and documents surrounding it, the adviser should also make sure they know the opponent's case thoroughly. This will enable the adviser to engage knowledgably with their opponent, to see any gaps or flaws in their opponent's case and to take advantage of those to the benefit of their client. It will also allow the adviser to advise their client better on the strengths and weaknesses of their case which will in part arise from strengths and weaknesses in their opponent's case.

For example, Cathy Clark may have informed her adviser that the nursery had said that if they no longer had any work for her there was no point in her working out her notice period. Ada may need to point out to the nursery that she knows that this is their case or part of their case and she has advised her client that she is nevertheless entitled to either work out her notice or be paid her notice pay in lieu. She will state that they have wrongfully terminated her employment contract

---

*   For more on the various courts and their structures and powers see chapter 18

a week before it should have expired, which gives rise to a potential claim by Cathy for her notice pay.

Case study: preparation for Cathy's case

Ada has now begun to move forward with both Cathy's housing case and her employment case. We saw in chapter 10 that Cathy's landlord had refused to accept her offer to pay off her rent arrears. We have just seen that Ada has written to Cathy's ex-employer seeking the payment of wages and notice pay owed to Cathy.

Ada now needs to plan how to progress both these matters further, if necessary, as far as a court case.

Cathy does not want there to be a court order made in relation to her rent arrears. She also wants Ada to start the case against her employer for the unpaid wages and notice pay if they refuse to pay her the money she is owed.

Ada will therefore do the following, all with Cathy's agreement.

Housing case	Employment case
With Cathy's consent write to the landlord again to try to avoid a court case	Obtain from Cathy all the details of her wages paid and any payslips or other documents to show what she was usually paid
Research the law on possession orders for rent arrears	
Prepare a statement for Cathy as to the reasons for the arrears and how she intends to make up the shortfall	Wait a period of three weeks from the date she sent the letter to Kidglove (to allow for post) and then start a claim in the small claims court on Cathy's behalf for the monies owed, using the correct procedures
Collect a bundle of Cathy's documents showing rent paid and missed	Prepare a statement for Cathy saying why she believes she is owed the money and how much she is owed
Obtain a doctors' letter to confirm her illness when the rent was unpaid	Prepare a set of Cathy's documents (payslips, letters etc), if any, about her employment at the nursery

continued

Housing case	Employment case
Prepare a schedule of Cathy's income and outgoings for the landlord and the court if the court case goes ahead	Attend with Cathy at her small claims hearing where Cathy will read out her statement and show the court her documents
Prepare a letter for Cathy to take to the court, if there is someone there (such as a court duty adviser) who can speak for her in court, or alternatively arrange to accompany Cathy to court on the day of her court hearing	Advise Cathy on the outcome of the case and if successful how much she can recover
Advise Cathy on what will happen at court and on the likely outcome of her case	If the employer fails to pay the judgment advise Cathy on how she can ask the court to enforce the judgment

CHAPTER 16

Negotiating, mediation and alternative dispute resolution

16.1   Introduction: ways of resolving cases

As part of the process of resolving a client's case, advisers will have a range of options for possible resolution. They may seek in letters or telephone calls to persuade an opponent or an organisation to agree to what their client is seeking, such as money or a change in a policy which might benefit them. They will learn negotiating skills as part of that process, which will be looked at in more detail below. They may seek to resolve the case by initiating a court case or tribunal which will be looked at later.

There are also other ways of resolving cases which essentially involve the parties attempting to put aside their differences in order to try to find a way of reaching a resolution. These alternative approaches are now being used more often. They will usually involve using a set procedure designed to bring the dispute to an end or using a middle person such as a mediator. This chapter will focus on using negotiating skills to reach a helpful conclusion for the client as well as the procedures used in the alternative methods of resolving a client's case. In the following chapter, examination will be made of the more traditional methods of resolving a client's case.

16.2   Negotiation: skills and tactics

Persuading the other party to agree to your client's outcome

Negotiating is an important aspect of all advice work. An adviser will need certain skills to engage confidently with another party on behalf of their client in order to achieve a successful outcome for the client. The process of negotiating can mean that the adviser reaches an outcome by persuading someone else to agree to do what the client wants. In our case study, for example, Ada Adams has been attempting to negotiate with the client's landlord in order to persuade them to accept the offer her client Cathy is making to pay off the rent arrears. She might use a number of arguments to persuade them. For example:

- if they accept the offer now then the arrears will start to be paid much sooner than if they wait for the outcome of a court case;
- if they accept the offer it may be that when Cathy is working she will be able to increase it;
- if they insist on going to court they are risking an uncertain outcome or one which would not be what they wanted;

- if the court makes an order for her to pay off the arrears in instalments it will be for a fixed amount with no obligation on the part of the tenant to increase it.

All these arguments could be used to negotiate an agreement whereby the landlord finally accepts the client's offer to pay off the rent in the amounts put forward by Ada on Cathy's behalf. The arguments may be put forward in discussion on the phone or in further correspondence or e-mails.

Negotiating a settlement of differences

In this meaning of the process of negotiation, the adviser is dealing with an opponent and both parties are putting aside their differences in order to try to reach a resolution which they can both accept.

The resolution will not necessarily be the outcome which either party wanted at the start but it will be an outcome which both parties can accept without losing face. The aim of a good negotiator is to learn how to achieve a result which their client will accept. They will reach that point by a blend of putting forward persuasive arguments in favour of their client's case but accepting the case made for the client's opponent. In doing so they are likely to concede points which were in their favour and reach a compromise. This is often referred to as settling a case. Where the case is due to go to court or tribunal it will be referred to as settling out of court if an agreement is reached either before or during a hearing.

Advisers new to negotiating will often expend too much energy in the negotiating process in repeating their client's case to an opponent and seeking to convince the other party of it in order to persuade them to give the client what they want. This is unlikely to persuade an unwilling opponent to see things from the client's viewpoint. A more constructive approach to negotiating a settlement will involve the parties knowing what their opponent's case or arguments are but seeing if in spite of that any common ground can be found to resolve the matter in a different way.

'Without prejudice' discussions

In court or tribunal cases, negotiations which attempt to reach a settlement will take place 'off the record' and are referred to by lawyers as 'without prejudice'. Any attempt to achieve a resolution different from the case put by the parties should be agreed between the parties as being done either 'without prejudice' or 'off the record'. The reason for this is to allow a free discussion without prejudicing the client's case as it has been formally set out to an opponent or a court. In court cases a judge should not be told of any discussions which might have taken place between the two parties in an attempt to settle the case out of court. If discussions aimed at settling a case have been recorded or conducted in writing, the letter or e-mail must be headed 'without prejudice' and should not be shown to a court or tribunal if the hearing goes ahead after all.

Tactics of negotiating

The negotiation process (whether conducted by letter, phone or in person) will normally involve utilising the following tactics:

- *Client's case.* Stating the client's case and inviting the opponent to agree on what it is.
- *Opponent's case.* Taking note of the opponent's case and agreeing on what it is.
- *Common ground.* Seeing if the parties can find any common ground – such as the fact that the client is owed a sum of money (but the amount owed is in dispute).
- *Reason to settle.* Agreeing any common reason or reason which each party might have for wishing to dispose of the case by settling it. The most common reasons are usually to save cost and time.
- *Conceding ground to achieve a settlement.* Whether or not there is any common ground but both parties wish to achieve a settlement, agreeing on what aspects each party might be willing to move ground on. This can be done without the parties conceding their case.
- *Knowing the limits of what can be achieved.* It is important for the adviser to ensure that whatever they agree to on behalf of a client is what the client wants and what the client has instructed them to settle for. Sometimes negotiations will involve starting the process by putting forward a higher figure for a money settlement than the figure which the client is actually prepared to accept to settle a claim. This will allow the negotiations to continue so that it appears that the client is conceding to their opponent if a lower offer is then made (which in reality will be the figure the client is seeking). This tactic will feature in the case study example overleaf.
- *Receiving offers and discussing with the client.* Once an offer is made to an adviser to settle their client's case it will need to be discussed with the client before any indication is given that it is appropriate or will be accepted. Even if the adviser thinks the offer is a good

one they must first discuss it with their client. All offers need to be discussed and advised on. This should not only be done in the context of how near to or far from the client's desired outcome the offer is but also in the context of the risks of rejecting it. No matter how strong a client's case appears to be, there are always risks inherent in going on with a case and achieving the ideal outcome. These will range from the risks of placing the client at the mercy of a court to the risk of a client letting themselves down by lack of persuasive evidence or by (understandable) nerves or forgetfulness.

• *Recording.* Often negotiations can begin without warning, say as part of a telephone conversation ostensibly made for some other purpose. In addition, once a settlement appears likely there may be frequent calls or conversations to 'fine tune' the settlement. It is important that all these transactions are recorded, not only on the adviser's file, but also in writing to the client, so that the client is fully up to date with the progress of the negotiations and is in a position to be able to give instructions as to how they want their adviser to proceed.

The negotiator's skills

Hopefully it will be seen from the exchange of correspondence overleaf that both parties are stating their own case, acknowledging the other party's case and seeking to find a middle ground for a stated reason. From the nursery's point of view, the goal will be to pay Cathy less than the court might order them to pay and to avoid court proceedings. From Cathy's point of view, the aim will be to ensure that she gets some money rather than none, is paid sooner than if she waited for the outcome of a court case and avoids the possibility of a possibly expensive or wasted court case should the nursery go out of business.

As well as using these common tactics, the adviser should be aware of the skills involved in negotiations which settle a dispute between two parties.

Preparing a client

Even if there is no indication from a client that they want to settle a case, the adviser should always discuss this as a possible option and seek the client's instructions as to what they would agree to accept by way of a compromise should the opportunity arise. This will involve having advised the client of the risks involved in setting out to achieve their desired outcome in full.

Case study: negotiating a settlement

In our case study in chapter 15, Ada contacted the owner of Kidglove Nursery to ask for Cathy's back pay and notice pay. She has claimed two-weeks' pay of £260 on Cathy's behalf, one for the week in hand and one for the notice pay, based on a figure of wages of £130 a week which Cathy says was her weekly take home pay.

In response, the following letter is received from the nursery:

Kidglove Nursery
2 The Brents
North Side
Middleton

3 August

Dear Ms Adams

Re Catherine Clark

I refer to your letter of 28 July in which you claim on behalf of Ms Clark that we owe her a week in hand and a week's notice pay based on a weekly sum of £130 take home pay. We accept that her weekly take home pay was £130.

However, you should be aware that we did not keep back any pay from Ms Clark at the outset of her employment. We believe she may have confused sick leave with a week in hand. A week after she started the job she went off sick and was not paid as she did not claim statutory sick pay when we invited her to. We did, however, pay her for all the time she worked for us.

We did not pay notice pay. This was because Ms Clark told us when we said there was no more work for her that she may as well sign on. We therefore saw no point in her being paid by us and the benefit office at the same time. There was no mention in our final telephone conversation of paying her a week in hand.

You say in your letter that Ms Clark intends to take this matter to the courts. You should be aware that the nursery has very little money at present due to a downturn in custom. Although we believed we were correct in not paying notice pay, as a gesture of good will we are prepared to pay her a week's notice pay of £130 in full and final settlement of all your client's claims against the nursery.

Yours faithfully,

Brenda Brown
Director, Kidglove Nursery

Ada talks to Cathy about this letter. She advises Cathy that if the nursery goes out of business she might never recover her money. Cathy is quite sure she was promised her week in hand. She recalls being off sick but only for three days, and was told by Brenda Brown that she would not be entitled to statutory sick pay as she would only be entitled to it if off sick for more than three days. Ada advised her that if this occurred it would be correct. Cathy wants to get two week's pay but will settle for £200. So Ada writes a reply:

Compass Advice Centre
6 East Avenue
West Side
Middleton

13 August

Dear Mrs Brown

Re: Catherine Clark Nursery Assistant – Without Prejudice

Thank you for your letter of 3 August. I have discussed it with my client. She informs me that she was off sick in the second week of her employment for three days and as such was advised by you that she would not qualify for any statutory sick pay. She accepted therefore that she would not be paid for that period.

However, she does believe she is owed a week in hand. She has no pay slip for the first week she worked. Furthermore her clear recollection is that you promised it to her on the telephone when you told her that you no longer required her to work for you. She is, however, aware that you now deny this part of the conversation.

I have advised her that in addition she should have received a week's pay in lieu of notice whether or not she put in a claim for benefits following the termination of her employment.

She would, however, be prepared to settle this matter without the necessity of a court case and in order to bring this dispute to a swift resolution. She would be prepared to reduce the amount she is claiming to £200 in order to save the time and costs of a court case.

Yours faithfully

Ada Adams
Compass Advice Centre

The letter produces a short response:

Kidglove Nursery
2 The Brents
North Side
Middleton

17 August

Dear Ms Adams

Re Cathy Clark: Without Prejudice

Thank you for your letter of 13 August.

I am prepared to increase my offer to £150. This offer remains open for the next seven days.

Yours faithfully,

Brenda Brown

Cathy realises that 'a bird in the hand is worth two in the bush'. If the money is forthcoming she will receive it much sooner than if she went to court and it will help her to pay off her rent arrears and other debts. She instructs Ada to accept it on her behalf on the basis that it is paid within 14 days from the date of Ada's reply.
   So Ada writes a letter in those terms and Cathy then awaits her payment.

Being on top of the case

Negotiations can be initiated by either party, often by an unexpected telephone call being received. The adviser needs to ensure they are at all times on top of their client's case and understand the way their opponent's case is being put so that they can be ready to deal with negotiations at any time. This preparedness will show them to be in control of the situation should they receive an unexpected offer to negotiate a settlement.

Displaying confidence in the client's outcome

There will inevitably be weaknesses in a client's case. Even where the client presents a set of facts which they wish to rely on (such as the fact that they are owed money by an ex-employer) there may not be the evidence to support this. They may not have kept payslips, letters or bank statements. There may have been evidence produced which contradicts what they say. In spite of this the adviser will present a confident approach to their opponent. If the adviser gives the impression to an opponent that they believe their client's case to be weak there will be no incentive on the other party to offer any concessions to settle the case.

Adopting a conciliatory approach

On the other hand, if the adviser takes a robust and unyielding approach to their opponent they will not necessarily be able to reach any form of compromise. It is quite possible to display faith in the strength of a client's case at the same time as indicating that in spite of that the client will be willing to reach a compromise position. A lot of negotiation can be described as 'posturing' as both parties are engaged in using the best aspects of their client's case and playing down the worst aspects to try to reach a point where they each will accept a middle way.

Being professional and courteous

In all conflict situations it should be possible to maintain a position in opposition to someone else's at the same time as showing that person courtesy and adopting a professional and impartial approach. This is nowhere more true than when negotiating a compromise of a client's case or position. No positive result will be achieved by adopting a combative approach or indeed by responding to like with like. If an opponent becomes annoyed or difficult, the best approach is to suggest ways of resolving the case, using some ground rules to help both parties to move forward. These may include not interrupting or not frequently contradicting the other person.

16.3 Alternative dispute resolution (ADR)

Meanings and processes

A process of using an alternative method of resolving disputes between two parties is becoming more embedded into our legal and disputes arena as time goes on. It is becoming more common for parties to be encouraged to resolve them outside the medium of a traditional court case.

In the civil court system there is now a Protocol (see page 221 note 10) which requires parties to observe good practice in the context of actively considering using alternative dispute resolution to resolve their case. The courts and tribunals now see this as a part of the process of resolving disputes. In the employment field, employment tribunals will not be able to hear certain cases if the employee has failed to use a grievance procedure in the workplace prior to starting their employment tribunal claim.[1]

Advisers should be aware of these alternative methods of resolving a dispute which are generically known as ADR. There are now four main strands of ADR in existence. They are:

- arbitration;
- conciliation;
- ombudsman;
- mediation.

All these processes have in common the concept of using outside help in trying to resolve a dispute. There are a number of organisations which give further information about these processes and which guide individuals towards their use, the most relevant of which, for the advice sector, is ADR Now.[2] Each process will be examined briefly for how it operates, with mediation looked at separately below as it is the fastest growing area of ADR.

Arbitration

For many years this was the only alternative way of resolving a dispute outside court. It is also the process which is the nearest to a court decision as the arbitrator will make a decision at the end of the process which will be legally binding on both parties. The arbitrator is given the role of deciding on the dispute and will then make a decision in favour of one party or another.

Arbitration began as a process in the commercial world and is still commonly used in relation to commercial contract disputes. Many of these contracts will have in them an 'arbitration clause' whereby, if there are disputes as to how any part of the contract should or has operated, the parties will be required to go to an arbitrator to resolve the matter. Unlike other ADR methods, arbitration will involve the

1   See Employment Act 2002 s32(4).
2   www.adrnow.org.uk.

use of arbitrators whose actions will be governed by law.[3] Arbitration also exists as a process in some employment disputes. There are some types of unfair dismissal claims which can be referred by the parties to an ACAS [4] arbitrator. This is also governed by law.[5]

The process of arbitration will involve a hearing or meetings or a series of meetings with both the parties in dispute and the arbitrator (or sometimes a panel) inviting each party to state their case and then decide on the outcome for them. The rules of evidence which apply in court hearings will not apply in these hearings but it will be possible for witnesses to be called and for documents to be put before the arbitrator as part of the party's evidence.

Although normally concerned with commercial matters, knowing of the possibility of arbitration in some areas will be of benefit in the advice sector. For example, if there is a holiday dispute involving a company governed by ABTA[6] it will be useful to know that this organisation offers a free e-mail arbitration service. In addition, the ACAS arbitration service referred to above in relation to unfair dismissal claims, although not used very frequently, is a service to be aware of in advising on these claims.

Conciliation

Conciliation is a less formal approach than arbitration in that the latter will result in a decision being made by the arbitrator which both parties will be required to abide by. In conciliation, the conciliator will be used by the parties as a medium for them to try to reach a compromise or a decision which one of them or both of them agrees to put into action. The decision will be reached by the parties and not by the conciliator. Furthermore, the decision will not be legally binding on either party and so it involves more of a leap of faith on the part of the parties.

Conciliators do not have to possess any particular legal or other professional expertise or qualifications, which is usual for arbitrators. However, they will often have received training or have a relevant background which will enable them to talk knowledgeably to each party about the issue and to use powers of persuasion to see if the

---

3   The Arbitration Act 1996.
4   Advisory Conciliation and Arbitration Service – see www.acas.org.uk.
5   ACAS Arbitration Scheme (Great Britain) Order 2004 SI No 753 (also extends to Scotland).
6   Association of British Travel Agents.

parties can reach an acceptable compromise. Conciliation has a particular role in some disability disputes[7] and in the process of compromising employment claims.[8] There are also legal requirements which must be followed in compromising employment claims which have been settled with the help of the ACAS conciliation service and ACAS will advise as to how these will operate.[9]

Another field in which conciliation takes place is in the public sector. Many health authorities and local authority services will encourage aggrieved individuals to use their conciliation services and the outcomes may result in changes of policy as well as admissions of below-standard services or unnecessary delays. These are matters which a court cannot always address and may be useful for a client with concerns about public services.

Ombudsman

The ombudsman service is a process whereby someone who has no legal redress can seek a review of their case and seek a finding of maladministration (improperly using their powers) in relation to a business or public body. The relevant ombudsman will investigate what the organisation has done to handle the person's complaint or case and can recommend compensation as well as deciding if there has been poor practice or maladministration.

This service takes us more into the realms of a complaints process. Most organisations who deal with the public will have their own complaints process and if this has not produced a satisfactory result for a client they may be able to go to the relevant ombudsman assisted by their adviser. There are time limits for using the ombudsman service and the process involves leaving it entirely up to the ombudsman officer to ask whatever questions or seek whatever documents they decide they need in order to reach a decision. Someone who goes to an Ombudsman for redress will be required to show that they have first of all exhausted the complaints procedure of the organisation their complaint is about. Banks, local authorities and other public bodies all have their own ombudsman service. The full range can be seen on the website of ADR Now.

---

7   See for example the Disability Conciliation Service.
8   See ACAS Conciliation.
9   See note 4 above.

16.4   Mediation as an option

Mediation is a growing area of ADR. There is now a range of mediation services, including those especially for local community organisations to use. Mediators do not have to have any particular qualifications but many have attended intensive training which they regularly update.

Mediation is now available for many disputes which would otherwise involve court orders and costs. Some examples of the areas where it is used are set out below. It can also be used where there have been no litigation or court proceedings but there are apparently intractable disputes between two parties. It may be used as an agreed alternative to going to court or arbitration.

As indicated above, civil courts will expect any party entering that system to resolve a dispute to consider ADR and to signal that they have actively done so.[10]

Advisers should be aware of this tendency in the court system as well as knowing of any community mediation services they can use to assist their client in resolving a dispute. Mediation is usually available in one form or another for the following types of disputes:

- housing and property;
- family;
- consumer;
- neighbour disputes;
- education; and
- business disputes.

In addition, where a client has a small claim in a local county court, many courts now offer a mediation service to try to avoid the case being decided in front of the judge.

Mediation does not produce a legally binding result for the parties but it does have many advantages. A trained or experienced mediator (which will include a judge in the court system) will enable the parties to speak freely but constructively about their differences and will help them to explore any common ground they might have.

---

10 In the civil court system there is a Protocol Practice Direction – part of the process of following the court's procedures – which requires a party to consider ADR, and which may extend to a requirement to use a form of ADR – there can be costs penalties for parties who appear to have ignored that requirement: http://www.justice.gov.uk/civil/procrules_fin/contents/practice_directions/pd_protocol.htm.

The process

Mediation will take place in the form of a meeting or series of meetings in which the mediator will seek to enable the parties to find some common ground and to reach a helpful outcome. The mediator will remain impartial and their approach will not so much lie in helping the parties to argue their differences better or to understand their respective weaknesses, but to assist them in seeing an end to the dispute by opening up the channels of communication and being a lever to allow for changes in a person's position to be made in a positive way.

The process can take some time, possibly a number of days spread out over a period of time. It will usually take place in a neutral setting or an informal room in a court building set aside for mediation purposes.

Many mediation services will involve each party paying the mediator. In the county court mediation system, where mediation services exist in some courts in relation to a small claim (worth up to £5,000), there are set fees payable if both the parties decide to opt for mediation. They may also have been encouraged to mediate by a judge at a preliminary meeting to discuss the case or once he or she has read the parties' case papers.

There are also free mediation services[11] which can be used in the local community and, where there is any dispute in relation to a matter where mediation is an available service, an adviser should always be considering it as an option in terms of resolving the client's case.

---

11 For a directory of these see www.intermedial.co.uk.

CHAPTER 17

Other ways of resolving the case

17.1   Letters, phone calls and meetings

In the previous chapter we saw how it might be possible to involve a third party in seeking to resolve the client's claim. This route may be followed as well as attempts to resolve the issue in dispute by more traditional means. This chapter will explore a number of these other ways in which the adviser will be able to reach a resolution for their client.

It is quite common for the adviser to be able to resolve the client's problem using the traditional tools of communication: letter writing, telephone calls or attending meetings with or on behalf of their clients. This will often be the route to resolution where the problem will be one which will not require consideration of too many complex issues or documents.

Effective letter writing

It will nearly always be the case that the new client will instruct their adviser to write a letter on their behalf in an attempt to obtain their desired outcome. In writing such a letter the adviser needs to exercise the skills of clear communication. They should write letters which are not too lengthy, which have a professional style and which clearly state the case for the client and say why they believe the client's case to be correct.

These initial letters are very important as they are the first signal the adviser puts out to others on behalf of their client. The letter therefore should confidently and accurately relay a client's instructions, knowledgeably put the case for the client, and clearly state the outcome being sought. Before such a letter is sent out it will have been carefully checked by the adviser and approved by the client. It is quite often the case that the client will want to comment on or make suggestions about the contents of draft letters, and time and care should be taken to explain why certain things are being put as they are, and always to ensure that the client's wishes are fully complied with in terms of what goes into the letter.

It should also be borne in mind that if a letter fails to resolve the problem, and the adviser and client then move forward to other ways of resolving the case, early letters can form the backbone of that subsequent case.

Some pointers towards the type of letters which produce results follow.

Length

A lengthy letter is less likely to be read in detail than a letter which gets across its points succinctly. Paragraphs and sentences should be short and concise. Using three words where two will do will mean that the letter lacks the necessary focus to get to a resolution.

Flow

The letter must be seen to flow from one point to another. It will usually be the case that the letter will follow the patterns of:

- introduction of the adviser to the recipient;
- brief outline of facts as put to the adviser by their client;
- statement of the way in which the recipient of the letter has wronged the client;
- any relevant law which confirms that wrongdoing and how it applies to the current situation;
- what remedy the client is seeking;
- any time limits the adviser is imposing on the recipient to resolve the matter in the manner indicated in the letter; and
- any action which the client seeks to take if the recipient does not resolve the matter in the manner indicated.

It may even be worth using short headings in a letter which reflect these different stages of the letter.

Style

The letter will be couched in a professional, business-like way, avoiding slang or abbreviations. It will not seek to judge, criticise or condemn the recipient unnecessarily. Any comment about how the client feels about their loss or treatment will be made in a factual and not an emotive setting. The letter should be written in plain English and not legal jargon.

E-mails

E-mails have changed the way we all function in the workplace. They are used as a matter of course for internal communications within organisations and are now being used more frequently by advisers to communicate with clients and with their client's opponents.

The use of e-mail as a means of communication is inherently informal. Many people do not believe it necessary to keep to the formal letter writing mode or to use full sentences or paragraphs. Forms of address are also often less formal than in letters. Overall, the effect of e-mail is to speed up communication, which has led to more messages being sent.

If advisers use e-mail they should always bear in mind its informal and swift nature. Decisions and agreements taken on behalf of clients should be carefully thought out if to be reached via e-mail communication. Copies of e-mail messages should be printed off for the file and care taken as to whom any message is copied to. In addition, the use of the 'reply' button is to be avoided as long strings of messages can easily be sent to the wrong person or can mean replies are made without careful thought and planning.

Telephone calls

Like e-mail, the telephone call has a more temporary and less formal character than the letter. Both e-mails and telephone calls do, however, serve to resolve client's problems and their advantage is that they are much more immediate than a letter.

The same guidance as to how to set out the client's case and the remedy being sought will apply to the telephone call or e-mail. In terms of style it is important to keep a professional approach and steer away from any attempts to personalise the matter in the way the adviser addresses the recipient.

Furthermore, it will be important not to be drawn in telephone calls into any change of approach which is not in the adviser's remit and is beyond instructions. Many opponents will use a range of tactics to persuade an adviser to shift their client's position. Examples are:

* indicating that the adviser is not aware of certain matters relating to their client which place their client in a bad light;
* indicating that they do not have the means or the ability to meet the client's stated remedy and offering an alternative one instead;
* indicating that they or their client have already spoken to the adviser's client and reached a different resolution; or
* indicating that as professional advisers they know better than their respective clients and that they can therefore reach a resolution in a more helpful way. This often translates as a way more favourable to the opponent.

No matter how unprepared or surprised an adviser is by the contents of a telephone call, they must be clear that they cannot shift any ground at all without their client's consent. They should be ready to hold their ground politely and argue their client's case in spite of any different scenarios thrown at them. Finally they should ensure that the telephone call is properly concluded. If a resolution is proposed or agreed it will need to be clearly understood by each party and the adviser will then indicate that they will take their client's instructions on whatever has been discussed or proposed and thereafter record it in writing with the client's opponent. Whatever the outcome of the call, the adviser needs to make a full note of it on the client's file and report back to the client.

Meetings

It may be the case that a relatively informal meeting can resolve a client's problem. The meeting may be with a housing department or a benefit agency or a school. The adviser may accompany their client or may go on behalf of the client. It is likely that the meeting will in any event be conducted away from the adviser's office and be controlled by the organisation which the client is alleging has caused them the problem they are complaining about.

The adviser therefore needs to ensure that they are prepared for the meeting in advance. They will need to allow plenty of time to get to the venue. They will need to take with them any papers or files which they will need to refer to and ensure that these are kept safely throughout the time they are away from the adviser's office. They will need to check in advance who will be at the meeting, their names and their role in the organisation. Finally they should try to find out how long has been planned for the meeting by the organisation concerned which will help the adviser to plan or to negotiate with the organisation for a different timing if they feel the meeting should last longer.

Many organisations are reluctant to allow individuals to be accompanied by professional advisers at meetings and, where they do allow it, will expect the adviser to abide by their procedures. They may exhibit a defensive approach to a professional adviser which the adviser will have no choice but to accept if they are to focus on their client's best interests.

The adviser will need to accept the rules of the organisation holding the meeting but politely and firmly put the client's points across. If the client is asked questions during a meeting, the organisation will usually expect the client and not the adviser to reply. They will expect the adviser to make points or submit arguments on their client's behalf but not to speak for them. In these situations, sometimes the client may say unexpected things in answer to questions in meetings and the adviser should therefore prepare very carefully with their client in advance of a meeting in terms of what the client will say at that meeting.

The adviser should make careful notes at a meeting and should keep those notes thereafter on the client's file. Once the meeting is concluded and before the participants depart, the adviser should check

- if all present are agreed on the outcome of the meeting;
- who will record the outcome – the organisation or the adviser; and
- whether that record will be sent out to all interested parties and by what date.

17.2   Client takes action

In many advice-giving situations, the adviser will be able to give the client the necessary information and support in order for the client to resolve the matter themselves.

Sometimes the adviser will only have the resources or the capacity to offer this approach to resolving the client's problem. They will have an advice service which is tailored to the client resolving matters themselves.

Sometimes an advice centre or agency will offer a core service which includes advice and representation for clients but will also run a satellite advice service, where the advice is often given by volunteers (usually legally qualified) coming in order to deliver free advice for that agency's clients. These advice sessions are often specifically geared to the concept of providing clients with a self-help service.

The volunteer advice service helping the client to resolve their problem

The advantage of the volunteer advice service is that more clients can be helped, as less time and fewer resources are utilised in relation to each client. Furthermore, the aim is to assist the client in resolving the matter themselves once they have had some preliminary advice and assistance. The disadvantage is that some clients will still find it hard to resolve their own problems and will realistically find the limited help they are offered insufficient, a situation which a volunteer adviser will be all too often aware of and unable to remedy in the limited time which they have to offer to the advice service.

In either of these contexts the client may be offered more than one appointment so that they can be supported as they progress their own case to resolution. This service will be suitable for clients who are for example using the small claims court in the county court to resolve dispute over money claims or consumer matters.* It may also be used for clients using a tribunal service such as Leasehold Valuation Tribunals, or benefits tribunals.

A typical pattern of a volunteer advice service

If an agency does run a service which is geared towards assisting clients to resolve their own problems, the following approaches will usually be employed in that process:

1. *An initial advice session takes place.* This is likely to be the key interview and may last up to an hour or even longer. The client will usually have telephoned or e-mailed in advance with an outline of their problem and will have been told that the adviser will offer advice and assistance to help the client to resolve the problem themselves. At the interview the client will give a full account of what they are seeking advice and assistance on. They will then be given information about the law, advice on the merits of their case, advice on how to resolve the case and advice on likely outcomes of following a given approach to resolving the case. The interview will in effect serve as the main advice route for the client to resolve their problem.

2. *A detailed letter of advice will be sent to the client by their adviser.* The letter will confirm the content of the interview. In particular it will make clear any steps the client needs to take to protect their interests, and the time limits within which any steps will need to be taken. The letter will make it clear that all actions to be taken from that point on will be taken by the client and this will include taking responsibility for complying with any deadlines. Furthermore the client will be reminded that they will need to take responsibility for all subsequent steps and should not name the advice organisation as being their legal representative to any third parties. This is important since, if a client erroneously holds an organisation out as being their legal representative, there could be serious implications in terms of the steps that organisation might

---

* See chapter 18 for an explanation of county court claims.

then be expected to take on the client's behalf. Furthermore, the organisation is unlikely to be insured in the self-help context to do any more than advise.

3. *A letter may be drafted by the adviser for the client to send to the organisation or individual with whom they have a dispute.* This will often be drafted by the adviser for the client. It will be written setting out the client's case and at the same time seek a resolution.

4. *The client will aim to be able to resolve the matter directly with their opponent.* The letter drafted by the adviser may produce the desired outcome or the client may be able to steer their way into the county court or a tribunal system using leaflet and on-line guidance to help them understand the process. Many individuals find the process of resolving their own case or problem is empowering and gives them back a sense of control over an area of their lives which was causing them stress or unhappiness. Others do not fare well in the legal or another similarly formal system, and the statistics show that these are more likely to outnumber those who do when clients are acting on their own behalf. In general, clients will need to be advised that courts and tribunals should only be used as a last resort.

17.3   Courts and tribunals

In chapter 18 there is an overview of the English and Welsh legal system to enable advisers to form an understanding of the structure as a basis for giving legal advice and to advise clients how each jurisdiction works.

This is one way in which problems with a legal resolution may need to be resolved. Prior to advising a client that this is the right option the adviser needs to address the following questions.

Time limits

What are the time limits for a particular claim to be brought and can the client comply with those time limits? Has a court or tribunal already required a client to take any steps within a required time limit and can the client comply with that time limit? Note that time limits will be relevant to all civil court and tribunal claims. An adviser should be aware of what these are by checking the relevant court or tribunal rules and procedures.

Fees and costs

What are the financial implications for the client in entering into this particular process? Will the client need to pay any court fees at any stage and will the client be at risk of having to pay any legal costs to an opponent at the end of the process?

The general rule in the civil court system is that 'costs follow the event'. This means that the loser of a court case is required to pay not only their own legal costs but the legal costs of the winning party. There are exceptions to this such as claims in the small claims court of the county court (claims up to the value of £5000) where costs are not normally awarded, and in most tribunals. In the employment tribunal, costs can be awarded where the tribunal believes they should be, in terms of the way in which the case has been conducted or its relative merits. In addition, clients who receive public funding towards their legal adviser's costs in the main court system are usually precluded from paying their legal costs or those of the other party, win or lose.

Procedures

Is the adviser confident about the procedure to be followed in the relevant court or tribunal and can they explain the various steps to the client as they are due to take place? Have they advised the client as to their role in the process, in particular the process of giving evidence to a court or tribunal? Is there any guidance, fact sheet or booklet that can be given to the client as background reading so that they can familiarise themselves with the process?

Likely outcome

Has the adviser carefully advised the client on the likely outcome of the case? Whatever the adviser feels about the merits of the client's case they will need to add in to their advice the 'uncertainty factor'. Courts and tribunals will sometimes produce a different outcome from that predicted by advisers. This can be due either to unforeseen developments occurring during the progress of the case, or simply due to the court deciding to see things in a different light or taking a different tack in approaching the issues. This is why all advice on outcomes needs to be relatively cautious and why there are always risks inherent in embarking on, or being involved in, court or other legal procedures.

These are the basic issues to be covered prior to embarking on a court or tribunal claim. It may of course be that the client has no choice

and has come to see their adviser because they have been threatened
with court action themselves or are facing a court or tribunal hearing
in the near future. Nevertheless all the above preliminary points will
still be relevant and necessary to cover.

Is court the right option for the client?

Overall, where there is a choice as to whether to start court proceedings or not, the question of how far a court case will go to producing
both the desired result and a sense of real satisfaction for the client is
an important one for the adviser to address.

For clients who succeed in court or tribunal claims there will be
a sense of justice done and of achievement at having come through
the process. It is, however, a stressful process and some will give up,
feeling overcome by the stress of the proceedings.

Those who do not succeed in court claims or who have been unable to successfully defend claims made against them will have a
range of reactions. Some are philosophical and often say at the end
of the process that they had a sense that they may not succeed. This
may be due to advice given to them as to their prospects of success,
coupled with advice about the difficulty of predicting accurately the
likely outcome of a court hearing.

Others may feel bitter and angry at what they perceive to be unjust treatment. This can also arise where they have been successful
but have witnessed their opponent behaving in what they regard as
a reprehensible manner, or where they are unable to recover money
ordered by a court or tribunal to be paid to them.

A victory in a court or tribunal will not always mean that the opponent will accept that decision or abide by it. Some court and tribunal
decisions will be taken further by way of an appeal by a losing party
and this will mean a long delay. The process of an appeal will usually
be quite legalistic which can have the effect of locking the client out
of the process unless they are able to grasp the legal issues.

For all these reasons, courts and tribunals should probably be seen
as the last resort, and any other approaches to resolving a client's case
should be thoroughly tested out first.

17.4   Resolutions leading to change

There are occasions when a case or claim is resolved either in the
context of a policy being applied by a public body or in terms of a court

Case study: resolution

In our case study we saw in the last chapter that Cathy decided to settle her claim against her ex-employer for £150. If the employer does not honour that settlement Cathy will need to make a claim for her unpaid wages and notice pay either in the employment tribunal, if she can do so within the necessary time limits, or in the county court as a 'small claim'.

However, if she is still not paid by the nursery even after obtaining a court judgment or order, she may then need to enforce any order or judgment she receives. This will involve her paying fees to the court to institute ways of enforcing the judgment. One method of enforcement would be to use the court bailiffs. Hopefully Cathy will be paid her money to save her the stress and cost of trying to recover this money in other ways.

In terms of her housing problem she found that the landlord decided to apply to the court for a possession order on her property. She was very distressed about this. Even though she had been advised by Ada that the court would be likely to postpone the possession order if she was paying off her rent arrears in instalments, she did not want to face the stress and publicity of having to attend court. She also did not want a court order to be made against her as she was worried that it would affect her future ability to obtain credit.

When she told her parents about this decision on the part of her landlord they offered to pay off all her rent arrears and to come to a private arrangement with her whereby she would repay them in instalments. Ada was able to assist therefore in the satisfactory conclusion of the case involving Cathy's rent arrears.

Note that in real life such a helpful outcome for Cathy may not be so easily achieved. Part of the adviser's role will be to continue to assist and support clients where there is a continued lack of resolution.

case where the resolution of the case will affect a large number of people. In legal terms these can be referred to as 'test cases'.

For many years, Law Centres® or other specialist advice agencies have conducted cases like these, often acting for groups of individuals, as it fits their aim of developing social welfare law to enable more people on lower incomes to have access to justice. Examples of the types of cases which have been conducted in this way have included those where the clients have challenged their rights to certain state benefits, including public sector housing accommodation, or clarifying that their treatment comes within the definition of discrimination law, or to clarify the circumstances in which an individual can claim asylum.

Many of these specialist organisations employ experienced lawyers to ensure that the aims of the organisation include developing legal and social justice rights. Clients who are involved in these cases may find that they can take a long time to resolve but once resolved will not only benefit that client but that category of individual exercising the same rights in the future. The map of advice agencies, including those especially committed to challenging the law for individuals whose rights they represent, is provided in more detail in chapter 1.

PART 5

Using the law

CHAPTER 18

Legal systems, courts and tribunals in England and Wales

18.1   Introduction: navigating the legal system

For a new adviser, understanding how our legal system works can be just as problematic as for a client who has been plunged into the system for the first time and who wishes to access it to right a perceived wrong.

For the adviser it will be necessary to be familiar with the court and tribunal system since an important part of legal advice is about being able to explain what will happen if a court or tribunal takes over the resolution of the problem which the adviser has been asked to try and resolve at first hand. Even if the adviser only practices in one area of law where usually they will only be using one court or tribunal, it will be useful to understand the whole map of the legal system in order to see where the court or tribunal they use fits in, or what happens if decisions made in that court or tribunal are challenged or appealed.

Each part of the legal system in England and Wales deals with different types of claims. These will be looked at below. There are, however, a number of common features about the system, some of which may be obvious, others not.

Formality

The legal system is formal and that extends to tribunals. Those using the legal system for the first time find that they are required to comply with the formality of court proceedings. Many find some aspects of the court system outdated and at odds with how the other public bodies function. There are many features of the language used in the legal system which are not plain English. Clothes are worn by Judges and advocates in a fashion which dates back many hundreds of years, and there is sometimes a perception that most judges and barristers appear to come from the white middle class group in our society.

The court system is conscious of these trends and while it remains formal for many obvious reasons, it is addressing its image and is more accessible also in terms of how people can use the system than was the case five or ten years ago. Websites have been set up to help people to understand what goes on in court and podcasts and other modern communication tools are used to provide information about how things work.[1] Efforts are being made to provide a more diverse

---

1   See eg Her Majesty's Court Service (HMCS) at www.judiciary.gov.uk describing the function and work of judges.

legal profession including careful scrutiny of who is appointed as a judge and how this process takes place. Oddly enough, one aspect of going to court which seems likely to survive is the mode of dress worn by lawyers and judges.

Fees and costs

The civil court system will usually require fees to be paid before an individual can enter into that court system and in some cases as they progress through it. There are some exceptions to this, most notably where an individual is using the small claims court, or where they are in receipt of certain state benefits (eg, Income Based Jobseekers Allowance or Tax Credit, which means they are in a low income bracket).[2]

Costs are a major feature in the civil court system in that the court will usually order the losing party to pay the winning party's legal fees and expenses (which they will have to pay in addition to paying their own costs and expenses). As we have seen in the previous chapter this is known as costs following the event. There are exceptions to this and where, for example, a low income client has public funding the rules about costs are different. In the criminal system, costs and financial penalties are a regular feature of the outcome of a criminal case. This is one aspect of the court system which advisers need to be aware of and they should familiarise themselves with the costs rules in the part of the legal system they are using.

Tribunals do not charge fees for those wishing to use the relevant tribunal. Nor do they have a system of costs following the event. Some tribunals do have a discretion to order costs to be paid which advisers should familiarise themselves with.

Procedure and Rules

The criminal and civil legal systems have Rules which judges follow in hearing cases and which advisers and advocates are expected to know. The Rules in the civil court system (known as the Civil Procedure Rules (CPR) were completely overhauled in the late 1990s and now contain many key themes in relation to how claims should be prepared and presented. They are constantly under review and there are

---

2   For a useful explanation of how exemptions and remissions operate in relation to court fees see Her Majesty's Court Service (HMCS) website at www. hmcourts-service.gov.uk/infoabout/fees/exemption/exemption.htm.

regular updates to them. They provide a comprehensive framework of procedure at the same time as underpinning the power of a judge to exercise their discretion in how they arrive at a just decision.

In the criminal system, rules and procedures are contained in a number of statutes. The Courts Act 2003 deals with many, but not all, procedural aspects of the criminal justice system.

In both the civil and criminal systems, rules of procedure guide the judiciary in the process of the exercising of justice. The judiciary forms an integral part of the constitution and as such has powers and discretion to examine a wide range of issues including, on some occasions, how Government is exercising its lawful duty. These powers give the judiciary independence to interpret our laws and how they operate.

Tribunals on the other hand are created by Acts of Parliament which give them the ability to function. They are known as 'creatures of statute'. Each tribunal has its own rules and procedures which dictate what the tribunal can and cannot do. They are inferior to the main court system and not part of it but are governed by The Council of Tribunals.

18.2 The court structure in England and Wales

The legal system in England and Wales is divided into civil and criminal law. A flowchart showing the structure of the criminal and civil systems is shown opposite.

The criminal system

Although this book does not deal with advice on criminal matters, it will be helpful to see how the criminal system functions. The 'lower' courts are at the foot of the flowchart and the 'higher' ones at the top. However, it will be seen that the European Court of Human Rights sits over to the left as it is a court to which any person may be able to apply if they believe that their human rights have been infringed by any public body (including the Government), court or tribunal. The court sits in Strasbourg and the judges are drawn from all the countries which are signatories to the European Convention on the Protection of Human Rights and Fundamental Freedoms.

The 'lowest' court on the rung in the criminal system is the magistrates' court. It will be seen from the flowchart that the court will also hear civil cases either relating to family matters (care orders,

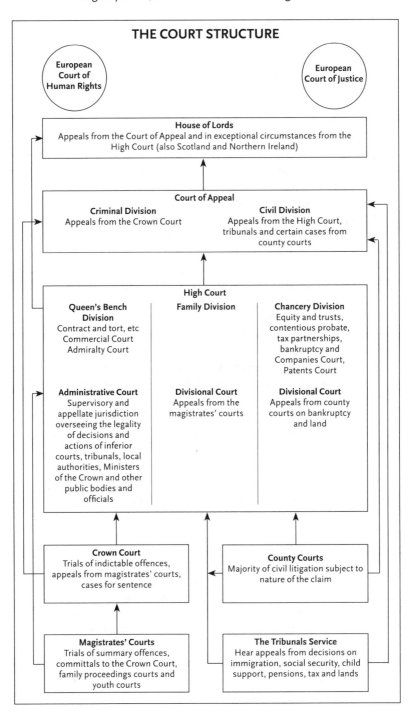

THE COURT STRUCTURE

European Court of Human Rights

European Court of Justice

House of Lords
Appeals from the Court of Appeal and in exceptional circumstances from the High Court (also Scotland and Northern Ireland)

Court of Appeal

Criminal Division
Appeals from the Crown Court

Civil Division
Appeals from the High Court, tribunals and certain cases from county courts

High Court

Queen's Bench Division
Contract and tort, etc
Commercial Court
Admiralty Court

Family Division

Chancery Division
Equity and trusts, contentious probate, tax partnerships, bankruptcy and Companies Court, Patents Court

Administrative Court
Supervisory and appellate jurisdiction overseeing the legality of decisions and actions of inferior courts, tribunals, local authorities, Ministers of the Crown and other public bodies and officials

Divisional Court
Appeals from the magistrates' courts

Divisional Court
Appeals from county courts on bankruptcy and land

Crown Court
Trials of indictable offences, appeals from magistrates' courts, cases for sentence

County Courts
Majority of civil litigation subject to nature of the claim

Magistrates' Courts
Trials of summary offences, committals to the Crown Court, family proceedings courts and youth courts

The Tribunals Service
Hear appeals from decisions on immigration, social security, child support, pensions, tax and lands

residence orders etc) and to a range of other civil matters, most commonly non-payment of council tax, or TV licences.

The magistrates also hear a range of criminal cases. Cases involving young people (under the age of 18) are heard in the youth courts which are a part of the magistrates' court but the hearings take place in smaller, less formal rooms.

Although the starting point for a criminal case will be the magistrates' court, some cases of a more serious nature will be heard by a judge and jury sitting in the Crown Court. Alternatively, the magistrates' court will send a case to the Crown Court to be heard from the outset where the defendant has asked for a jury trial, which they can do for certain types of offences being tried.

Appeals from the magistrates' courts take a different route depending on whether they come from the family or civil cases heard, or from the criminal cases tried. The Crown Court is where a person appeals against their criminal offence sentence passed on them in the magistrates' court or against their conviction there. Decisions taken in the Crown Court can be appealed further to the court of criminal appeal and ultimately to the House of Lords, but permission has to be given by the court making the decision to continue the case with a further appeal.

Appeals from the magistrates' court on civil or family cases will go to the relevant division of the High Court civil system, for which see below.

Above the magistrates' court is the Crown Court where more serious criminal offences will be heard. A decision to bring a prosecution will always be made by the Crown Prosecution Service once the police have referred the case to them. The famous Old Bailey court is a Crown Court but cases heard there will be serious ones where the judge sitting with the jury to try the case is a High Court judge rather than a circuit judge who sits to hear less serious cases in the Crown Court.

It is hopefully sufficiently well known that cases heard in the Crown Court are decided on by a jury who are all members of the public required as part of their civic duty to sit on a jury. At the end of a criminal trial the members of the jury will receive guidance from the judge on the legal issues and the way in which they should consider the evidence they have heard in terms of what the law says, but the decision rests with them. Their role is to decide on the evidence they have heard whether the defendant is guilty or not guilty. That is their verdict. They will not decide on sentence to be passed once they hand up a guilty verdict; that is for the judge to decide.

The civil system

Whereas a criminal case is a case brought by the state ('the Crown') against an individual to punish them for their offence against the state, civil claims involve private claims between two individuals. Although it is often the case that a crime, such as robbery, assault or blackmail will affect another individual's life, the state decides which actions amount to a crime which it has the right to punish perpetrators for committing. The Government sets out the laws of the land and all individuals in society are bound by this 'rule of law'.

The civil system on the other hand deals with a range of matters which individuals can seek a remedy or decision on in relation to everyday life and their dealings with each other. Claims range from disputes in business dealings, consumer's claims about quality of goods or workmanship, disputes between neighbours, accidents in public places causing injuries and family or matrimonial disputes or problems.

Like the criminal system there is a hierarchy of courts dealing with cases in the civil court system. It will be seen from the flowchart on page 241 that the European Court of Human Rights (ECtHR) sits to the left. It is a body to which any individual may have recourse in relation to a breach of their human rights. Indeed, since the passing of the Human Rights Act 1998 all courts and tribunals must take human rights issues into account when hearing cases and deliberating and deciding on outcomes.

The European Court of Justice

It will also be seen on the flowchart that the European Court of Justice (ECJ) sits at the top to the right. The ECJ (which sits in Luxembourg) encompasses all the other courts in the civil system as a sort of 'umbrella' court. This is because the ECJ may be required by any court to assist in reaching the correct decision by interpreting a law or ruling in line with European law (European law being equally applicable and as much a part of UK law as the laws passed by the UK government). Either a court or an individual can in principle ask the ECJ for a ruling on a relevant issue. Usually the referral will be made by the court. Furthermore, tribunals can also refer questions to the ECJ for a ruling. For example, referrals have been made to the ECJ on pension and benefits rights and on employment law rights from the relevant tribunal hearing these types of cases. There are quite complex rules for how these referrals may be made but in terms of the structure of our legal system the ECJ is nevertheless a court to which an individual in the UK can have recourse.

Lower court: the county court

The court at the lowest end of the civil system is the county court, which, like the magistrates' court, is a local court. There are county courts in every district of the country where people will go with their individual disputes. Many simple and lower value claims are heard in the small claims court. This is part and parcel of the county court but running on a different speedier 'track' than other claims heard in the county court. Here claims are heard relatively soon after they are commenced with fewer formalities and will relate to money issues worth less than £5,000 (or £1,000 in the case of personal injury claims). Such claims will be heard by a district judge in his or her chambers (a private informal room in the court). The district judge hears claims in open court as well, where claims worth over £15,000 are heard by a circuit judge, who is more senior.

County courts also hear landlords' or mortgage providers' claims for repossession of residential property, for example based on a history of arrears payments of the rent or mortgage. Simpler or uncontested claims are heard by the district judge with the contested claims heard by the circuit judge. It should be noted that any claim which goes before a judge to decide on a dispute will be called a 'trial' (to be 'tried' by the judge) just as it will be in a criminal case where the case is tried by a jury. The difference in the civil system is that the two opposing parties in a case are usually private individuals whereas the two parties in the criminal case will be the State (or 'crown') against a private individual.

The High Court

Where personal injury claims are worth over £50,000 they will be started in the High Court. Other civil claims worth over £15,000 can be started in the High Court. Most civil claims in the High Court are heard in the branch of the High Court known as the Queen's Bench Division. As is seen in the flowchart, the High Court divides its business into three areas, or divisions, with differing cases heard in each of those areas. Judges who sit are therefore specialists in the areas of law they hear cases on. In brief, most civil cases (contract disputes, injury claims and other legal wrongs such as nuisance or negligence) are heard in the Queen's Bench Division.

The Family Division deals with a range of family issues including divorce and claims concerning the welfare of children include wardships. This court also hears appeals from the family decisions made in the county courts and the magistrates' courts.

A third division, the Chancery Division, hears cases relating to business matters, wills and probate (proof of who will inherit a person's property) and a range of other business-related legal claims.

The High Court also has a Queen's Bench Divisional Court which in part deals with cases of administrative law. These are cases where an individual will be challenging decisions made by public bodies, such as local authorities, as being wrongly exercised or beyond their powers. This is also known as public law. It involves the court considering decisions which are made which have affected one person but which could also have an impact on a sector of society. Examples are decisions about planning, school admissions policies or care provisions. The Public Law Project[3] is a national agency which specialises in identifying issues of this type on behalf of members of society who lack the means or ability to pursue such cases, which can be costly and complicated.

Parties who wish to appeal decisions made in the High Court will do so by way of appeal to the Court of Appeal (Civil Division) and from there to the House of Lords.

Tribunals

There are a large number of tribunals which deal with a range of matters including mental health review panels, lands tribunals, criminal injuries compensation, and tax. They all now come under the Tribunals Service set up in 2006. As the name tribunal indicates, hearings will usually be conducted before a panel of three people and usually there are two lay (not legally qualified) people on the panel, with the chair being a qualified lawyer.

Although tribunals are not part of the main civil system, they do overlap with it in many respects. Some tribunals will allow for an appeal system to operate. Some types of tribunals (such as the Asylum and Immigration Tribunal (AIT) exist to hear appeals against decisions made by the Government. The AIT, for example, hears appeals from decisions of the Home Office in relation to asylum-seekers or concerning immigration rights.

Others, such as the Special Educational Needs and Disability Tribunal will allow for their decisions to be appealed to the High Court or the Court of Appeal. The Employment Tribunals have their own appeal court which is part of the High Court, the Employment Appeal Tribunal (EAT), and from there further appeals can be made to the Court of Appeal and from there to the House of Lords.

3   www.publiclawproject.org.uk.

Statutes, case-law and precedent

In chapter 19 we will be looking at how to do legal research as part of advice skills. Here we will need to examine what courts and tribunals are basing their decisions on.

Statutes

Most of the laws which the courts enforce derive from statute (Acts of Parliament) – or supplementary legislation (statutory instruments (SIs)). There are, however, some unwritten laws, known as common law. Some, such as the crime of assault, are also described in various statutes; others, such as the civil wrong relating to the injury of another person, are not described in statutes but there are statutes or regulations which describe how such claims will operate, for example who should be sued and how blame or damage may be apportioned between various defendants. An adviser needs to be aware of the core statutes and regulations relating to the area they are advising on and where they are applicable to their client's case.

Case-law and precedent

The legal cases are just as important. Judges have the power to interpret a law when they are trying cases which come before them. Their decisions can have the effect of clarifying what the statute or common law means or how it should be interpreted in certain circumstances. Once a higher court has carried out this exercise of interpretation or guidance, the decision will then become precedent or guidance to be applied when similar issues are looked at by a court in the future.

The hierarchy of the court system is a fundamental part of this precedent-based approach to our laws. The decisions of a higher court will be binding on a lower court. In other words a decision made in the Court of Appeal will need to be applied and followed by a judge in the High Court and the courts below when the case to be heard is on the same or similar facts. This concept of precedent-based law is sometimes called 'judge-made law' or case-law. The judge-made decisions which are the most binding are those made in the House of Lords.

We will see an example of how a precedent is made in chapter 19. There we will look at a case heard by the House of Lords in the 1930s which looked at the facts of a case and, arising from its consideration of those facts, gave guidance for how the courts should in future approach the question of when someone may be found liable for a wrong or injury caused to another person by their actions.

Judges in the European Court of Justice will also interpret our legislation by answering specific questions as to what the European laws (Directives) mean and how each member state should apply them in their own legislation. A decision of the ECJ will bind the Government of the member state from where the reference to the ECJ came. Although in some circumstances it is possible to ask the European Court for a remedy (compensation) in relation to what an individual regards as the failure of a UK court to implement their rights properly,[4] the usual approach of the European court is to hand down its opinion on the law it has been asked to interpret to the state concerned.

18.3 Judges and staff in the court system

Court staff

Most people who approach a court or tribunal will initially be put in touch with the administrative staff who support the running of the court. They are usually called clerks. Any processing of the necessary paperwork which gets a case into that court's system will be done by them. They will process fees and other monies paid to the court, ensure forms are correctly completed and arrange the timetable of hearings in consultation with the judges who sit at the court.

Cases in all parts of the legal system are allocated case numbers and references. When you contact the court you will always need to know that reference and quote it to the clerk or court administrator if you have a query about the case. You will usually be referred to the rules or procedures of that court in reply to a query. The court clerks will not be able to advise you how to proceed with a case you are involved in nor can they give any legal advice. If you have an administrative question, such as checking the date for a hearing you are involved in, you might be asked to put your question in writing.

When you arrive at a court to attend a case or hearing you will be guided into the room by an usher who ensures that the formalities for running the hearing are adhered to. That person, for example, will ask those in the court room to stand when a judge or the magistrates come into the room or leave it. In the magistrates' courts and the higher courts, the courts will also have a clerk who sits with the magistrate or judge. These individuals are there to guide the panel or

---

4   Often referred to as *Frankovich* claims following the case of *Frankovich v Italy* [1992] IRLR 84.

judge and to assist them in the smooth running of their lists of cases. They have different functions depending which court they sit in and are different also from the court office clerks in that their primary function is to assist the person hearing the case, whereas the court clerks are there to ensure the smooth running of the court or tribunal as a whole.

Magistrates and judges

Magistrates

Most magistrates are not legally qualified. Anyone who is over 18 can apply to sit as a magistrate, who are also called Justices of the Peace (JPs). They sit as a panel of three (usually called a 'bench'). They are guided on the law by a clerk who sits with them at all times (the magistrates' clerk). This person is legally qualified and well versed in the law the magistrates are asked to deal with. The clerk will confer with the bench during a hearing and will offer advice on the law relevant to each case being heard. The clerk does not, however, take any part in the decision-making process. There are also legally-qualified magistrates called district judges (magistrates' court) and these will try the same sort of cases as the bench and will also hear more complex cases in the magistrates' court. They will always sit alone to hear a case.

Judges and tribunal chairs

Judges and tribunal chairs (who are a part of the judiciary) are now all appointed by the Government department, the Ministry of Justice (MoJ). The most senior judge is the Lord Chief Justice (up to April 2006 this position was occupied by the Lord Chancellor). All judges are experienced lawyers, either solicitors or barristers, of a minimum required number of years' practice in law. They receive comprehensive training in their functions, as well as in the law they are required to deal with. The training continues on a regular basis throughout the time they sit as judges.

Advisers who meet judges in court are often uncertain how to address them. The same is true of the individual litigant. Some guidance is offered opposite.

Although not all the judges in the court system are set out in the table, it nevertheless offers guidance on how to address the judges an adviser is most likely to come into contact with. Knowing the correct mode of address to a judge will show courtesy and will give the

Court or tribunal	Title of judge	Form of address
Tribunal Chairman	Chairman (whether male or female).	Sir or Madam (or Madam Chairman)
Magistrates	Justice of the Peace (JP)	Your Worship (but usually Sir or Madam or Madam Chairman)
District Judges (county court)	District Judge (Jones etc)	Sir or Madam
Circuit Judges (bigger cases in the county court)	His or Her Honour Judge Jones	Your Honour
High Court Judges	The Honourable Mrs Justice Jones	My Lady, My Lord
Court of Appeal Judges	The Right Honourable Lady Justice Jones	My Lady, My Lord

adviser confidence to engage with the judge if asked questions by him or her.

As might be guessed, if we were to carry on higher through the court system, we would see that judges would continue to have more extended (and exalted) titles. Nevertheless, any more senior judges not referred to here will be addressed in court as My Lord or My Lady. Most advisers, likely only to attend a tribunal, county court or magistrates' court should therefore be safe in knowing that the person they address will be addressed as either Sir or Madam, unless they are before a circuit judge in the county court who will wear a purple robe and who will be addressed as Your Honour.

18.4 Using the court system: protocols, tips and tactics

In this section the emphasis is on some aspects of protocol when using courts or attending a hearing. An important part of using the court system is knowing how it all operates in order to make it easier to use. As we saw at the beginning of this chapter the legal system is a formal one and a serious and courteous approach to using that system will assist.

Communicating with court staff

- Be ready with the case number and any additional reference initials of a case you are involved in each time you contact the court or tribunal. Put it at the top of all correspondence with the court or tribunal and have it to hand when making telephone calls to the court office.

- Be prepared to put even the simplest request in writing. Court files are still in paper version and the clerks will be required to show each and every step that has been taken on the file.

- Be firm but polite with court clerks when trying to make progress. If you have waited a long time for a reply to a letter or a date for a hearing you should receive an explanation. However, you may be dealing with someone who has no knowledge of your case or more importantly less knowledge than you have in relation to the law or the legal procedures. You will need to bear in mind that the function of court clerks is to manage court business and not to help you to resolve your client's case.

- Be aware of how to deal with cases on the telephone. Some civil court hearings now take place on the telephone. Even if you are acting for a defendant you may have to take responsibility for organising the hearing in advance if your opponent is unrepresented. Make sure you know the exact process of preparing for the hearing by checking the relevant CPR.

Complying with deadlines

All courts and tribunal hearings have deadlines and time limits for when you need to be ready with certain aspects of the preparation of your case. It is not always possible to meet those deadlines, not least because of a problem coming from the direction of the client. Nevertheless, the penalties for failing to meet a deadline can be severe. They can include costs orders made against the defaulting party or, in some cases, an individual even being prevented from defending a case or continuing with a case. This is usually referred to as being struck out.

If an adviser is faced with a missed deadline, perhaps due to ignorance or stress on the part of their client, no delay must occur in contacting the court or tribunal concerned and, where appropriate, the opposing party. Any application to seek more time or to 'turn the clock back' in some way will need to be made as soon as possible and will always need to be made in writing, no matter what the venue is for the case. No court or tribunal will be able to meet a request to delay or adjourn on the telephone.

Attending a court or tribunal

Checking in, case listing and waiting

If you or your client have not attended the venue before, make sure that you allow plenty of time to get there and to locate the room you need to go to. A receptionist will often combine a security check with a check of which case you are here for, so the case reference and number should be kept handy as you enter the building.

Most court buildings have a daily case list pinned to a notice board near the entrance, indicating the names of the parties, the times of the hearings and where in the building hearings will take place. There will usually be waiting areas or waiting rooms. Be prepared to wait. A lot of courts and tribunals will list a number of cases to be heard at the same time. This is for the simple reason that there are often last minute changes which lead to cases being removed from the list. Instead of the court having blanks at various times of the day, they will work their way down the list of all those who are ready to proceed at the time the case is listed, usually at 10.00 am or 10.30 am. It is rare for cases to be listed in the afternoon although they may not be heard until the afternoon. Warn your client that they may have to wait for some time and suggest that they cover their childcare or other domestic arrangements.

On the subject of children, unless a child is the subject of a case or is directly involved in it, clients will find that courts and tribunals are, on the whole, not particularly child-friendly. Unless the child is part of the case, the court will not usually allow children under the age of 14 in court. There are waiting facilities but, owing to the length of time often involved in waiting for a hearing, this will usually amount to inadequate provision for a small child. It is rare that drinks machines or refreshments are situated in courts or near the waiting areas of a court or tribunal. If at all possible, therefore, clients should try to make other arrangements for young children. If they need to bring them to court they should try to have someone with them who can take over the care of the child for the client as they go into their hearing. From 1 July 2007 all courts and tribunals are non-smoking venues.

18.5   Court etiquette and language

Dress and behaviour at court

Dress

Court staff responsible for getting people in place for their hearings are called ushers. They will often wear formal dress, sometimes a floor length black robe over their day wear. They will address parties by the family names and will be polite and helpful. Although being at court can be very stressful, it is always useful to remind the client of the formality of the court system and to suggest that they dress soberly and conservatively. Lawyers or other legally-qualified practitioners who have a right of audience in various levels of the legal system will be required to observe a dress code. Barristers, for example, will wear a wig and gown in some courts.[5] A right of audience in the courts will have been obtained as a result of qualifying as a barrister or solicitor or by obtaining a relevant qualification to appear in certain courts. An adviser who does not have that right will not be able to address a court although they do regularly go to tribunals to represent their clients. They should dress according to the seriousness and formality of the environment they are functioning in.

Courts will also expect people to converse quietly while they wait so as not to disturb the conduct of the cases being heard. They will not allow the use of mobile phones in the court but will allow them to be used in a court building.

Once in court, behaviour should be as follows:

- Stand up each time a judge or magistrate enters or leaves the room – usually an usher will ask all in court to 'rise'.
- Wait until the magistrate or judge has sat down before sitting down.
- Switch off mobile phones or put into silent mode.
- Do not speak to or address the judge or magistrate from the seating area of the court.
- Do not talk to others in court unless absolutely essential and then only whispering. Clients should whisper if they need to talk to their representative in court.
- Do not react (facial expressions or vocal reactions) to what is said during a hearing.
- Do not eat, drink or chew gum in court.

5   As from 2008, gowns will be worn in the civil courts, and wigs and gowns will continue to be worn in the criminal courts.

18.6 Language

We have already outlined how to address judges and other members of the judiciary in the legal system. Although the courts have spent considerable effort in ensuring that they communicate with their users in plain English, it still remains the case that judges and lawyers do use language which is often quite different from everyday speech. In some cases Latin will be used to describe a form of claim or order and this can be very intimidating for a lay user of the court system and can confuse an adviser with no formal legal training. The answer is probably to try to familiarise yourself with some basic expressions. At the same time you should not be afraid to ask politely for an explanation of an expression or 'Latin tag' used in a hearing.

It would be problematic and probably off-putting to set out here all the Latin tags which may be used in court. Nevertheless, a short glossary of some basic but unfamiliar expressions which arise in the course of a hearing taking place is offered. A few Latin phrases have crept into this list but only on the basis that they are used very regularly in the context of hearing a case:

Addressing the court. This is usually by way of invitation by a judge who will invite a party or representative to make a speech. The speech will often be made at the end of a hearing where a representative is invited by the judge to sum up his or her client's case and put forward their good points.

Adjourning. Putting a date back which the court has already fixed for a hearing to take place. A decision to adjourn can only be made by the court or tribunal and could in theory take place at any stage either in the prior stages, in the preparation for a hearing or during the hearing itself. A party can ask for an adjournment for whatever reason but cannot force the decision on to the court.

Being minded or being of a mind. This expression is sometimes used by judges to indicate how their thinking is going and in what direction in relation to a particular issue. It is sometimes used by lawyers in discussing cases with their clients or with other lawyers.

Being without instructions. This refers to a lawyer or representative who cannot take any steps on behalf of their client as they have no instructions from the client to do so. This is different from a situation which often arises in court where there is a new development and a representative needs to take instructions on that new development. In those circumstances they will take instructions. The instructions may be that the client is not happy to proceed. However, if a representative is without instructions there is nothing they can do. Where this situation persists for some time the representative may have no option but to withdraw from the case. An example of this was given in chapter 3 in the letter terminating the adviser/client relationship in section 3.5.

Closing speech. A closing speech is given by a party's representative in a court or tribunal. The representative will be addressing the court. They will have prepared that speech before the hearing and will then need to adapt it to the way the evidence has gone. It will be a speech summing up the evidence and highlighting for the judge or jury the best analysis of that evidence in order to argue that their clients' case is the one which should succeed.

Cor (Coriam – 'cor-ee-am'). This Latin word will appear at the foot of a barrister's brief when they record the outcome of a hearing. When that brief is handed back to the adviser who has asked the barrister to attend they will see the word Cor, meaning 'in the presence of' and the name of the judge who heard the case.

Costs in the cause. In the main civil system, costs applications may be made prior to the completion of a hearing. If a judge is unwilling to commit to a costs order at an early stage, he or she may order that all costs will ultimately be borne by the party who the trial judge orders to pay costs. The question of who pays the costs therefore is decided at the end of the case and earlier costs orders of 'costs in the cause' are added to that party's requirement to pay. As previously indicated, costs in the court system are complex but relevant and people using the court system will need to be aware of their application, of which this is just one example.

Counsel. This simply refers to a barrister representative but is often used in the third person in the context of a court hearing (eg, 'Counsel may wish to make a separate application').

Ex parte ('ex-pah-tey'). Another Latin expression used. It refers to applications as well as hearings which a judge hears and where only one party will be required to attend. A typical example of this will be an application heard by a judge in a matrimonial or child-care context with only one of the parties being present. Since the introduction of the Civil Procedure Rules (the CPR) courts are meant to refer to 'without notice' applications or hearings rather than use the Latin words 'ex parte', but this expression still survives.

Executing. This word is used in a range of different contexts in court parlance. It means 'carrying out' or putting into effect. It can be used to mean that a person with a judgment against them might have their goods seized (executing a writ or court order to seize goods). It is also used to describe the process of writing out a person's will (executing a will).

Finding for or against. This expression is sometimes used when a legal representative is discussing a point they are making in court. They may put the point on the basis that the judge may decide in their favour or not. This will be known as a finding. At the end of a case the judge will find for one party or another. A finding can also be made on part of an issue being tried. So the judge might find that the defendant owed the claimant some money but not the actual amount claimed.

First open date. When a court decides either to list a case or to adjourn a hearing they will usually refer to the first open date, meaning the first date when the court staff will be able to allocate that case to a judge for a hearing.

Inter alia ('inter-ay-lee-ah'). This means 'among other things' and will be used both in court and in court pleadings (see below) to make it clear that this item is one of a number. For example, a landlord may claim that the tenant has caused damage to his property and may refer to the fact that damage was caused, inter alia, to the furnishings and fittings.

Making submissions. This is what a representative or a litigant will do when summing up their case at the end of a trial. The submissions will refer to the evidence heard and state how it assists that party's claim. There will also be references to case-law which supports the party's position (see chapter 19).

My (learned) friend. A barrister in court will refer to his or her opponent (representing the other party in the case) who is not themselves a barrister as 'my friend'. When the barrister's opponent is also a barrister they will refer to that person as my learned friend.

Obiter dictum ('oh-bit-er dict-um'). More Latin. This phrase refers to a part of a judgment which is not the main reasoning of the case decision, but is a reference to similar situations or to other cases which are relevant. A judge may decide in favour of one party, applying the law. He or she might then state how the law might apply in similar circumstances. This is not regarded as part of the judgment but is an 'aside' made in the context of giving the judgment.

Opening speech. This is made by a representative who will be leading off with their case in court, either because they are prosecuting a criminal case or because they are claiming against a defendant in a civil case. They will outline the facts briefly, refer to the issues which the judge has to decide on and sometimes, in a civil trial, ensure that the judge is aware of the history of any earlier hearings and has access to all the relevant documents.

Part heard. This is a civil case where the hearing has begun but has not been completed and will need to be completed at a later date.

Pleadings. These are the statements made by a claimant and a defendant on the relevant court forms relating to a civil claim. The claimant sets out the facts and the basis of the legal claim which they are bringing, and the way in which the defendant has caused them wrong. The claimant will also state what they are asking the court to do: award them compensation or another remedy. The defendant will write out the ways in which they might be disputing the claim and why. The pleading will form the basis of a civil claim and will be frequently referred to when witnesses are giving evidence in court. They are also referred to in the civil court system as 'a statement of case'.

Prima facie ('pry-ma-fay-see'). Latin. This literally means 'at first sight'. It is usually used in the context of looking to see if the evidence in a case will stand up to proof. Is it enough to show that there is a case? For example, if there is a prosecution for burglary, there would have to be some evidence that the accused person was at the premises at the relevant time and took the missing goods. This evidence may be by way of witnesses, security cameras or forensic evidence. If there is no prima facie evidence then there can be no case.

Reasons. This word has a stronger meaning in the context of giving out a decision or judgment at the end of a hearing than in every-day language. It is important for any court or tribunal to give reasons for their decisions so that they can be clearly seen to be properly addressing the case before them and have reached a properly deliberated judgment. A court will find in favour of one party or another and then will go on to give reasons why they have done so, taking into account the evidence heard and applying the relevant law.

Reserved judgment. Sometimes a judge or panel will indicate at the end of a case they have heard that they will not make a decision that day but at a later date and will therefore reserve their judgment which will then be sent out in writing once it is ready or is handed out or read out at a future hearing.

Skeleton arguments. These are an outline of the legal arguments which each party will be making to the judge or panel at the end of the hearing of a case. They are traditionally regarded as being drawn up by barristers. However, in any court or tribunal it will be a useful exercise to prepare to represent a client by drawing up a short document which summarises the law and any previous decided cases which are relevant and helpful to the client's case. The argument then runs through how the facts of the case are supported by the law referred to in favour of that particular party.

Statement of truth. Various documents used in the context of court proceedings will be required to be endorsed by a statement of truth. Relevant documents include a witness statement, an expert's report or a pleading (now usually called a statement of case).

The statement of truth should use the following words at the end of a statement of case:

I believe that the facts stated in this document are true.

The statement of truth at the end of a witness statement should say:

I believe that the facts stated in this witness statement are true.

Those instructing [me]. Used by barristers in court to refer to solicitors or other legal advisers who will relay to the barrister what their client would like the barrister to achieve for them. Sometimes it can refer to the client themselves.

Witness statements. A witness statement is the evidence of that witness which is put into a statement and signed by the witness. It should be signed and dated but not witnessed by anyone. It then stands as the witness' evidence and before they go into the witness box the witness will swear on a holy book (eg Bible or Koran) or affirm to the court that what they are about to say will be the truth. They will then read out their witness statement to the court or panel.

Doing legal research

19.1   Subject areas

It will always be necessary to do background research as part of advising. Even if an adviser does not think of themselves as a legal adviser they will need to be familiar with procedures and policies they are advising on and how these change and develop. It is rare, in fact, for advice work not to involve some measure of law even if it is about getting some form of support in the community for an older person, or helping benefits claimants to complete forms. Both these activities will include consideration of that individual's rights to care or support, or the possible legal consequences of not completing forms or completing them incorrectly.

It will always be necessary for individuals who advise to be aware that those they advise will set great store by what they are told and will accept it as being accurate and informed. This means that the adviser should be regularly updating their knowledge of their subject area and having a system in place for doing so. Recipients of advice not only wish to know what action can be taken to resolve their problems but what their rights are and where these rights are contained.

An adviser will usually specialise in one subject area. If, for example, you advise in welfare benefits you will become familiar with the rules and regulations which govern how these rights can be exercised as well as with the process of applying for benefits or appealing a refusal to award a benefit. You will be aware of these rules by access to handbooks which set them out and which are regularly updated,[1] as well as a range of other resources.

Often it will be hard, if not impossible, to limit advice to this topic alone. Claimants of benefits will often need advice on practical topics such as support in their community for their needs as a disabled member of the community, or grants or other services for parents of young children, as provided for in the Government's Sure Start programme.[2] In addition, they may find that the delay in receiving benefits has meant they fall behind with payments for consumer goods or rent which will have an impact on their liabilities and rights as a consumer or a tenant.

Advisers therefore often need to have a broad approach to how they advise. They should be aware of the different aspects of a client's problem. Where an adviser is familiar with more than one area of

---

1   See eg, *Child Poverty Handbook: Welfare Benefits and Tax Credits Handbook*, 9th edn, 2007–2008: available on-line at www.cpag.org..uk/onlineservices.

2   www.surestart.gov.uk/surestartservices.

advice, the organisation they work for may not have funding to offer advice on a wide range of advice topics. In this situation, advisers may need to refer clients with 'multi-claims' to other organisations for assistance with other aspects of their claims. Nevertheless, the adviser who is aware that their specialism may involve consideration of a wider problem will be able to identify how other organisations and resources can assist their client.

One way of seeing the whole picture in an advice context will be for an adviser to subscribe to magazines or electronic publications which discuss and update readers on the whole range of social welfare topics being practised. An example is the monthly magazine, *Legal Action*, published by the Legal Action Group. An example of a free on-line newsletter covering all aspects of welfare rights is Rights Net.[3]

19.2 Where to find the law

In this section, a range of the possible sources of reference for researching the law, procedure and policy on an adviser's specialist topic will be introduced, with suggestions as to who they will most benefit and how. In later sections, suggestions will be offered on how to research a given subject area using some of these resources. Although this section is aimed at the adviser in practice, it will also be of benefit to someone studying the skills of advice-giving.

Internal reference systems and websites

There are some national organisations, such as Citizens Advice, which have their own intranet bank of reference systems where an adviser working there can find out what the current legal position is on a matter they are advising about. The pages give an accurate and up-to-date outline of the legal position in an accessible and 'non-lawyerly' fashion. In addition, they, and other voluntary organisations concerned with the provision of advice, have websites which can be used by the lay person or the legal adviser and which will be able to give an in-depth analysis of the law often by referring to statutes or decided case-law. Other examples are the Disability Rights Commission[4] or Public Concern at Work,[5] who advise on whistle-blowing claims.

3 www.rightsnet.org.uk.
4 www.drc.org.uk.
5 www.pcaw.co.uk.

Search engines

There is nothing more amazing than the ability of a search engine to throw up a topic or an article you wish to find out more about. The links will be varied and sometimes appear to be random and it may be a time consuming exercise to discover the exact point being researched. The search engine method of research should really only be used to clarify the point of a decided court case or the name or details of an organisation which offers a service which would be useful in the context of the advice being offered. Although it is possible to check a number of sources of relevant information using a search engine, it will rarely lead into any articles or documents which will give in-depth analysis or information about a legal topic as these are usually only available for subscribers.

Books

There is no shortage of books on the various topics an adviser may need to advise on. In the areas of law more traditionally practised by solicitors in private practice, such as conveyancing, probate or commercial client work, books are usually in the form of an outline of the relevant law in some considerable detail and are fairly specialist, designed for those who already know some law or are already familiar with the law in that area.

There are other categories of book which have a practical approach to resolving a legal problem arising in the context of that subject, or which are overviews of one branch of a legal topic, such as books on running small claims in the county court or calculating compensation for personal injury claims.

There is also a range of books on specific topics which are aimed specifically at the student market, especially students studying for professional examinations to qualify as solicitors or barristers. These books are usually concise, accessible and accurate as they are updated each year for a new intake of students. They often form a useful introduction to a particular legal subject or practice area.

There is another category of short books, which may be regarded as 'crammers' or very short versions of a legal topic. Sometimes they are so concise they will not be able to explain fully the body of knowledge that underpins the legal topic. Their main function is to summarise an area of law which had already been studied in depth, to aid in revising for examinations or assessments.

Magazines, subscriptions or articles

A regular subscription to a magazine in a given area of law is an excellent way of keeping up to date with that topic as the contributors are always experienced practitioners in their field. This also goes for e-mail alerters provided by some journals as a supplementary resource, or provided by solicitors firms or barristers' chambers, all of which are a useful way of keeping practitioners and advisers up to date with changes in the law or policy developments.

Some advisers and practitioners will also make sure they read reports of ongoing cases or trials in the press to keep abreast generally of how the courts are interpreting the law.

It is necessary for anyone who advises on a legal topic to be aware of recent case-law developments and to be watchful for decisions which will create or refine precedent-based law. It is possible to subscribe to some of these case reports on-line. *The Times*, for example, regularly reports on cases in the three divisions of the High Court, the Asylum and Immigration Tribunal and the European Courts. These reports are known as The Times Law Reports and appear in the newspaper each week or can be accessed on-line via subscription. Specialist areas of law also have their own law reports. Examples are the Housing Law Reports (HLR) and the Industrial Relations Law Reports (IRLR). How case reports are written up and codified is discussed in more detail in section 19.5.

Statutes and regulations

If an adviser needs to read a statute or, more likely, a section of a statute they can do so on-line by going to Her Majesty's Stationery Office website (The Office of Public Sector Information).[6] It is also possible to buy the statute or regulation in paperback form for a reasonable price from the HMSO Bookshop: they can be ordered on-line or by telephone.

Some legal books are also in the form of statutes and/or regulations all of which relate to one particular topic. Some have commentary on these statutes but usually law books are divided into either textbooks or statute books. Some books replicate statutes, which usually means the book is more affordable, but care should be taken to ensure that it is up to date is and fits the purpose. In some advice

6   www.opsi.gov.uk.

areas it will be very useful to have a handy statute book which high-lights the most common part of the statute for reference purposes.

19.3   Statutes and statutory instruments explained

Statutes

A statute is simply another word for an Act of Parliament. Statutes and statutory instruments are usually referred to as legislation. Parliament has unlimited powers to introduce Acts of Parliament which will regulate all areas of public life and some areas of private life. These will include all the statutes concerned with criminal justice, to freedom of information laws, matrimonial laws or consumer laws regulating fair consumer practices. Most Acts of Parliament are known as 'public acts' but there are some 'private acts' which relate solely to the function of a specific body or corporation, for example the legislation dealing with the development of various Channel Tunnel projects by certain companies.

Acts are processed through the parliamentary system on their way to becoming law, and there are various preliminary stages, including committees and debates. The draft of an Act (which will usually start life as a White Paper and then a Bill) will be debated in the House of Commons and must be ratified by the House of Lords before it is given Royal Assent by the Queen. Sometimes the House of Lords will amend or reject a Bill and it may fail to become law. The House of Commons is nevertheless entitled to re-introduce it in the next session of Parliament.

There are some Acts of Parliament, but not many, which were brought into being on the initiative of one Member of Parliament. In the preliminary or debating stage these are known as Private Members' Bills. Once a statute becomes law it will normally be incapable of challenge by an individual or a court.

Some legislation has been subject to challenge by the courts where it has been argued that it contravenes a European Directive or human rights legislation, which initially derived from Europe. A Directive is also legislation and member states should not pass legislation which contravenes European law in any way as it has sovereignty over all our legislation. Many examples of this European sovereignty can be found in everyday life. For example, a local authority or a company will keep pace with European law in the way in which they carry out their statutory functions, such as waste disposal or health and safety.

Statutory instruments

Statutory instruments (SIs) are usually also known as Regulations. They may also be called Rules or Orders – see, for example, the Civil Procedure Rules 1998. An SI will be given a date and a number, relating to where it comes in the series of SIs passed in any particular year. An SI does not have to be debated in Parliament in order to become law. It is often described as secondary legislation.

The SI will usually be a supplementary to a statute and will provide additional provisions relating to that statute. An example is a key statute on health and safety at work, the Management of Health and Safety at Work Act 1999. This Act has given rise to a range of SIs dealing with specific workplaces and types of health and safety hazards. An example is the Provision and Use of Work Equipment Regulations 1998 whose subject matter is hopefully self-explanatory.

Another use of SIs is to pass law which needs to be passed to comply with a European Directive. An example of this is the Working Time Regulations 1998 which were passed to comply with the European Working Time Directive and which provide, as the Directive does, for minimum paid holidays, rest breaks and maximum hours of work for all workers and employees.

Often a statute will indicate that in respect of parts of that statute the Secretary of State will be allowed to lay down, or enact, Regulations dealing with that aspect of the statute. Some statutes could even be referred to as 'empty boxes' waiting to be filled in terms of an SI providing the full details of the relevant legislation. The advantage to the government of enacting law through an SI rather than a statute is speed and efficiency. However, for an adviser it can often mean having to be sure that not only are they aware of the main piece of legislation and what it covers but that also any SI is known about as it will usually complement or complete what the statute has set out to do.

Format

A statute is categorised by its title and the year in which it was introduced, for example the Freedom of Information Act 2000. The same is true for a statutory instrument which is given a number as well as a year, for example the Working Time Regulations SI 1998 No 1833.

A numbered paragraph of a statute is always referred to as a section and usually abbreviated to 's' (eg Housing Act 1988 s21). A numbered paragraph of a statutory instrument will be referred to as a reg or regulation (eg regulation or reg 21 of the Working Time Regulations 1998).

An adviser should know the key statutes relevant to their area of law, what they cover and what, if any, regulations supplement those statutes. The adviser will from time to time be checking exactly what a specific piece of legislation says. Sometimes statutes are hard to understand as the wording of legislation is concise and the proper meaning occasionally hard to fathom. Some statutes have a useful 'explanatory note' at the end. Some books will contain statutes and will explain by way of footnotes and commentary the meaning of some sections of the statute. More commonly, the meaning and practical operation and effect of statutes are set out in legal books.

19.4   Using books

Statutes in books

If the adviser needs to have regular access to statutes or SIs they may check these on-line or have shortened versions of them set out in a book which contains the key statutes or SIs they need to know. However, it is often hard to judge whether the parts omitted from a shortened statute book are indeed less frequently applicable. For those new to law or advice, there will certainly be some advantage to knowing the key statutes in your areas and having on hand a copy of that statute or at least key statutory provisions. Free downloads of statutes can be seen at statutelaw.gov.uk, a website developed by the Ministry of Justice. Note, however, that the latest amendments to these may not always be up to date.

Judges will often refer in detail to specific sections of a statute when making decisions, and this is because it is their function to ensure that when they apply the law to the facts of a particular case they are referring to the relevant statute or SI and ensuring that they interpret it correctly.

It will not necessarily be helpful for an adviser to sit and read large chunks of legislation and to memorise it. What they will need to do is to ensure that they are aware of key provisions and know what they mean, if necessary by having a book which helps them to interpret and understand legislation. Furthermore, they should have a system to help themselves keep up to date with any changes. In order to ensure their knowledge of legislation is accurate, they will use a combination of the statute source itself, a book which helps them to understand its meaning and application, and a search engine or updater to ensure that they are up to date with changes.

The application of law in a book

The type of book which deals with a legal topic in detail will be useful to the experienced adviser or practitioner and will also be helpful for students. Large tomes such as *Archbold: Criminal Pleadings, Evidence and Practice* or *Chitty on Contracts* will usually be on the bookshelf of a specialist lawyer in these areas of law. These works are regarded as the cornerstone book, the 'Bible', in the areas of law they cover and new editions are published on a regular basis. Some of these detailed works will be in multi-volume loose-leaf format (often called Encyclopedia). The publisher will regularly send updates of the pages to be replaced to match changes in the law for readers to insert. Increasingly these detailed books can be subscribed to on-line.

An overview of law in a book

A book which gives an overview of the law in a certain area will be useful for beginners, non-legal advisers as well as experienced advisers and practitioners looking for a quick reference guide or an aide-mémoire. These books are usually in paperback form and are relatively affordable. They will explain how the law operates and discuss how courts or tribunals have interpreted it in the recent past. They will often give practical suggestions on how to advise on or represent clients on that area of law.

Such a book will initially be read right through as an introduction to a subject or a new subject and then kept for regular reference. An adviser or organisation will need to ensure that the book was recently published or updated as the law is changing all the time.

Student books and revision aids

As indicated above, student books aimed at postgraduate students studying for professional examinations will often provide a concise and up-to-date overview of a particular area of law. They are designed for someone who is aware of the general legal principles and who is approaching a legal topic perhaps for the first time. It will therefore discuss how the general legal principles apply to that topic, which means that the book will assume that the reader has a good grounding in legal thinking and analysis.

These books cannot, however, stand in place of a detailed practitioner's reference source (a book dealing with the application of the law), as they are intended primarily to bring the reader up to the level of someone who is about to embark on postgraduate legal training with the support and supervision which that entails. The adviser new to a legal topic would probably need to supplement this type of book with a more detailed analysis of the subject they are looking to advise on.

Some advisers or students may be tempted to buy or borrow a short summary text on a particular legal topic in order to help them grasp the essentials. This is likely to be the wrong approach as these books are usually more geared towards being revision aids for someone who already has a good grounding in their legal knowledge of that subject and who wants to recall key concepts or cases.

Unfortunately there is no substitute for studying law and some hard work will need to be done to understand and apply your legal topic before you are at the point where a summary of it will help you to recall its main components. As revision aids or reminders, however, these short books do of course have great value.

19.5   Case-law

Relevance

The English legal system is based not only on statute but also on 'judge-made law'. In some countries, the law of the land will be codified and the court can only apply the code to any claim made in the court. In our constitution, Parliament will write the legislation but the judges are given constitutional powers to interpret them, so that their decisions are also part of the law of the land. This is how case-law is formed.

We saw earlier that the higher the court is in the legal system the more binding the cases are on lower courts. In other words, a lower court should follow the interpretation of the law set out in a decided case by a higher court where the facts of that case are the same or very similar. This is usually referred to as a 'precedent' as it paves the way for future decisions in that area. When giving a decision in a case, the judge or judges will come to the 'nub' of their decision by clearly stating how the law should be interpreted as well as going on to explain why, in the light of their interpretation of the law, they have come down in favour of one of the parties appearing before them. The nub of their decision is still referred to as being the 'ratio' of the case or to give it its full expression, the 'ratio decidendi' ('ray-tee-oh dessi-den-die'). The nearest translation of that Latin phrase is the 'decided reasoning' of the law upon which the judge is basing his or her decision.

Application

Perhaps the most well-known example for law students of a ratio (decided reasoning) in a legal case is in the case of *Donoghue v Stevenson* finally decided in 1932 in the House of Lords.

The facts of the case concerned a woman who drank a bottle of ginger beer and found the remains of a snail in the bottle. She then suffered severe gastroenteritis and wanted to claim for her injuries. Mrs Donoghue had not formed a contract with the shop as she had not herself bought the bottle of ginger beer. Could she sue the manufacturer, Mr Stevenson, even though she had no contract with him?

The court looked at the law of negligence in deciding in her favour and made a ruling that set out the way in which future claimants could base a similar claim. It ensured that anyone who takes action which might ultimately affect another individual should be aware of that possible effect and the damage it might do and it therefore established the 'neighbourhood principle' in the law of 'tort' or civil wrongs between private individuals. Lord Atkin said:

> There must be, and is, some general conception of relations giving rise to a duty of care, of which the particular cases found in the books are but instances ... The rule that you are to love your neighbour becomes in law you must not injure your neighbour; and the lawyer's question: Who is my neighbour? receives a restricted reply. You must take reasonable care to avoid acts or omissions which you can reasonably foresee would be likely to injure your neighbour. Who, then, in law, is my neighbour? The answer seems to be – persons who are so closely and directly affected by my act that I ought reasonably to have them in contemplation as being so affected when I am directing my mind to the acts or omissions that are called in question.

This 'neighbourhood principle' still endures today and reverberates in claims concerning injuries, faulty goods and many other unintended but foreseeable effects on others of an individual's actions which have caused loss or damage.

Using case-law as an adviser

An adviser will need to be aware of the relevant case-law in their field of advice. Many advisers who are not legally-qualified will know the principles of the law without necessarily knowing in detail the case-law which that principle is derived from. If an adviser does wish to ensure that they are up to date with their law they will need to ensure that they are up to date with case-law.

In order to research case-law it will be helpful to know how it is codified or described. All cases will be described by reference to the names of the two parties involved in the case, for example *Donoghue v Stevenson*. The 'v' stands for the Latin word 'versus' which means 'against'.

There are some exceptions to this however. For example, a case in which an individual is challenging a public body's decision-making powers as being wrongly exercised will be brought in the name of the Queen. These claims are known as judicial review proceedings as they are asking a High Court judge to challenge legal authority given by Parliament to a public body, such as the Government or a local authority in relation to the way it has been used on a particular occasion. They will be heard in the Queen's Bench Divisional Court.

The title of this type of case is in the format of

'*R on the application of Jane Jones v The Public Body*'.

The Queen ('Regina' being Latin for Queen) is the first party, the name of the individual, Jane Jones, who has been affected by the decision and the public body (eg, the Secretary of State for Education), whose decision Jane Jones is asking the administrative court to scrutinise.

Cases in books will usually set decided cases out in bold or italics with their titles, the year they were decided and reported, which of the higher courts made the decision and the number of the case, eg:

Donoghue v Stevenson [1932] 1 All ER 123, HL

This needs further explanation. As we know, this was a decision made by the House of Lords. Hence the abbreviation 'HL'. The phrase All ER refers to The All England Law Reports and the volume of those reports in the year in which the case was reported. In most years there are three volumes of All England case reports. As we shall see below, the High Court now has a different system for describing and codifying decisions. However, decisions are still transferred into one or the other of the Law Reports.

All court decisions in full can now be read on the relevant court's website not long after the decision has been made or 'handed down' as it is usually described. There are solicitors and barristers who are commissioned to sit in court, write out the summary of a case and to set out the judgment, the nub or ratio of the decision, for the purposes of law reports. We have already seen a reference to The Times Law Reports. There is a range of other law reports. In the civil system, the two most common law reports reporting cases in the higher courts are called the Weekly Law Reports (WLR) and the All England Law

Reports (All ER). Some decisions will be reported in each of these reports, which are bound and available for sale. Others may only appear in one and still others will not be reported but can still stand equally as judge-made law.

Due to the law of precedent, it will not be usual for decisions of the lower courts, such as the county court, to be reported or referred to (or 'cited') in later cases when arguing a particular point. These decisions are, however, written up and available.[7] They are sometimes of assistance in understanding a judge's reasoning or why a higher court has overruled that judge's decision. There will also be instances when a decision of a lower court is the only decision or the nearest most helpful decision available on a particular point of law. It will not have the force of a decision made in the higher courts in attempting to sway a judge to decide in your favour however.

Some years ago the High Court set out some guidelines for how cases should be described and referred to in later hearings. There is now a consistent series of numbers and descriptions of each case heard in the higher courts which will, if reported, have added to it the reference as to where it will be found in the law report.

The system has been set out by the court[8] for codifying or 'citing' (referring to) cases as follows:

Judgments will be numbered in the following way:

Court of Appeal (Civil Division)   [2000] EWCA Civ 1, 2, 3 etc.
Court of Appeal (Criminal Division) [2000] EWCA Crim 1, 2, 3 etc.
High Court (Administrative Court)   [2000] EWHC Admin 1, 2 etc.

Under these ... arrangements, paragraph 59 in *Smith v Jones*, the tenth numbered judgment of the year in the Civil Division of the Court of Appeal, would be cited: *Smith v Jones* [2001] EWCA Civ 10 at 59.

The neutral citation will be the official number attributed to the judgment by the court and must always be used on at least one occasion when the judgment is cited in a later judgment. Once the judgment is reported, the neutral citation will appear in front of the familiar citation from the law report series. Thus: *Smith v Jones* [2001] EWCA Civ 10 at [30], [2001] QB 124, [2001] 2 All ER 364, etc. The paragraph number must be the number allotted by the court in all future versions of the judgment ...

---

7   See for example www.courtrecordsandreports.org as a tool to look up any court reports.

8   This is taken from a High Court Practice Direction: Practice Direction (Judgments: Form and Neutral Citation) 2001.

Citation of judgments in court

For the avoidance of doubt, it should be emphasised that both the High Court and the Court of Appeal require that where a case has been reported in the official Law Reports published by the Incorporated Council of Law Reporting for England and Wales it must be cited from that source. Other series of reports may only be used when a case is not reported in the Law Reports.

This explains what the courts will expect when cases are referred to them in court and also what the abbreviations mean in terms of whether cases are 'reported' or not and if so where they can be found. Advisers who need to be familiar with immigration case-law, employment case-law or welfare benefits decisions will be looking for the law reports relevant to that tribunal which also have numbering systems relevant to the year they were heard and the page number of the report for that year.

If an adviser needs to read case-law regularly they will hopefully be working in an organisation which can subscribe to the case-law reports relevant to that area of advice work. They should find case reports fairly accessible and easy to understand but will need to practice reading case reports until they are familiar with the language and logic. Some case-law reports are very accessible and others less so, which is usually linked to the complexity of the matter which the judge has been required to deal with.

Advisers who need to keep pace with changing case-law should take out a subscription to a journal or e-mail alerter or on-line case reporting service.[9]

19.6   Keeping a reference system

Some organisations will have a well-stocked and up-to-date reference system for their advisers to use. Larger organisations will have on-line or intranet reference systems. They may also subscribe to on-line or paper law reports, legal or advice journals, and regularly review what books are on the market and buy them for their advisers to refer to.

Organisations with fewer resources will need to be selective about what they can afford to buy. Careful thought should be given to the possibility of purchasing an on-line handbook, or system of law reports which can be used by more than one user in the organisation. There are often financial concessions made for a group of users to

---

9   Such as Justis (www.justis.com) or Casetrack (www.casetrack.co.uk).

access an external system. Furthermore, the subscription may also come with automatic updates.

A new adviser, or one who is starting out, should at the least have an up-to-date 'overview' book which they use as a reference for their advice subject, and a subscription to a journal which keeps them in touch with developments in their area of law and related areas. They may, in addition, use search engines to research areas on free sites which they need to check as they advise.

Whichever reference system the adviser or the organisation adopts, they should ensure that the sources they use are:

- *User friendly*: capable of being read by an adviser, a volunteer or an experienced lawyer coming in to run a free advice session;
- *Up to date*: in terms of the law and any policy or procedure being discussed;
- *Easily accessible*: capable of being accessed at short notice perhaps even during a client interview;
- *Properly filed*: there is nothing more frustrating than not knowing where to find your references, either because they have no home or because another colleague is using them. Even if there is nothing as comprehensive as a library, there should be a basic system which provides for where books or journals are kept and who might be using them at any given time. This can be just in the form of a notebook kept near the book shelf in which people can record what they are using and when they took it.

The adviser's own system: keeping up to date

Even where there is a good reference system, the adviser will often have their own system to assist them in keeping up to date. This will vary from one person to another and will depend on what area of advice or legal advice they cover. Some examples are set out here.

A paper file of recent cases

The adviser may keep a paper folder of recent cases, articles about cases or case reports which they have recently read about, perhaps in e-mail alerter or in journals or newspaper reports, which are of particular relevance to the work being done by that adviser. They may have a case running for a number of months on one topic, such as disability discrimination, and will keep a record of all they read on that topic during that period as background reference.

A precedent file

This may be kept in the adviser's computer or be in a paper form. Where the adviser is writing letters which are essentially the same or preparing claims for court hearings which are in outline the same, on a regular basis, they may build up a 'bank' of precedents which will be the letter or claim in outline. Some organisations' case management systems have these built into their system for use by all the advisers in the organisation. They will of course have been initially drafted by someone and then will be saved for use by all. Either way it will be a useful approach to the idea of good practice and will save time in repeating the same outlines each time there is a new client or case.

Peer reviews or mentoring

This can be done informally in the context of team meetings or in contact with other similar organisations and their staff who might be in the local community. Views and information can be exchanged about how law or policies are developing in the adviser's practice areas which is a way of networking, gaining casework support and keeping up to date with recent developments.

Keeping up to date with legal research

Advisers will develop a number of habits and strategies for keeping up to date with their advice work subject and ensuring that they are aware of current developments.

Reading and meetings

It can be hard for a busy practitioner to keep up to date with all the inevitable changes which come in to this area of work. Many subscribe to weekly or monthly journals which give updates and news of developments or forthcoming changes.

In many areas of advice work there are organisations which function as information exchanges and which hold regular meetings for practitioners and advisers to meet and discuss a topic or hear a speaker talk on a topic. Examples are the Housing Law Practitioners Association (HLPA) or the Immigration Law Practitioners Association (ILPA). These organisations do not confine themselves to lawyers (although there are some practitioners groups who do, for example the Employment Lawyers Association (ELA)), and will usually meet once a month. Unfortunately, most of these national organisations tend only to hold meetings in London which can make them inaccessible for some people.

Continuing education and training

Some advisers will combine their practice with ongoing development by taking courses or qualifications, as discussed in chapter 2. Many courses in advice work skills, casework management or legal knowledge can now be taken part time or in the evenings and are also an invaluable way of keeping up to date with law or legal advice.

Some advice practitioners (usually qualified lawyers) will be required to have continuing development points (CPD) obtained by attending training courses and will need to attend a minimum number of hours' training each year. Other advisers will use training courses of one day or less as a way of keeping up to date with their subject area of advice. Training courses are also a useful way of meeting colleagues advising in similar fields and informally exchanging experiences.

19.7 Using legal research in preparation for advising or representing clients

The whole function of ensuring that research is up to date and accurate is to provide the best possible service to a client seeking advice. Many organisations will in any event have quality control procedures in place which require them to demonstrate to their funders or managing bodies that they have systems in place which enable advisers to give up-to-date and accurate advice.

An adviser who is preparing for an interview with a client will need to approach their preparation for that interview with a view to ensuring that they are prepared for the discussion by having satisfied themselves that they are familiar with the topic the client has come for advice on.

This preparation will not always be complete as the adviser will often find that the client has not properly described in advance the exact nature of their problem or that they come to an interview with supplementary or different information which will affect the nature of the advice to be given.

In these circumstances the adviser should explain that they have researched a legal or other advice-related point based on what information they had at the time. They should tell the client what that information was and offer to do any further necessary research either as the interview progresses (if time will allow or they feel confident to do this) or after the interview has concluded, which means that any advice offered in the context of the interview will be subject to those later researches.

In any event, in preparation for an interview an adviser can bear in mind the following checklist:

Checklist: preparing to give legal advice

Topic
- What is the topic the client wants advice on – is it, for example, housing law, welfare benefits advice or a combination of more than one topic?
- Have I understood and clearly set out for myself the facts of the client's case as known to me at present?

Legal issue
- How do those facts relate to any legal issue? For example, if my client has indicated that they are owed money what is the possible basis for their claim? Do they have a contract, for example, with the person they say owes them money?

Statute law
- What does the law say about these types of circumstance? Do I need to check out any statute or regulation to find this out?
- What does that statute or regulation say about this situation? Do I understand what it says or do I need to check this, perhaps by reference to a book or by talking to a colleague or supervisor?

Case-law
- Is there any case-law relevant to this situation? If so, how do the decided cases help my client?
- Do I need to check if there are any more recent cases than the ones I am thinking of – should I take a copy of what those cases say to the interview to refer to when I discuss this with my client?

Preparing to advise
- Am I properly prepared to advise on the legal aspects? Am I aware of the legal issues which are relevant to this claim so that I can ask relevant questions and then if necessary research the law in more depth once I have taken full details from my client in the interview?

Preparation such as this should ideally be done before every interview with every client. Even an experienced lawyer will always prepare to see a client by ensuring that they have done the appropriate background research and are ready with their legal analysis of the client's problem. Even though a client may be distressed or unable to communicate well with their adviser due to language or other differences, they will still be ready and able to assimilate any legal advice they are given as long as it is well-expressed, concise and relevant to their problem.

PART 6

An introduction to social welfare law

CHAPTER 20

Overview of social welfare law topics

20.1   Meaning of social welfare law

20.2   Areas of social welfare law commonly practised

20.3   How and where to learn more

20.1   Meaning of social welfare law

This is a short introductory chapter which will lead into the next two chapters, where some analysis is offered of two key areas of social welfare law, employment law and housing law, to complement the case study in chapter 9 and following chapters.

There have been references throughout the book to 'social welfare law' and so perhaps a short explanation of what is meant by this and who practices it would assist.

The traditional way of describing what is known as social welfare law is to describe the areas being practised as areas where basic social rights are being fought for, such as the right to stay in the country lawfully, to challenge discrimination at work, to be properly educated or to be housed. A significant proportion of individuals in society suffer disadvantage by being denied these basic rights and will often need a champion to assist them in obtaining these rights or redress where they have been denied. Certain organisations, most notably free advice agencies in the voluntary sector, will advise on and practise in social welfare law to give access to justice for those individuals in our society.

In addition, a feature of some, but not all, areas of traditional social welfare law is that they receive no public funding. For example, virtually all tribunals (with the exception of some immigration tribunals) will be free to access but no state funding is available to help to pay legal fees for advice or representation for those using the tribunals.

Examples are representation in tribunals such as social security, educational special needs or employment. Where an individual is on a low income, such as state benefits, it is unlikely that they will be able to pay a solicitor for advice and assistance on a matter where there is no public funding available to help pay a solicitor's legal fees. Free advice agencies, where no fees are payable for the service (which will pay for its service by external funding sources) can fill this gap and offer to assist or represent the low income client in these areas of law.

Some advice agencies will advise and represent in the traditional areas of social welfare law where public funding is available (for example housing cases for tenants or judicial review cases). They will use the public funding they receive as a source of income and will be able to allow clients to keep monies they recover in court cases on the basis that the service they offer to clients is free.

20.2 Areas of social welfare law commonly practised

Traditionally, therefore, certain legal areas are practised in the advice sector either to fill the gaps in public funding or to work for the benefit of people denied these basic rights. The most common areas practised, listed in the research referred to in chapter 2, are welfare benefits and debt, housing and employment. Some organisations will also advise on consumer rights, immigration and education.

Organisations more geared towards legal representation, such as Law Centres®, will be looking to see if they can run a case for a client which might also be for the benefit of a larger group of individuals. There are many examples of this occurring over the past few decades. These include cases to establish rights for pregnant employees, asylum-seekers and the homeless.

20.3 How and where to learn more

Advisers who work in the advice sector will need to be experienced in their field of law. In addition they will be honing their skills as advisers, some of which have been examined in this book

As we saw in chapter 2, qualifications in the skills of giving advice are offered at different levels by a variety of organisations.

Many of the newer courses in the higher education sector referred to in chapter 2 include teaching and learning in these social welfare topics. Some will also offer courses in criminal law and justice, human rights and family law.

Law degree options will often include some of these topics; for example, there are Masters degree courses in Paralegal Advice[1] which specialise in the teaching of these topics. In addition, when students study for their postgraduate professional qualifications in order to train as a solicitor or barrister they can take up options outside the core modules which include employment law and asylum and immigration law.

There is also a variety of short courses and certificate courses provided within the voluntary sector, as well as the commercial and education sector, in many of these topics. All in all there is no shortage of options for studying these subjects and, as with all legal topics, there is also a selection of books on all of these areas.

1   See for example the course of that title which has been run by the London Metropolitan University for some years. It is not necessary to have a law degree to enrol on the course. See appendix B for details.

In the next two chapters an overview is offered of some aspects of two of these topics, which will hopefully have the effect of clarifying the way in which the case study ran and introducing the reader who may want to study these topics to some aspects of them.

CHAPTER 21

Giving employment advice

21.1   Introduction: the National Occupational Standards

The National Occupational Standards (NOS) are a recently-developed framework of the key elements of legal knowledge which are practised in the advice sector. The legal topics covered will be familiar to those who give advice in the voluntary, charitable or public sector. These topics include housing law, employment law, immigration law, consumer rights, debt advice and welfare benefits rights.

How knowledge in these areas is acquired will vary from one person to another. As we have seen, there is currently no national pattern of qualifying to advise in the key areas of social welfare law. There are currently higher education institutions that run foundation degree courses and honours degree courses[1] as well as a range of training courses and short course qualifications, all aimed at giving learners the tools to advise in these areas of law. One of the aims of designing and launching the NOS in Legal Advice was to provide a framework or blueprint for learning skills standards in these areas of legal advice for teachers, learners and employers.

Parts 2–4 of this book covered what NOS refers to as the Generic Standards of advice-giving, namely the range of skills from client care skills, good case management and the skills of good advice-giving and of promoting a satisfactory resolution to the client's case. These standards underpin the legal knowledge that the adviser is trained to impart to their clients.

This legal knowledge is expressed in the NOS for Legal Advice as a 'suite' of Knowledge Units covering the main areas of social welfare law. This chapter and the next will serve as an introduction to some of the Knowledge Units in two key areas of social welfare law, employment and housing, as well as a brief look at how some of the generic standards will operate in giving advice in these areas of law.

As the book progressed up to chapter 17, the case study of Cathy dealt with some areas of both employment and housing or, as it is sometimes known, landlord and tenant law, as well as the procedures and processes in which Cathy and her adviser had to engage in order to reach a helpful outcome for Cathy.

The law relating to these procedures will be discussed in the next two chapters. It will not cover all areas of law in either topic but it is hoped that the 'taster' offered into these two areas will encourage readers to enrol on courses or refresher courses to familiarise them-

---

1   See appendix B.

selves fully with these and other areas of law practised in the advice sector.

21.2 Employment advice: generic NOS standards

In giving employment advice the adviser will be practising a range of the generic standards set out in the NOS framework. These will range from client care and communication skills to case management skills and to ways of resolving the case, all of which have been explored in chapters 3–17. To illustrate how the generic standards will be used by the adviser in the context of giving employment advice, a few examples are given below of typical employment issues with the appropriate generic standard being operated in that context.

Develop and manage interviews with clients: generic standard LA3
Enable client to explore their problems and concerns: generic standard LA3.1

We have seen in chapter 8 how advisers will prepare for and conduct interviews. In this context, one of the key features in any employment case is the question of job security. This concern will be paramount for the client in this area of advice and law.

For those who feel they have been wronged by being dismissed or have been discriminated against and thereby severely disadvantaged, the resultant insecurity can be emotional as well as financial. Job loss can have a severe effect on lifestyle, often leading to debt and stress-related illness. In contrast, the employer's perspective will often translate into concerns about workplace disruption and the cost and time involved in dealing with claims.

The employee adviser needs to focus on their client's best chances of a helpful resolution knowing that their client's agenda will be different from that of the employer.

The employee client's adviser will need to exercise their client care and counselling skills in order to deal with that situation, as they will rarely be able to offer the client any outcome which will have the effect of turning the clock back and restoring them to a job they have lost or which has turned sour on them. In advising on this area, therefore, the adviser will be realistic with the client in exploring the most likely outcome to their problem.

Provide information to clients: generic standards LA5
Provide information to meet the needs of clients : generic standard LA5.2

It is the case that only around 25 per cent of employment tribunal claims go to a hearing. The rest are either withdrawn or a settlement is reached between the parties. This will need to be explained to an employee client. There are aspects of resolving an employment case in ways other than the outcome of an employment tribunal hearing which are of particular benefit to the employee client. A resolution which leads to a reference being provided by an employer and/or a sum of money paid to settle a claim avoids the stress and uncertainty of a tribunal hearing.

Negotiate on behalf of clients: generic standard LA 16

In chapter 16, the skills of negotiating were examined as part of resolving a problem or case. A negotiated settlement of an employment law dispute may also include an agreement on the part of the employer to provide a reference for the employee to assist in job hunting, an outcome which an employment tribunal is unable to provide. There may also be a form of wording negotiated in a settlement document which gives the employee the satisfaction of knowing that they did the right thing to challenge whatever the issue was. It should be said, however, that even where an employer agrees to settle a claim, they will rarely agree to apologise or admit that they were wrong as part of that settlement.

21.3   Employment advice: knowledge units

Introduction

Employment law is a large and often complex topic. It is also subject to frequent change, due not only to case-law developments, but also to the regular introduction of new legislation giving increased rights in the workplace or moderating employer and trades union or other collective types of workplace relationships.

Any student or practitioner of employment law needs to know the structure of the subject, a contract between the employer and employee, as well as the ever-increasing number of statutory rights and obligations with which that basic contract structure is garnished and which make up a broad and complex framework of rights. There is also a stream of case-law which interprets contractual and statutory rights as well as a need to know how claims are pursued in the civil courts and the employment tribunals and how these procedures operate. An adviser in employment law must keep up with changes which can be frequent and occasionally radical.

The employment contract and statutory rights

The legal basis of a workplace relationship is a contract between the employer and the employee. At its most simple level, the employer contracts to provide work and pay to the employee who contracts to provide his or her service to the employer in return. There are, however, a range of permutations on this basic contractual relationship.

Furthermore, since the mid 1970s, legislation has been introduced on a regular basis which has overlaid this basic arrangement, and has given employees, and people who provide services in the workplace, rights at work ranging from the right not to be unfairly dismissed or discriminated against at work, to the newer rights such as the right to paid holidays or the right to take leave for family-based reasons.

First Line Employment Advice: Knowledge Unit LA45

NOS LA45 is the Knowledge Unit for First Line Employment Advice and refers to the contractual and statutory frameworks which form the basis of employment law and the requirement to understand these in order to provide sound basic employment law advice.[2] Although there are other Knowledge Units dealing with employment law,[3] LA45 will form the basis of the employment law knowledge standards set out in this chapter.

Other employment law knowledge units deal with discrimination in more depth and also provide for a requirement to understand the basic knowledge units in more detail and to practise in the core areas of employment law to a higher level.

There are thirteen required Knowledge Units in LA45. In order to demonstrate that they are familiar with these units the employment

2   See Skills for Justice National Occupational Standards for Legal Advice: Knowledge Units: Unit Title LA45 First Line Employment Legal Advice. See appendix C.
3   Unit LA34 First Line Discrimination Legal Advice; Unit LA35 Discrimination Legal Advice and Casework; Unit LA46 Employment Legal Advice and Casework.

adviser will need to show that they have the knowledge and understanding of the following:

1. Employment law legislation and how it all fits together.
2. Different categories of employment status and what they mean – examples being the difference between an 'employee' and a 'worker'.
3. The different rights for different categories of people at work, such as part-timers or young workers.
4. The main statutory rights given to people in work and who is protected by each right. Examples are minimum wage, paid holidays and family leave.
5. The difference between rights under the employment contract and rights given by statute.
6. The main contractual terms and how to interpret them, eg pay, variations, and hours of work and notice clauses.
7. The key areas of discrimination law protection (age, gender, sexual orientation, race, religion or belief and disability).
8. How discrimination law operates to protect individuals in the employment context, including safeguards for and obligations towards disabled employees.
9. Definitions of dismissal, wrongful, unfair and constructive.
10. Rights on termination of work, eg the right not to be unfairly dismissed and the right to redundancy pay.

In addition advisers must be able to advise on and assist in preparing grievances, employment tribunal claims, and be aware of employment tribunal procedures, time limits and the lawful methods which are employed in resolving an employment tribunal claim without a hearing.

The above areas of employment law are the basis for any employment law advice, and these core elements will be found in many legal professional courses, certificate-based qualifications for non-lawyer advisers, or advice-based employment law training courses.

21.4   A working example: Cathy's employment law problem analysed

It will be recalled that Cathy came to see her adviser Ada about two employment law problems she had. Cathy had worked as a nursery nurse for the Kidglove Nursery for three months. She was telephoned by her employer as she was due to return from a week's holiday and dismissed. She was advised by Ada Adams that she had a claim for her notice pay and her first week's wages as she was paid a week in hand when she began. She was claiming £260 based on two weeks' pay at £130 a week. As we saw in the case study these two claims were eventually compromised by Cathy with her ex-employer and she instructed her adviser to indicate that she would settle them for a total of £150.

In order to advise Cathy properly on these two claims, Ada, her adviser, needs to have the following knowledge about her rights in employment law:

- Was Cathy an employee of the nursery? Only employees will have certain rights and in particular only employees will be able to claim notice pay.
- Did Cathy have a written employment contract? In particular did it refer to her agreement to work her first week in hand and to any rights to being given notice whenever her employer decided to terminate her contract?
- If Cathy had no terms in her contract, written or oral, relating to notice, what are her statutory rights to notice and what legal enactment are these to be found in?
- How can Cathy enforce her claim to be paid her first week's wages? What are her rights not to suffer an unlawful deduction in wages and how and when must she exercise those rights?
- Alternatively, as not being paid is also in breach of her contract which entitled her to be paid for the work she does, how and when can she enforce that failure to pay her as a breach of contract claim?

The key elements in Knowledge Unit LA45, excepting discrimination law, are inherent in this situation, namely

- employment legislation relevant to this case;
- employment status;
- rights under an employment contract;
- an example of a statutory right;
- the interpretation of a main contractual term;
- enforcing employee rights, time limits and remedies.

To illustrate the employment law issues, Ada's file contains a note of the legal research she has done on Cathy's' case which is set out overleaf.

Ada's File Note: Legal Issue on Cathy's Employment Case

Employment legislation relevant to Cathy's case

In looking to see what Cathy's rights are to notice pay I have looked at the main employment statute, the Employment Rights Act 1996 in which section 86(1) states that an employer is required to pay a week's notice pay to any employee who has worked for them for longer than a month.

Cathy's employment status

It will be necessary to confirm that Cathy is an employee of the nursery. Her history of employment has all the hallmarks of a contract of service. Cathy was required to work under the control of the nursery; she received payslips showing employer's deductions. I have checked the legal tests for employee status and have read recent case-law on this topic and can find nothing inconsistent with her being an employee. An example of that would have been an ability to refuse to work and there is no evidence here of any such arrangement. I can therefore confirm that she enjoys rights as an employee including the right to claim notice pay. As she had not worked for her employer for a year or more she cannot claim unfair dismissal and I would need to advise her of this.

Cathy's' rights under her employment contract

Cathy has not been provided with anything in writing by her employer to confirm any contractual arrangements which might have existed. I have discussed her contractual rights with Cathy and she was never told anything about how much notice she was to be given. Nor was she told that she would have to wait a week before she received her first pay cheque. I will need to advise Cathy that an employment contract does not need to be written and that once fully formed she is entitled to be paid for the work she does for her employer. I will also advise her that under section 1 of The Employment Rights Act 1996 she should have been provided with key particulars of her terms of employment within the first two months of her employment. These should have included any contractual terms relating to notice pay, if there were any.

An example of a statutory right

The law allows for employees to be given minimum periods of notice upon termination of their employment. For an employee who has worked more than a month and less than two years the law provides for them to be given a week's notice (see section 86 of the Employment Rights Act 1996). Cathy is entitled therefore to claim a week's pay instead of (in lieu of) notice. I will also advise Cathy that the failure to pay notice is usually referred to as a wrongful dismissal as the employer has wrongfully terminated the contract prior to its proper termination. It should properly terminate only once notice has been worked out by the employee.

An interpretation of a main contractual term

Given that there is no evidence by way of any contractual arrangement that Cathy agreed to her first week's pay not being paid to her, and given that it has never been paid to her then I will need to advise Cathy that this is a breach of her employment contract under which she is entitled to be paid for the work that she does. Furthermore I will need to advise her that the withholding of that money amounts to an 'unlawful deduction of wages' under section 13 of The Employment Rights Act 1996 and gives rise to a claim on Cathy's part in respect of that deduction. I will need to advise her that the same sum therefore can be claimed under the contract as a contractual right or under section 13 of the Employment Rights Act 1996 as a statutory claim.

Cathy's remedies

The usual remedy for employment disputes is a claim made to an employment tribunal by the employee or the person claiming a breach of their workplace rights (who will not always need to be an employee). This will be the procedure which the employee will start off. This is a free service but there are powers to order costs to be paid at the end of the case in certain specific circumstances relating to how a case has been conducted or how strong a case it was. There are strict time limits for conducting cases (usually three months) and there are also certain steps which need to be taken for some claims prior to starting a claim off in order for claims to be accepted or to avoid extra compensation being paid as a penalty.

In claims involving a breach of contract the employee can choose to take the claim to a civil court, the county court in this case. This will avoid concern about pre-action steps not having been taken and the time limit is considerably longer (six years). In this case I will advise Cathy that this will be her best option as she came to see me after her time limits had expired for her tribunal claim. She will have to pay a fee to start her claim and there are usually no costs awarded at the end of a small claim case.

21.5 Developing further knowledge of employment law

The two previous sections do no more than begin to give an overview
of some key aspects of advising on employment law.

An adviser who wishes to learn employment law from scratch (and
this may include a law graduate who has never studied employment
law) should perhaps take a 'taster' one day training course. A number
of professional course providers will run courses on the essential employment law elements.[4]

If they find that this is a helpful starter and that it is a subject they
are enthusiastic about, they can enrol on evening certificate courses
or do part-time foundation degree or honours degree courses which
have employment law as a module element. Many advisers begin
their practice with a base of legal knowledge such as a degree or they
may have already practised legal advice in other areas. They start to
read some of the excellent books on this topic and begin to observe
an experienced employment law practitioner giving advice and/or
representing at an employment tribunal. This person may be their
supervisor or it may be a colleague from a nearby advice agency or a
barrister who is taking on a client's case free of charge ('pro bono').

There are many experienced qualified lawyers who will give their
services to the voluntary sector in order to assist clients to resolve
legal disputes and observing how they advise and resolve cases can be
a very useful aspect of learning a new advice topic. There is, however,
no substitute for a new adviser ensuring that they are studying their
subject and applying their newly-acquired knowledge of that subject
to the skills of advice-giving which this book is designed to address.

---

4   See for example Legal Action Group's 'Essential Employment Law' one day
     course run once or twice a year: www.lag.org.uk. See appendix B.

CHAPTER 22

Giving housing advice

22.1   Housing advice: generic standards

Chapter 21 described the National Occupational Standards and re-ferred to the relevant standards in relation to employment advice. This chapter highlights the relevant generic standards in relation to a client facing a threat of eviction, as in Cathy Clark's case study.

Develop and manage interviews with clients: generic standard LA3
Enable client to explore their problems and concerns: generic standard LA3.1

One of the most common areas of housing advice work is dealing with clients who are threatened with eviction. As is explained below, there are many steps that a landlord must take before a tenant can be evicted and a client may approach an adviser at an early stage, when the landlord first contacts the tenant, or much later in the process, when an actual eviction is imminent. Most clients facing the threat of eviction will be feeling extremely stressed and fearful about the pros-pect. For clients facing eviction because of non-payment of rent, this will often be part of a wider problem of debt or an inability to manage the household finances. The adviser will need to allow the client to explain the reason for the arrears and their fears about their future housing. This will enable the adviser to offer the most appropriate advice to the client about reaching a realistic agreement regarding repayment, and about seeking help from other organisations, such as money advice agencies.

Provide information to clients: generic standards LA5
Provide information to meet the needs of clients: generic standards LA5.2

The client's fears about a threatened eviction may be allayed by the adviser explaining the necessary steps a landlord must take before an eviction can be carried out. Clients who believe, often wrongly, that an eviction is imminent and inevitable may believe that there is no point in trying to repay arrears and may even stop paying current rent. Giving advice about the legal process of eviction and the way in which the courts consider such cases will enable a client to put forward a proposal to repay arrears in order to persuade the landlord not to take further action. If a claim for possession has already been started, the client's proposals may persuade the court that no possession order should be made or that a postponed order should be made to give the client the chance to repay the arrears and avoid eviction. Even at a very late stage, after a possession order has been made, a realistic offer to repay arrears may prevent an eviction.

Clients who are anxious about the prospect of an eviction sometimes wish to put forward unrealistic or unreliable proposals (for example Cathy Clark's proposal that she borrow money from her boyfriend). An adviser can assist the client to ensure that any proposal is realistic and affordable by advising the client about the way in which the courts deal with such cases (for example, ordering people who are on benefits to repay arrears at the rate of £2.95 per week).

In all cases, the adviser must be familiar with the client's legal rights as a tenant. Some tenants have strong rights and can avoid eviction provided they are willing to enter into an agreement to repay any arrears by instalments. Other tenants, mostly with private landlords, have very limited rights and cannot prevent an eviction, even if all arrears are repaid (or even if there have never been any arrears). The adviser must therefore be able to identify the kind of tenancy the client has at an early stage. If the tenant has limited rights and cannot prevent an eviction, the adviser will need to be familiar with the law relating to homelessness and the way in which social housing is allocated.

Negotiate on behalf of clients: generic standard LA16

The adviser will often take on the role of negotiating with the landlord to reach an agreement so as to persuade the landlord not to pursue the claim for possession. This avoids tenants who are upset and fearful being placed under pressure to agree to pay more than they can afford. It also enables the adviser to demonstrate to the landlord that they are familiar with the law relating to possession and to the way in which the courts treat such claims – most courts being willing to permit tenants to repay arrears at a low rate in order to avoid an eviction. Landlords are often more willing to accept arrangements put forward by advisers who can reassure the landlords that they are advising the tenants of the consequences of not keeping to the agreement and are also assisting the tenant in relation to their finances and/or benefit entitlement to help ensure that the arrears are repaid.

22.2 Housing advice: knowledge units

Introduction

'Housing law' is a term used to describe the law relating to tenants' rights, the rights of those seeking accommodation and the law relating to housing standards, ie the condition of accommodation. In Cathy's case an adviser will need to be aware of her rights as a tenant and, if she were to be evicted, her right to obtain alternative accommodation from the local authority.

Knowledge Unit LA39

The NOS Knowledge Unit LA39 is the Knowledge Unit for First Line Housing Legal Advice.[1] There are nine required knowledge units in LA 39 and to meet the national standard advisers must know and understand the following:

1. The law relating to private and social housing, in particular the different rights and responsibilities of different kinds of tenants and other occupiers. The rights and responsibilities of landlords and the law on housing standards: the landlord's responsibilities for repairs and the powers of local authorities in relation to environmental protection, health and safety and housing standards.
2. How social housing is allocated, who is eligible and how decisions can be challenged.
3. Occupier's rights in relation to harassment and unlawful eviction by landlords.
4. The implications of environmental, health and safety requirements and their impact on housing.
5. Housing options generally, including awareness of the rules relating to people from abroad. The availability of accommodation in the private and social sectors and the options available on relationship breakdown.
6. How homelessness law works and how decisions are challenged.
7. A broad understanding of the benefits system in relation to paying for housing and maximising income.
8. The procedure for possession in both the private and social sector, and in relation to action by landlords and mortgage providers.
9. Complaints procedures, including the Ombudsman.

---

1   Reproduced in appendix C.

22.3 A working example: Cathy's housing problem analysed

The law relating to the rights of tenants is usually referred to as 'landlord and tenant' law and is found in both the 'common law' (established through previous legal cases) and statutory law (set out in legislation). Some of the tenant's rights will be found in the law of contract as a tenancy agreement is a legal contract between the landlord and the tenant. Each party has certain legally binding obligations: for example, the tenant must pay rent and the landlord must allow the tenant to enjoy the premises without interference. In addition, some of the tenant's rights are found in the principles of 'land law'. A tenancy is a legal 'interest' in land and can, in some circumstances, be transferred to someone else or inherited by a family member.

In addition to the rights and obligations set out in the contract, there are very important statutory rights given to tenants. The most important of these are 'security of tenure' and 'protection from eviction'. Both are very important in Cathy's case.

Security of tenure: grounds for possession

Security of tenure refers to a tenant's right not to be evicted from their home unless there is a good reason. Before a landlord can evict a tenant with security of tenure the landlord must prove to a court that a 'ground' for possession exists. Most tenants with private landlords do not have security of tenure after the first six months. Most tenants with social landlords (local authorities and housing associations) do have security of tenure. To find out exactly what Cathy's rights are, an adviser will need to know what kind of tenancy Cathy has. Different statutes set out the rights of different kinds of tenants. In Cathy's case, because of who her landlord is and when her tenancy started, she will either be an Assured or an Assured Shorthold Tenant. She will have security of tenure if she is an 'Assured Tenant' but not if she is an 'Assured Shorthold Tenant'. The rights of both Assured and Assured Shorthold Tenants are set out in the Housing Act 1988. As we saw during the first interview, she has an 'Assured Tenancy Agreement'. This means that Cathy cannot be evicted unless there is a 'ground' for possession. The most common ground for possession is that a tenant has failed to pay the rent. In Cathy's case this is admitted.

All of the grounds for possession are set out in the statute that is relevant to that particular kind of tenancy. In Cathy's case, the grounds for possession that can be used against her are set out in the Housing Act 1988. The Act also sets out the powers of a court when a landlord is asking for a possession order. An adviser will need to be aware of the fact that there are three possible grounds for possession against an assured tenant who has failed to pay rent. They are:

Ground 8: if a tenant who pays rent weekly has at least 8 weeks arrears of rent, when a formal possession notice is served, and at the date of the court hearing, the court must make an order for possession.

Ground 10: if a tenant has some rent arrears at the date when the formal possession notice is served and at the date of the hearing, the court may make an order for possession if it is reasonable to do so.

Ground 11: whether or not a tenant has arrears at the date of any hearing, if a tenant has persistently delayed in paying rent, the court may make an order for possession if it is reasonable to do so.

It will be essential therefore to find out from Cathy what her weekly rent is and how much her arrears are. An adviser will then be able to advise Cathy about the grounds that the housing association can rely on if they decide to take court action against Cathy.

Protection from eviction

The term 'Protection from Eviction' usually refers to the procedure a landlord must follow before a tenant can be evicted lawfully. Most tenants have protection from eviction even if they do not have security of tenure. This means that the landlord must give notice to the tenant, must apply for a possession order from the court and must use the court bailiffs to enforce the possession order. As Cathy has security of tenure she has stronger rights. An adviser must, however, be able to advise Cathy of the procedure a landlord must follow before she can be evicted.

Procedure

The Rent Arrears Protocol

For social landlords there is a 'Rent Arrears Protocol' which should be followed by a landlord before applying to the court for a possession order. This can be found in the Civil Procedure Rules which are available on the website of the Ministry of Justice at www.justice.gov.uk. As Cathy's landlord is a housing association, they should follow the protocol. The protocol says that a landlord must tell the tenant about the arrears as soon as possible and must try to reach an agreement for the tenant to repay the arrears. The protocol also says that the landlord must help a tenant with housing benefit problems if possible and, if the person is receiving welfare benefits, should help them to arrange for the rent and arrears to be paid direct from their benefit.

Notices

The adviser must be aware of the different kinds of possession notices served on different kinds of tenants before possession claims can be made. As Cathy is an assured tenant her landlord must send her a 'Notice of Seeking Possession'. This Notice sets out the grounds on which the landlord will ask the court to make a possession order. Some social landlords do not use Ground 8 even if the arrears are high. The adviser may be able to find out in advance whether the housing association's policy is to use Ground 8. If not, it will be clearly stated on the Notice of Seeking Possession which grounds are being used. The Notice of Possession must also give details of the rent arrears and state the earliest date that a claim for possession can be started. In Cathy's case this is two weeks after the date of the Notice but many social landlords give a tenant 28 days before making a claim for possession.

Possession hearings: the court's powers

Cathy will want to know what the likely outcome is if her housing association apply to the court for a possession order. The adviser will need to know what the powers of the court are and this will depend on which grounds for possession the housing association may rely on. If the housing association uses Ground 8 and Cathy is unable to bring her arrears below eight weeks before the hearing, the court must make a possession order. The court's powers are very limited: if Ground 8 is proved the court have no power to suspend or postpone a possession order and can only delay the possession order for six weeks if Cathy can show that she would suffer extreme hardship.

If the housing association is relying only on Ground 10 and/or Ground 11, the court has wide powers when considering making a possession order. The court can adjourn the claim or can make an order postponing the landlord's right to possession on condition that Cathy makes regular payments to clear the arrears. The most likely outcome at court in Cathy's case would be the making of a postponed possession order. Such an order will set out the payments Cathy must make to repay her arrears. Provided she makes those payments she will not lose her tenancy. If Cathy fails to make the payments her housing association can apply to the court for a date to be fixed which will mean that her tenancy ends on that date. Cathy will have the chance to explain to the court why she has not paid and the court may postpone the order again. Even if the court makes an order fixing the date for possession, the housing association must apply for a bailiff's warrant to carry out an eviction. Even at that stage Cathy can ask the court to suspend the warrant to give her time to repay the arrears. Cathy can also ask the court to vary the possession order or even to discharge it when she has repaid her arrears.

As will be clear, if advising and assisting Cathy through the process of a possession claim, an adviser must be aware of the law relating to Cathy's rights as a tenant and the procedure a landlord must follow, as set out above. In addition, at the stage when Cathy first seeks advice about her rent arrears, such knowledge is necessary to advise her realistically about what is likely to happen and what steps she should take. It is also necessary to enable an adviser to negotiate with Cathy's landlord to reach an agreement to avoid court proceedings. In particular, the following knowledge will inform the advice given to Cathy:

Procedure

Cathy will be advised that there are several steps a landlord must take before evicting a tenant and that this will give Cathy some time to sort out her finances and reduce or clear her arrears. In particular, the housing association must follow the Rent Arrears Protocol before serving notice. If notice is served Cathy will have at least 2 weeks before a claim can be sent to the court. The court rules also say that a tenant should have at least 21 days notice of any possession hearing. So Cathy can be advised of the likely time before any court hearing.

The Rent Arrears Protocol

Cathy will be advised that the landlord has an obligation under the protocol to try to reach an agreement and to make an application to court only as a last resort.

Ground 8: if Cathy's arrears are more than 8 weeks, she must be advised of the importance of reducing the arrears to below 8 weeks before any hearing. If she cannot do that she will almost certainly lose her home. If she can do that, the court will only make a possession order if it is reasonable and has the power to adjourn the claim or postpone the possession order. This will give Cathy the chance to pay off her arrears and avoid losing her home.

22.4 Developing further knowledge of housing law

Many specialist housing advisers are employed by local authorities as they have a statutory role in giving housing advice in the local area. It is also a function of homeless persons' units to give housing advice to applicants to prevent homelessness where possible. In addition, there are many voluntary agencies that provide specialist and general housing advice, often funded in part by local authorities. Shelter and Citizens Advice are national organisations that employ housing advisers in centres around the UK. In addition, there are many local independent advice agencies, most of which will offer housing advice at some level.

Many of the housing advisers employed by such agencies will start their employment with little or no experience of giving housing advice and will begin their job with an intensive programme of training including shadowing experienced advisers and attending courses. If the person is employed by a national organisation such as Shelter or the CAB they will be able to attend in-house training courses. Others will be able to attend the same training courses for a fee. In addition, the Chartered Institute of Housing operates a full programme of courses for housing advisers and other housing professionals. The Legal Action Group also offers one day courses on a range of housing law topics.

Meetings and seminars are also arranged by organisations such as the Housing Law Practitioners Association and the Social Housing Law Association.

The training programmes offered by all of these organisations can be viewed on their web-sites and comprise both introductory courses and up-date courses for more experienced practitioners.

Many institutions offering the Legal Practice Course now offer a housing law option for those seeking to qualify as solicitors. In addition, a number of higher education institutions now offer courses in advice-giving which will usually include housing law as an option.

APPENDICES

Useful organisations

Government departments and agencies

Communities and Local Government
Eland House
Bressenden Place
London SW1E 5DU

Tel: 020 7944 4933
Website: www.communities.gov.uk

Department for Business, Enterprise & Regulatory Reform (formerly DTI)
Victoria Street
London SW1H 0ET

Tel: 020 7215 5000
E-mail: enquiries@berr.gsi.gov.uk
Website: www.berr.gov.uk

Department for Children, Schools and Families (formerly DFES)
Sanctuary Buldings
Great Smith Street
London SW1P 3BT

Tel: 0870 000 2288
E-mail: info@dfes.gsi.gov.uk
Website: www.dfes.gov.uk

Department of Health
Richmond House
79 Whitehall
London SW1A 2NS

Tel: 020 7201 4850
Textphone: 020 7210 5025
E-mail: dhmail@dh.gsi.gov.uk
Website: www.dh.gov.uk

Home Office
2 Marsham Street (for centralised administration)
London SW1P 4DF

Tel: 020 7035 4848
Minicom: 020 7035 4742
E-mail: public.enquiries@homeoffice.gsi.gov.uk
Website: www.homeoffice.gov.uk

See www.ind.homeoffice.gov.uk for Immigration and Nationality Directorate

Ministry of Justice
Selborne House
54 Victoria Street
London SW1E 6QW

Tel: 020 7210 8500
E-mail: general.queries@justice.gsi.gov.uk
Website: www.justice.gov.uk

Government agencies and legal services

Community Legal Service
Tel: 0845 345 4345
Website: www.clsdirect.org.uk

Consumer Direct
Tel: 0845 404 0506
Website: www.consumerdirect.gov.uk

Council on Tribunals
81 Chancery Lane
London WC2A 1BQ

Tel: 020 7855 5200
Website: www.council-on-tribunals.gov.uk

Court Service
5th Floor
Clive House
Petty France
London SW1H 9EX

Website: www.hmcourts-service.gov.uk

See website for court telephone numbers and addresses.

Employment Appeal Tribunal
Audit House
58 Victoria Embankment
London EC4Y 0DS

Tel: 020 7273 1040
Website: www.employmentappeals.gov.uk

General guidance on EAT procedure plus venues listings, appeal forms and judgments.

Employment Tribunals
Tel: 0845 795 9775
Website: www.employmenttribunals.gov.uk

General guidance on ET procedure plus venues listings and forms.

Health and Safety Executive
Tel: 0845 345 0055
Website: www.hse.gov.uk

Legal Sevices Commission
85 Gray's Inn Road
London WC1X 8TX

Website: www.legalservices.gov.uk

National organisations

ADR Now (Alternative Dispute Resolution)
See Advice Services Alliance. This is not an ADR service but provides an overview of the options available.

Website: www.adrnow.org.uk

Advice Now
See Advice Services Alliance.

Website: www.advicenow.org.uk

Advisory, Conciliation and Arbitration Service (ACAS)
Brandon House
180 Borough High Street
London SE1 1LW

Tel: 020 7210 3613
Helpline: 08457 47 47 47
Website: www.acas.org.uk

Advice Services Alliance
12th Floor, New London Bridge House
25 London Bridge Street
London SE1 9SG

Tel: 020 7378 6428
E-mail: info@asauk.org.uk
Website: www.asauk.org.uk

Advice[UK]
12th Floor, New London Bridge House
25 London Bridge Street
London SE1 9SG

Tel: 020 7407 4070
E-mail: general@adviceuk.org.uk
Website: www.adviceuk.org.uk

Age Concern England
Astral House
1268 London Road
London SW16 4ER

Tel: 020 8765 7200.
Helpline: 0800 00 99 66
Website: www.ace.org.uk

Bar Council
289–293 High Holborn
London WC1V 7HZ

Tel: 020 7242 0082
Website: www.barcouncil.org.uk

Bar Pro Bono Unit
289–293 High Holborn
London WC1V 7HZ

Website: www.barprobono.org.uk

Child Poverty Action Group
94 White Lion Street
London N1 9PF
Tel: 020 7837 7979

E-mail: info@cpag.org.uk
Website: www.cpag.org.uk

Childrens Legal Centre
University of Essex
Wivenhoe Park
Colchester
Essex CO4 3SQ

Tel: 01206 873820
E-mail: clc@essex.ac.uk
Website: www.childrenslegalcentre.com

Citizens Advice
Myddleton House
115–123 Pentonville Road
London N1 9LZ

Tel: 020 7833 2181 (admin only)
Website: www.citizensadvice.org.uk and www.adviceguide.org.uk

The main office is for central administration. See website for details of bureaux and regional offices.

Commission for Equality and Human Rights
Website: www.cehr.org.uk

The CEHR is operational from October 2007. The website is limited and at time of going to press continues to link externally to the CRE, DRC and EOC websites:
www.drc.org.uk
www.eoc.org.uk
www.cre.gov.uk

DIAL UK
St Catherine's
Tickhill Road
Doncaster
South Yorkshire DN4 8QN

Tel: 01302 310123
Textphone: 01302 310123
E-mail: informationenquiries@dialuk.org.uk
Website: www.dialuk.org.uk

Free Representation Unit
6th Floor
289–293 High Holborn
London WC1V 7HZ

Tel: 020 7611 9555
E-mail: admin@freerepresentationunit.org.uk
Website: www.freepresentationunit.org.uk

Joint Council for the Welfare of Immigrants (JCWI)
115 Old Street
London EC1V 9RT

Tel: 020 7251 8708
Advice line (for general civil contract holders): 0845 602 1020
E-mail: info@jcwi.org.uk
Website: www.jcwi.org.uk

The Adviser's Toolkit: giving legal advice / appendix A

Institute of Legal Executives
Kempston Manor
Kempston
Bedfordshire MK42 7AB

Tel: 01234 841 1000
E-mail: info@ilex.org.uk
Website: www.ilex.org.uk

Law Centres Federation
293–299 Kentish Town Road
London NW5 2TJ

Tel: 020 7428 4400
E-mail: info@lawcentres.org.uk
Website: www.lawcentres.org.uk

Law Society
113 Chancery Lane
London WC2A 1PL

Tel: 020 7242 1222
Minicom: 0870 600 1560
E-mail: contact@ lawsociety.org.uk
Website: www.lawsociety.org.uk

See website for details of regional offices and for the 2007 Code of Conduct.

LawWorks (formerly Solicitors Pro Bono Group)
10–13 Lovat Lane
London EC3R 8DN

Tel: 020 7929 5601
Website: www.lawworks.org.uk

Money Advice Association (MAA)
Tel: 01476 594 970
Website: www.m-a-a.org.uk

National Consumer Council
Tel: 020 7730 3469
Website: www.ncc.org.uk

National Mediation Helpline
Equity House
Blackbrook Park Avenue
Taunton TA1 2PX

Tel: 0845 60 30 809
E-mail: enquiries@nationalmediationhelpline.com
Website: www.nationalmediationhelpline.com

Refugee Council
240–250 Ferndale Road
London SW9 8BB

Tel: 020 7346 6700
Website: www.refugeecouncil.org.uk

These are the details for the head office – see website for regional and
specific offices and advice line contact details.

Refugee Legal Centre
Nelson House
153–157 Commercial Road
London E8 2DA

Tel: 020 7780 3200
Advice line: 0207 780 3220
Website: www.refugee-legal-centre.org.uk

These are the details for the head office – see website for regional and
specific offices and advice line contact details. RLC offer walk-in advice
sessions.

Rights of Women
52–54 Featherstone Street
London, EC1Y 8RT

Tel: 020 7251 6575.
Advice line: 020 7251 6577
Sexual violence legal advice line: 020 7251 8887
E-mail: info@row.org.uk
Website: www.rightsofwomen.org.uk

Shelter
88 Old Street
London EC1V 9HU

Tel: 0845 458 4590
Shelterline: 0808 800 444
E-mail: info@shelter.org.uk
Website: www.shelter.org.uk

See website for Shelter Cymru, Scotland and NI

Solicitors Regulation Authority
Ipsley Court
Berrington Close
Redditch B98 0TD

Tel: 0870 606 2555
Website: www.sra.org.uk

Youth Access
1–2 Taylors Yard
67 Alderbrook Road
London SW12 8AD

Tel: 020 8772 9900
Email: admin@youthaccess.org.uk
Website: www.youthaccess.org.uk

Practitioner associations

Employment Lawyers' Association
Tel: 01895 256972
E-mail: enquiries@elaweb.org.uk
Website: www.elaweb.org.uk

Discrimination Law Association
E-mail: info@discrimination-law.org.uk
Website: www.discrimination-law.org.uk

Housing Law Practitioners' Association
Tel: 020 7505 4693
E-mail: admin@hlpa.org.uk
Website: www.hlpa.org.uk

Immigration Law Practitioners' Association
Tel: 020 7251 8383
E-mail: info@ilpa.org.uk
Website: www.ilpa.org.uk

Resolution (Solicitors Family Law Association)
Tel: 01689 850227
E-mail: info@resolution.org.uk
Website: www.resolution.org.uk

Resources for legal information

British and Irish Legal Information Institute
www.bailii.org

Office of Public Sector Information
www.opsi.gov.uk

RightsNet
www.rightsnet.org.uk

The UK Statute Law Database (Ministry of Justice)
www.statutelaw.gov.uk

Courses and training

General

Skills for Justice
9–11 Riverside Court
Don Road
Sheffield S9 2YJ

Website: www.skillsforjustice.com

The standards-setting body for the justice sector. The Skills for Justice legal advice toolkit is available for download.

Vocational training

Advice^{UK}
12th Floor, New London Bridge House
25 London Bridge Street
London SE1 9SG

Tel: 020 7407 6611
E-mail: traininglondon@adviceuk.org.uk
Website: www.adviceuk.org.uk

The only advice sector based Advice NVQ Assessment Centre approved by City & Guilds.

Citizens Advice
Myddleton House
115–123 Pentonville Road
London N1 9LZ

Tel: 0114 389 5504 (for training enquiries)
Website: www.citizensadvice.org.uk

Institute of Legal Executives (ILEX)
Kempston Manor
Kempston
Bedfordshire MK42 7AB

Tel: 01234 841 1000
E-mail: info@ilex.org.uk
Website: www.ilex.org.uk

Legal Action Group
242 Pentonville Road
London N1 9UN

Tel: 020 7833 2931
E-mail: lag@lag.org.uk
Website: www.lag.org.uk

One-day courses in areas of social welfare law.

Academic courses

London Metropolitan University
London North campus
166–220 Holloway Road
London N7 8DB

Tel: 020 7133 4202
E-mail: admissions@londonmet.ac.uk
Website: www.londonmet.ac.uk

MA Advice and Paralegal Work (full time: one year/part time: two years)
and Foundation Degree in Legal Advice (full time: two years/part time:
three years)

Peterborough Regional College
Park Crescent
Peterborough PE1 4DZ

Tel: 01733 767366
E-mail : info@peterborough.ac.uk
Website: www.peterborough.ac.uk

Foundation Degree in Paralegal Studies (Part time (eve): three years)

Truro College
College Road
Truro
Cornwall TR1 3XX

Tel: 01872 267061
E-mail: heinfo@trurocollege.ac.uk
Website: www.trurocollege.ac.uk

Foundation Degree in law (FdSc Law) with business and advice based content (Full time: two years)

Staffordshire University
College Road
Stoke on Trent
Staffordshire ST4 2DE

Tel: 01782 294000
E-mail: admissions@staffs.ac.uk
Website: www.staffs.ac.uk

BA (Hons) Advice Studies (three years' full time study or up to eight years' part time: distance learning)

University of Central England
Faculty of Law
Perry Barr
Birmingham B42 2SU

Tel: 0121 331 5595
E-mail: info@ucechoices.com
Website: www.uce.ac.uk

Diploma in Professional Studies in Legal Advice and Representation (15-week course: part time study/work-based practice)

University of Wales
College Street
Lampeter
Ceredigion SA48 7 ED

Tel: 01570 424785
E-mail:enquiries@volstudy.ac.uk
Website: www.volstudy.ac.uk

Various certificate courses in voluntary sector studies and skills. Degree in Voluntary Sector studies taken over flexible periods

University of Wolverhampton
School of Legal Studies
Wulfruna Street
Wolverhampton WV1 1SB

Tel: 01902 322222
E-mail: enquiries@wlv.ac.uk
Website: www.wlv.ac.uk

LLB (Hons) Advice Work (three years' full time study)

APPENDIX C

National Occupational Standards for Legal Advice*

* © JSSL Ltd (Skills for Justice) 2006, NOS for Legal Advice. The full suite is available at www.skillsforjustice.com.

GENERIC STANDARDS (EXTRACTS)

LA3   Develop and manage interviews with clients

Summary

This Unit is for you if you are involved with establishing a supportive working relationship with clients and helping them to explain their needs. You will need to be able to make the client feel at ease and also be able to explore any additional information about the client, which may be important in providing appropriate help. You must also be able to recognise when there is a need to take immediate action and follow the appropriate processes for doing so. You may also have to cope with clients who may be abusive or violent and know how to do this safely.

The Unit requires you to:
- Enable clients to explore their problems and concerns
- Manage the interview process
- Bring interviews to an end

There are 3 elements:

No	Title
LA3.1	Enable clients to explore their problems and concerns
LA3.2	Manage the interview process
LA3.3	Bring interviews to an end

This is a new Unit that has been developed for the independent Legal Advice Sector. It has been developed in the format agreed for the NOS Legal Advice.

LA3.1   Enable clients to explore their problems and concerns

Performance Criteria

To meet the standard, you must be able to:

1. Create an atmosphere and environment in which clients feel comfortable enough to express their problems and concerns
2. Clarify if any other service is providing advice and support to client and follow organisational procedures if this is the case
3. Identify and recognise clients' circumstances, responsibilities and priorities
4. Provide clients with opportunities to explore their issues
5. Explore the issues raised by clients to establish their nature and scope
6. Summarise clients' issues and check own understanding with client
7. Identify any situations where immediate action is required to assist clients and take the appropriate action
8. Recognise and follow organisational procedures where the client may be excluded from receiving the service or not eligible to receive the service
9. Work within own area of competence
10. Comply with all relevant legislation, codes of practice, guidelines and ethical requirements, including potential conflict of interests

The skills you will need to enable you to deliver the service effectively are
- questioning

- active listening
- presenting information
- summarising
- reviewing/reflecting
- prioritising
- reviewing
- negotiating
- decision making
- challenging
- time management
- interviewing

Knowledge and Understanding

To meet the standard, you must know:

a) The types of atmosphere and environment that are appropriate to different clients

b) What situations could make clients feel uncomfortable and how to minimise them

c) Organisational procedures for when a client is receiving advice and support from another agency and why it is important to establish this

d) Why it is important to recognise clients' circumstances and priorities

e) Ways of providing opportunities to the client for exploring issues

f) The kinds of issues that might occur and how they should be explored

g) Ways of establishing the nature and scope of different issues

h) How to summarise issues

i) The kinds of situations that require immediate action and how to deal with them

j) Reasons why clients may be excluded from the service and organisational procedures for addressing the situation

k) Reasons why clients may not be eligible to receive the service

LA3.2 Manage the interview process

Performance Criteria

To meet the standard, you must be able to:

1. Provide suitable opportunities for clients to contribute to discussions and sustain the interview

2. Encourage clients to provide additional information on their situation or needs

3. Respond to clients' immediate needs at each stage during the interview

4. Provide suitable indications to reassure clients of continued interest

5. Provide responses according to the guidelines and procedures of the organisation

6. Identify any signs of increased client stress during interactions and establish their significance

7. Identify any problems with maintaining interactions during the interview and take appropriate action to address them

8. Ensure that all organisational health and safety and risk-assessment procedures are followed – including risk to self

9. Recognise and respond to difficult or challenging clients in a way that sustains the interaction and minimises difficult behaviour or end the interview safely using organisational procedures

The skills you will need to enable you to deliver the service effectively are

- questioning
- active listening
- assertiveness
- presenting information
- summarising
- reviewing/reflecting
- prioritising
- negotiating
- decision making
- challenging
- time management
- assessing risk
- interviewing

Knowledge and Understanding

To meet the standard, you must know:

a) How to provide opportunities for clients to contribute to the interview
b) The type of information that should be obtained from clients
c) Why it is important to respond at regular intervals
d) What type of indications of reassurance are appropriate
e) Organisational guidelines an procedures for providing client responses
f) How to recognise the signs of increased stress in clients and what the significance might be
g) The types of problem that could occur and how to address them
h) Why it is important to address problems and the implications of not addressing the problems
i) Organisational health and safety and risk-assessment procedures relating to different interview procedures
j) Ways that clients may display difficult or challenging behaviour and ways of minimising this
k) Organisational procedures for ending interviews with abusive or violent clients
l) Organisational procedures to adopt when limits of own competence is reached
m) The relevant national, local, professional and organisational requirements relating to equal opportunities, discrimination, health and safety, security, confidentiality and data protection; why it is important to comply with them; and the consequences of non-compliance

LA3.3   Bringing interviews to an end

Performance Criteria

To meet the standard, you must be able to:

1. Provide clear opportunities for clients to signal their desire to end the interview

2. Manage effectively any tensions between the time and resources that are available and clients' needs

3. Assure clients that their decisions will be respected after the interview

4. Summarise the discussions and the outcomes achieved or agreed and check client'sunderstanding

5. Follow organisational procedures to end the interview safely if a client becomes abusive or violent

6. Identify and clarify opportunities for providing further support for clients

7. Record the interview outcomes and agreed actions in the appropriate systems

The skills you will need to enable you to deliver the service effectively are

- questioning
- active listening
- presenting information
- summarising
- review/reflecting
- prioritising
- negotiating
- decision making
- challenging
- interviewing
- time management
- assessing risk
- recording and storing information

Knowledge and Understanding

To meet the standard, you must know:

a) How clients might signal their desire to end the interview

b) How much time and resources are available for interview

c) What type of tensions could emerge with clients

d) Why it is important to assure clients that their decisions will be respected

e) How to summarise interview outcomes and agreed actions

f) What further support might be available to clients

g) Organisational procedures for ending interviews with abusive or violent clients

h) Organisational systems and procedures for recording interviews, why it is important to use the systems and the consequences of not following them

LA5   Provide information to clients

Summary

This Unit is for you if your role is the provision of information to clients. The information may be in written format or may be provided orally. Other formats and communication methods, e.g. signing, Braille etc. may also be used according to the needs of the client.

The Unit requires you to:

- Identify the information required by clients
- Provide information to meet the needs of clients

There are 2 elements:

No   Title
LA5.1   Identify the information required by clients
LA5.2   Provide information to meet the needs of clients

This Unit has been imported from the National Occupational Standards for Advice, Guidance and Advocacy, managed by ENTO. It has been tailored in the format agreed for the NOS for Legal Advice.

LA5.1   Identify information required by clients

Performance Criteria

To meet the standard, you must be able to:
1. Enable clients to express their needs for information
2. Explore with clients the reasons for their information needs
3. Assess correctly clients' needs for information
4. Confirm the information required with the clients
5. Agree the provision of information with clients
6. Refer clients to additional or alternative sources of relevant information
7. Comply with all relevant legislation, codes of practice, guidelines and ethical requirements

The skills you will need to enable you to deliver the service effectively are
- questioning
- active listening
- presenting information
- checking understanding
- summarising
- reviewing
- reflecting

Knowledge and Understanding

To meet the standard, you must know:
a) How to encourage clients to express themselves
b) The difficulties that can occur when clients express their needs and circumstances
c) Factors that can affect the ability of clients to access information
d) The different reasons clients may have for seeking information
e) The kinds of information that may be sought
f) How to assess clients' needs
g) Why it is important to confirm the information required with clients
h) Why it is important to agree that the information will be provided
i) What other sources of information could help the clients
j) The relevant national, local, professional and organisational requirements relating to equal opportunities, discrimination, health and safety, security, confidentiality and data protection
k) Why it is important to comply with different requirements and the consequences of non-compliance
l) How to obtain information on the requirements

LA5.2 Provide information to meet the needs of clients

Performance Criteria

To meet the standard, you must be able to:
1. Agree with clients appropriate methods for providing the information
2. Retrieve the relevant information from the appropriate systems
3. Provide sufficient and suitable information to meet clients' needs
4. Ensure the information that is provided is current and capable of meeting a diverse range of needs
5. Check clients' understanding of the information
6. Assist clients to obtain other relevant information
7. Identify any problems with providing the information and take appropriate action to address them
8. Agree with clients any further activities that are necessary to meet their needs

The skills you will need to enable you to deliver the service effectively are
- questioning
- active listening
- researching information
- presenting information
- checking understanding
- summarising
- reviewing
- reflecting

Knowledge and Understanding

To meet the standard, you must know:
a) The different methods that are available for providing information
b) How information can be presented in different formats
c) Organisational systems for recording information and why it is important to use the systems
d) The procedures relating to the use of the systems
e) How much information should be provided for different clients
f) What type of information is suitable
g) How to check the currency, accuracy and suitability of the information that is provided
h) How to ensure the information is free from stereotypes and is not biased
i) How to check clients' understanding of the information
j) What other sources of information are available
k) What additional information is available
l) What type of assistance might be necessary
m) What are the types of problem that could occur and what actions can be taken to address them
n) Why it is important to address problems
o) The implications of not addressing the problems
p) What other activities might be necessary

LA8   Enable clients to act on their own behalf

Summary

This Unit is for you if your role involves you in working directly with clients to help them gain the skills and confidence to act on their own behalf. You may provide ongoing support for the client during the proceedings, which may involve you attending hearings etc, but not formally participating in the process.

The Unit requires you to:
*   Establish the nature of the client's needs and capabilities
*   Enable the client to act on their own behalf
*   Provide ongoing support for clients during the course of the action

There are 3 elements:

No	Title
LA8.1	Establish the nature of the client's needs and capabilities
LA8.2	Enable the client to act on their own behalf
LA8.3	Provide ongoing support for clients during the course of the action

This is a new Unit that has been developed for the Independent Legal Advice Sector. It has been developed in the format agreed for the NOS for Legal Advice.

LA8.1   Establish the nature of the client's needs and capabilities

Performance Criteria

To meet the standard, you must be able to:

1. Establish the individual's capability to undertake actions on their own behalf
2. Explain all options to the client including representation and referral
3. Establish with the client the nature of their need and expectations and who they should present their case to
4. Work with the client to ensure that their expectations are realistic and achievable
5. Explain to the client the nature and extent of the support services that you can provide and check their understanding
6. Ensure the client understands and agrees to the relevant legislation, codes of practice, guidelines, and ethical requirements of working together
7. Record details of the agreement in the appropriate systems

The skills you will need to enable you to deliver the service effectively are
*   questioning
*   active listening
*   providing information
*   negotiating
*   summarising
*   reviewing/reflecting
*   challenging
*   time management
*   recording and storing information

Knowledge and Understanding

To meet the standard, you must know:

a) Why it is important to establish the client's capability and ways of doing this

b) Why it is important to explain all options to the client and ways of doing this

c) The kinds of needs and expectations that clients may have

d) When it may be appropriate to provide support to help the client to act for themselves

e) What kind of initial help you can give the client

f) The kind of ongoing support that you can offer and why it is important to ensure client understanding of that

g) Relevant national, local, professional and organisational requirements relating to equal opportunities, discrimination, health and safety, security, confidentiality and data protection; the importance of complying with them; and the consequences of non-compliance

h) Organisational systems and procedures for recording client details

LA8.2 Enable the client to act on their own behalf

Performance Criteria

To meet the standard, you must be able to:

1. Establish with the client the nature and extent of the support you can provide and agree roles and responsibilities for taking actions forward

2. Assist the client to identify the information and support that they require

3. Work with clients to help them access and present information relevant to their case

4. Work with the client to ensure that their presentation meets the requirements set by others involved with their case, including timescales

5. Enable clients to present their case in the best possible way

6. Work with clients to enable them to explain their position and to ask and answer questions

7. Explain to the client the relevant legislation, codes of practice, guidelines and ethical requirements of working together in ways that facilitate their understanding

The skills you will need to enable you to deliver the service effectively are

- questioning
- active listening
- negotiating
- challenging
- summarising
- providing information
- reviewing/reflecting
- providing feedback
- decision making
- time management

Knowledge and Understanding

To meet the standard, you must know:

a) Why it is important to agree the organisation's and the client's responsibility and how to do this

b) The kinds of information and support clients may need and where to access it

c) How to enable clients to access information

d) The kinds of requirements that others involved with the case may have and how to help clients to meet them

e) The kinds of skills clients will need to enable them to present, ask and answer questions and how to help them acquire these skills

f) Relevant national, local, professional and organisational requirements relating to equal opportunities, discrimination, health and safety, security, confidentiality and data protection

g) Why it is important to comply with different requirements and the consequences of non-compliance

LA8.3   Provide ongoing support for clients during the course of the action

Performance Criteria

To meet the standard, you must be able to:

1. Agree with clients the nature and extent of the support that you will offer them on an ongoing basis

2. Monitor the progress of the action against agreed criteria and review progress with clients

3. Agree with the client the steps that need to be taken to progress action and who is responsible for taking them

4. Agree with clients when the action has reached a conclusion

5. Take appropriate steps to end the support to allow clients to take responsibility for future actions

6. Record details of the client interaction in the appropriate systems

The skills you will need to enable you to deliver the service effectively are

- questioning
- active listening
- summarising
- reviewing/reflecting
- decision making
- negotiating
- challenging
- recording and storing information

Knowledge and Understanding

To meet the standard, you must know:

a) The kinds of support that you are able to offer the client

b) Ways of reviewing progress against agreed criteria

c) Issues that can occur in progressing actions and how to address these

d) How to decide when the action has reached a conclusion and ways of working with the client to help them understand this

e) When it is appropriate to end the support and ways of doing this
f) Organisational systems and procedures for recording referrals and why it is important to follow them

LA11 Provide legal advice to clients

Summary

This Unit is for you if your role involves you in working directly with clients to establish their needs and expectations of the service and to provide them with appropriate and accurate legal advice.

The Unit requires you to:
- Explore and analyse the nature of the client's needs
- Research information relevant to the client's situation
- Provide appropriate and accurate advice to meet the client's needs

There are 3 elements:

No	Title
LA11.1	Explore and analyse the nature of the client's needs
LA11.2	Research information relevant to client's situation
LA11.3	Provide appropriate and accurate advice to meet the client's needs

This is a new Unit that has been developed for the Independent Legal Advice Sector. It has been developed in the format agreed for the NOS for Legal Advice.

LA11.1 Explore and analyse the nature of the client's needs

Performance Criteria

To meet the standard, you must be able to:
1. Explain clearly the kind of service you can offer and check client's understanding
2. Explore and agree with the client the nature of their advice needs and expectations
3. Agree with the client where a situation requires immediate action and take steps to implement this
4. Agree next steps with client
5. Explain the organisation's systems and procedures for working with the client and check understanding including the limits of service provision and when service may be withdrawn
6. Agree with the client the procedures, responsibilities and time limits for further actions
7. Review and analyse available client information relevant to their case
8. Comply with the relevant legislation, codes of practice, guidelines, and ethical requirements
9. Record client details and agreed actions using organisational procedures for recording and storing client details

The skills you will need to enable you to deliver the service effectively are
- questioning
- active listening

- negotiating
- summarising
- checking understanding
- decision making
- planning
- problem solving
- presenting information
- recording and storing information

Knowledge and Understanding

To meet the standard, you must know:

a) The reasons why it is important to discuss service provision with the client, including any limitations of the service

b) The kind of situation that may require immediate action and the organisational procedures for doing so

c) The kind of actions (next steps) that might be required from you and/or the client and why these are important

d) Organisational systems and procedures for working with clients, why it is important to follow these and why it is important to check the client's understanding

e) Why it is important to agree with the client the time limits, responsibilities and procedures for further actions

f) The kind of client information that may be available about the case and why it is important to review this

g) Relevant national, local, professional and organisational requirements relating to equal opportunities, discrimination, health and safety, security, confidentiality, data protection and conflicts of interest

h) Why it is important to comply with different requirements and the consequences of non-compliance

i) Organisational procedures for the recording and storing of client details

LA11.2   Research information relevant to the client's situation

Performance Criteria

To meet the standard, you must be able to:

1. Identify, review and access sources of information, both internal and external, relevant to the client's situation
2. Ensure the information obtained is accurate and up to date
3. Ensure that the information obtained is appropriate to enable you to advise the client
4. Analyse the information received from the client and the research process and formulate options that could meet client needs
5. Work within agreed organisational procedures and time limits for researching information

The skills you will need to enable you to deliver the service effectively are

- research
- decision making
- analysing
- planning

- problem solving
- time management

Knowledge and Understanding

To meet the standard, you must know:

a) The kinds of information sources, including relevant legislation, case law and national and local policies and practice and internal and external colleagues

b) Why it is important to check that the information is accurate and up to date and ways of doing this

c) Why it is important to check that you have obtained appropriate information and ways of doing this

d) Why it is important to consider organisational procedures and timescales for research

LA11.3 Provide appropriate and accurate advice to meet the client's needs

Performance Criteria

To meet the standard, you must be able to:

1. Present clients with information and possible options for action
2. Advise clients on the implications of possible options
3. Provide clients with advice in a manner and format that helps their understanding
4. Check the client's understanding of the advice offered
5. Agree any further action that needs to be taken by you and/or the client
6. Comply with the relevant legislation, codes of practice, guidelines and ethical requirements
7. Record client details and agreed actions using organisational procedures for recording and storing client details

The skills you will need to enable you to deliver the service effectively are

- questioning
- active listening
- negotiating
- persuading
- decision making
- planning
- problem solving
- presenting information
- checking understanding
- recording and storing information

Knowledge and Understanding

To meet the standard, you must know:

a) Why it is important to advise on the implications of possible options for action

b) Different ways and formats for providing appropriate advice

c) Why it is important to check client understanding and ways of doing this

d) What additional actions might be required and who will take them

e) Relevant national, local, professional and organisational requirements relating to equal opportunities, discrimination, health and safety, security, confidentiality, data protection and conflicts of interest
f) Why it is important to comply with different requirements and the consequences of non-compliance
g) Organisational procedures for the recording and storing of client details

LA12   Manage legal advice

Summary

This Unit is for you if you are involved in managing an ongoing case for a client. It may involve you in briefing someone outside the organisation to carry out some part of the case (eg, a barrister) but it will be your overall responsibility to ensure that the case moves forward.

The Unit requires you to:
• Establish the case file
• Progress the case
• Close the case

There are 3 elements:

No	Title
LA12.1	Establish the case file
LA12.2	Progress the case
LA12.3	Close the case

This is a new Unit that has been developed for the Independent Legal Advice Sector. It has been developed in the format agreed for the NOS for Legal Advice.

LA12.1   Establish the case file

Performance Criteria

To meet the standard, you must be able to:
1. Open a client case file, using organisational procedures
2. Establish and agree with the client the desired case outcomes and milestones
3. Establish the method of funding the case and ensure the client is aware of any cost implications
4. Explain the organisational systems and procedures for working, including confidentiality, and check client's understanding
5. Comply with the relevant legislation, codes of practice, guidelines and ethical requirements
6. Record client details and agreed actions using organisational procedures for recording and storing client details

The skills you will need to enable you to deliver the service effectively are
• presenting information
• active listening
• questioning
• oral and written presentation
• negotiating

- problem solving
- summarising
- checking understanding
- time management
- resource management
- recording and storing information

Knowledge and Understanding

To meet the standard, you must know:

a) Organisational procedures for opening and maintaining client case files

b) Why it is important to establish and agree the desired case outcomes and milestones

c) Different funding sources for the case and how to access them

d) Organisational systems and procedures for working with clients and why it is important to check client's understanding

e) Relevant national, local, professional and organisational requirements relating to the equal opportunities, discrimination, health and safety, security, confidentiality, data protection and conflicts of interest

f) Why it is important to comply with different requirements and the consequences of non-compliance

g) Organisational procedures for the recording and storing of client and case details

LA12.2 Progress the case

Performance Criteria

To meet the standard, you must be able to:

1. Take timely steps to initiate and progress agreed actions on behalf of the client

2. Brief other individuals required to progress the case

3. Ensure that the client is kept informed at all stages of the case of progress against milestones and outcomes

4. Ensure that all deadlines and key dates are met

5. Ensure the case file is maintained accurately and is up to date

6. Make best use of available resources in progressing the case

7. Review and evaluate case progress against milestones and outcomes

8. Comply with the relevant legislation, codes of practice, guidelines, and ethical requirements

9. Record client details and agreed actions using organisational procedures for recording and storing client details

The skills you will need to enable you to deliver the service effectively are

- presenting information
- recording and storing information
- active listening
- questioning
- summarising
- reviewing/reflecting
- oral and written presentation
- negotiating

- problem solving
- decision making
- evaluation
- time management
- resource management

Knowledge and Understanding

To meet the standard, you must know:
a) Actions that should be taken to progress the case
b) Why it is important to consult with and inform the client at each stage of the case
c) Who might need to be briefed about the case
- solicitor advocate
- barrister
- expert witness

and what information they will require
d) Why it is important to ensure that all deadlines and key dates are met
e) Why it is important to maintain the case file accurately
f) The reasons for making best use of resources
g) Why it is important to continuously review and evaluate case milestones and outcomes
h) Relevant national, local, professional and organisational requirements relating to equal opportunities, discrimination, health and safety, security, confidentiality, data protection and conflicts of interest
i) Why it is important to comply with different requirements and the consequences of non-compliance
j) Organisational procedures for the recording and storing of client details

LA12.3 Close the case

Performance Criteria

To meet the standard, you must be able to:
1. Review case progress against milestones and desired outcomes
2. Check any opinions/rulings and follow organisational procedures for progressing or closing the case
3. Evaluate the performance of externally briefed case workers for future reference
4. Ensure the client is made aware of any further actions they can take to progress the case
5. Explain reasons and procedures for closing the case and check client understanding
6. Agree with the client arrangements for case closure and close the case using organisational procedures
7. Comply with the relevant legislation, codes of practice, guidelines and ethical requirements
8. Record client details and agreed actions using organisational procedures for recording and storing client details

The skills you will need to enable you to deliver the service effectively are
- questioning
- summarising
- oral and written presentation
- negotiating
- problem solving
- evaluating
- reviewing/reflecting
- decision making
- checking understanding
- time management
- resource management
- recording and storing information

Knowledge and Understanding

To meet the standard, you must know:

a) Why it is important to review case progress and ways of doing this

b) Why it is important to consider any opinions/rulings and how to use them to decide further actions

c) The importance of evaluating the performance of externally briefed case workers and how to do this

d) The importance of keeping the client informed about the progress of the case, including plans for conclusion

e) Organisational requirements relating to equal opportunities, discrimination, health and safety, security, confidentiality, data protection and conflicts of interest

f) Why it is important to comply with different requirements and the consequences of non-compliance

g) Organisational procedures for the recording and storing of client details

LA16 Negotiate on behalf of clients

Summary

This Unit is for you if your role involves you in negotiating on behalf of your client with other organisations and agencies. This is not the same as representing the client in formal or informal situations, which is covered in Unit LA3: Act on behalf of clients in informal proceedings and Unit LA15: Represent clients in formal proceedings

The Unit requires you to:
- Exchange offers on behalf of clients
- Establish an agreement for clients

There are 2 elements:

No	Title
LA16.1	Exchange offers on behalf of clients
LA16.2	Establish an arrangement for clients

This Unit has been imported from the National Occupational Standards for Advice and Guidance revised by ENTO, December 2005, Unit AG11. It has been tailored in the format agreed for the NOS for Legal Advice.

LA16.1   Exchange offers on behalf of clients

Performance Criteria

To meet the standard, you must be able to:
1. Review the needs of clients
2. Identify a suitable negotiation strategy to achieve the needs of clients
3. Prepare suitable offers for clients that encompass their needs
4. Receive offers from other parties
5. Assess how far the offers achieve the needs of clients
6. Consult with clients on the offers that have been received
7. Recommend the next stages in the negotiations
8. Record details of the negotiations in the appropriate systems

The skills you will need to enable you to deliver the service effectively are
- questioning
- active listening
- presenting information
- negotiating
- persuading
- prioritising
- reviewing
- evaluating
- recording and storing information

Knowledge and Understanding

To meet the standard, you must know:
a) How to obtain information on clients' needs
b) What type of negotiation strategies are suitable for different types of issue
c) How to prepare offers over a period of time
d) When to present new offers
e) How to receive offers
f) How to assess offers and what different offers might signify
g) When to consult clients
h) The potential next stages in negotiations
i) When to conclude negotiations
j) What the systems are for recording negotiations and the procedures that relate to the use of these
k) Why it is important to use the systems

LA16.2   Establish an agreement for clients

Performance Criteria

To meet the standard, you must be able to:
1. Produce agreements that effectively meet the needs of clients
2. Incorporate all necessary details into the agreement
3. Ensure the agreement is capable of being implemented
4. Ensure the agreement complies with all relevant legislation, codes of prac-

tice, guidelines and ethical requirements

5. Confirm agreements with clients at appropriate points in the negotiation process
6. Provide a suitable rationale for any needs that cannot be met or any significant changes to the agreement
7. Produce the agreement in the required formats with the necessary supporting documentation
8. Record agreements in the appropriate systems

The skills you will need to enable you to deliver the service effectively are

- questioning
- active listening
- presenting information
- negotiating
- persuading
- prioritising
- reviewing
- evaluating
- recording and storing information

Knowledge and Understanding

To meet the standard, you must know:

a) What different types of agreement can be reached
b) What types of detail should be included in the agreements
c) How to check the feasibility of the agreement
d) What factors might affect the agreement
e) The relevant national, local, professional and organisational requirements relating to equal opportunities, discrimination, health and safety, security, confidentiality and data protection
f) Why it is important to comply with different requirements
g) What the consequences are of not complying with different requirements
h) How to obtain information on the requirements
i) When clients should be consulted during negotiations
j) What levels of detail clients require
k) What types of change to the agreement might be required
l) Why it is important to provide a rationale for any changes to agreements
m) What the different formats are for agreements
n) What types of supporting documentation might be required
o) What the systems are for recording agreements and the procedures for using these
p) Why it is important to use the systems

LA18 Obtain and provide legal information materials

Summary

This Unit is for you if you are responsible for providing legal information materials within your service. You will be involved in reviewing the use of and need for information materials and obtaining and supplying them. Legal information materials may be made available in a variety of formats (eg, posters, leaflets, newsletters, video) and can involve storage and dissemination using a range of media (eg, paper-based, audio, website, intranet). Legal information materials may be for use by practitioners within the service or by clients and members of the general public.

The Unit requires you to:
- Identify the need for legal information materials
- Obtain and supply legal information materials
- Review the use and effectiveness of legal information materials

There are 3 elements:
No   Title
LA18.1 Identify the need for legal information materials
LA18.2 Obtain and supply legal information materials
LA18.3 Review the use and effectiveness of legal information materials

This is a new Unit that has been developed for the independent Legal Advice Sector. It has been developed in the format agreed for the NOS for Legal Advice.

LA18.1   Identify the need for legal information materials

Performance Criteria

To meet the standard, you must be able to:
1. Review the legal information materials currently used by the service
2. Explore the future requirements for information materials, identifying any trends or developments in the ways in which such materials are presented and provided
3. Identify the range of users of legal information materials
4. Gather relevant information on the overall needs of users of legal information materials
5. Identify and confirm the specific needs of different client groups
6. Identify the life cycle of information materials
7. Assess how the information resources comply with relevant legislation, codes of practice, guidelines and ethical requirements

The skills you will need to enable you to deliver the service effectively are
- questioning
- active listening
- research
- decision making
- written and oral presentation
- recording and storing information

Knowledge and Understanding

To meet the standard, you must know:
a) What type of legal information materials are used
b) What format the legal information materials are presented in
c) Who should be involved in reviewing the information materials
d) What the potential future needs might be
e) How you might obtain information about future needs of users
f) The type of trends or developments that might occur

g) How to assess the potential impact of information and communication technologies on information material presentation and supply
h) How to identify who uses legal information materials
i) Who can provide information on users of legal information materials
j) How clients' requirements of information materials may differ from each other
k) How information materials will be used during their life cycle
l) How to calculate the life cycle of information materials
m) The relevant national, local, professional and organisational requirements relating to equal opportunities, discrimination, health and safety, security, confidentiality and data protection; why it is important to comply with them; and the consequences of non-compliance

LA18.2 Obtain and supply legal information materials

Performance Criteria

To meet the standard, you must be able to:
1. Specify the legal information materials that should be obtained within the constraints of available resources
2. Identify and use methods to obtain relevant legal information materials that comply with organisational procedures and timescales
3. Record and store information materials using appropriate systems
4. Maintain sufficient supplies of available legal information materials to meet the needs of users
5. Identify and use the most appropriate methods to supply legal information materials to users
6. Help users to locate the information materials they need or provide information on other relevant sources
7. Record the supply of legal information materials using the relevant systems
8. Ensure that the information resources comply with relevant legislation, codes of practice, guidelines and ethical requirements

The skills you will need to enable you to deliver the service effectively are
- recording and storing information
- active listening
- questioning research
- decision making
- written and oral presentation

Knowledge and Understanding

To meet the standard, you must know:
a) Who requires to know what legal information materials are being obtained
b) What resources are available for obtaining legal information materials
c) How to prioritise needs
d) What methods are available for obtaining information materials
e) What the organisational procedures are for purchasing information materials and the established timescales
f) What systems exist for recording and storing information resources and why it is important to use them

g) What quantities of information resources are required
h) What the variations in demand are for information resources
i) How often resources should be restocked
j) What methods are available for supplying legal information materials in the service
k) The most appropriate methods for providing different types of information resources
l) How to access different information resources
m) What other sources of information resources exist
n) What systems exist for recording the supply of legal information materials
o) The relevant national, local, professional and organisational requirements relating to equal opportunities, discrimination, health and safety, security, confidentiality and data protection
p) Why it is important to comply with different requirements and the consequences of non-compliance

LA18.3   Review the use and effectiveness of legal information materials

Performance Criteria

To meet the standard, you must be able to:
1. Review the way legal information materials are used
2. Confirm with users that the information materials provided are sufficient and appropriate to their needs
3. Review all the relevant information collected on the effectiveness of the legal information materials
4. Identify accurately any non-compliance with legislation, codes of practice, guidelines or ethical requirements
5. Identify any aspects of the information materials that could be improved
6. Identify and use relevant methods to improve legal information materials
7. Consult with all relevant people on planned improvements
8. Record information relating to use and effectiveness of legal information materials in the appropriate system

The skills you will need to enable you to deliver the service effectively are
- active listening
- questioning
- research
- decision making
- written and oral presentation
- recording and storing information

Knowledge and Understanding

To meet the standard, you must know:
a) Who the users of legal information materials are
b) The range of methods available for consulting users
c) What information is available and can be collected on the effectiveness of information materials
d) What the methods are for collecting information
e) How to assess the effectiveness of information resources

f) The relevant national, local, professional and organisational requirements relating to equal opportunities, discrimination, health and safety, security, confidentiality and data protection

g) What aspects of the legal information materials have potential to be improved

h) What methods and resources are required to implement different types of improvement

i) Who should be consulted on improvements to legal information materials

j) What systems exist for recording information relating to the use and effectiveness of legal information materials and why it is important to use the systems

LA19 Manage personal caseload

Summary

This Unit is for you if you are responsible for managing your own caseload of clients. Caseload management is an important part of ensuring that all cases are dealt with appropriately to achieve the outcomes required by the client within the timescales required by the service.

The Unit requires you to:
- Record and maintain case notes
- Review personal caseload
- Establish priorities for dealing with personal caseload

There are 3 elements:

No	Title
LA19.1	Record and maintain case notes
LA19.2	Review personal caseload
LA19.3	Establish priorities for dealing with personal caseload

This Unit has been imported from the National Occupational Standards for Advice and Guidance revised by ENTO, December 2005, Unit AG14. It has been tailored in the format agreed for the NOS for Legal Advice.

LA19.1 Record and maintain case notes

Performance Criteria

To meet the standard, you must be able to:

1. Record all key information about each case
2. Record all actions being undertaken for clients
3. Ensure case notes are accurate and an appropriate amount of detail is included
4. Ensure case notes are structured in a way that provides a clear case history
5. Ensure case notes are legible and clear
6. Use relevant documentation and systems to record the case notes
7. Comply with all relevant legislation, codes of practice, guidelines and ethical requirements

The skills you will need to enable you to deliver the service effectively are
- analytical
- prioritising
- decision making
- problem solving
- presenting information
- recording and storing information
- time management

Knowledge and Understanding

To meet the standard, you must know:
a) What type of information should be recorded about cases
b) Why it is important to record what is happening
c) How to confirm that case notes are accurate
d) How much detail should be included for different types of case
e) How case notes should be structured
f) Why it is important that case notes are legible and clear
g) What the systems are for recording case notes and the procedures relating to the use of these
h) Why it is important to use the systems
i) The relevant national, local, professional and organisational requirements that relate to equal opportunities, discrimination, health and safety, security, confidentiality and data protection
j) Why it is important to comply with different requirements
k) What the consequences are of not complying with different requirements
l) How to obtain information on the requirements

LA19.2 Review personal caseload

Performance Criteria

To meet the standard, you must be able to:
1. Review all relevant information on the personal caseload
2. Monitor the progress in achieving the required outcomes for the cases
3. Identify any obstacles in achieving the required outcomes for the cases
4. Identify any factors that might affect the structure or content of the caseload
5. Identify any improvements that can be made to the management of the cases
6. Exchange information on the cases according to the procedures of the service
7. Record the information on the cases in the appropriate systems
8. Comply with all relevant legislation, codes of practice, guidelines and ethical requirements

The skills you will need to enable you to deliver the service effectively are
- analytical
- prioritising
- decision making
- problem solving

- evaluation
- presenting information
- recording and storing information
- time management

Knowledge and Understanding

To meet the standard, you must know:
a) The types of information on personal caseloads that should be reviewed
b) How often information on personal caseloads should be reviewed
c) How many cases can be managed
d) How to monitor the progress of cases
e) What type of obstacles could occur in achieving the required outcomes for the cases
f) How the obstacles can be overcome
g) The factors that can affect the quantity of cases being managed
h) What types of improvements could be identified to the management of cases
i) What types of information are involved in different types of case
j) Who should be provided with information on cases
k) Who should provide information on cases
l) What the systems are for recording case information and the procedures relating to the use of these
m) Why it is important to use the systems
n) The relevant national, local, professional, and organisational requirements that relate to equal opportunities, discrimination, health and safety, security, confidentiality and data protection
o) Why it is important to comply with different requirements
p) What the consequences are of not complying with different requirements
q) How to obtain information on the requirements

LA19.3 Establish priorities for dealing with personal caseload

Performance Criteria

To meet the standard, you must be able to:
1. Establish criteria for setting priorities for cases
2. Assess cases against the specified criteria
3. Identify any immediate action required to meet deadlines
4. Specify clearly the cases that require highest priority
5. Inform all relevant people of the need to prioritise specific cases
6. Ensure high-priority cases are implemented and assigned the appropriate resources
7. Monitor the effect of the priorities on the entire caseload
8. Ensure all cases receive the appropriate attention within the timescales established by the service
9. Provide a clear rationale for the priorities

The skills you will need to enable you to deliver the service effectively are
- analytical
- prioritising

- decision making
- problem solving
- evaluation
- presenting information
- recording and storing information
- time management

Knowledge and Understanding

To meet the standard, you must know:
a) What types of criteria could be used for setting priorities
b) How to agree on the priority criteria
c) How to match cases against the priority criteria
d) What deadlines can occur
e) What the consequences are of not meeting the deadlines
f) How to specify the highest priorities
g) Who should be informed of the priorities
h) Who is responsible for implementing cases
i) Which resources should be assigned to implementing different types of case
j) What types of effect or distortion the priorities could have
k) What timescales are required by the service for different types of case
l) Why it is important to provide a clear rationale for priorities

KNOWLEDGE UNITS (EXTRACTS)

LA39 First Line Housing Legal Advice

Summary

This Unit is designed to equip you with a broad understanding of the knowledge required to provide clients with direct housing information and advice at the point of initial contact with the service and to decide when to refer a client on to more specialist sources of advice.

This is a new Knowledge Unit that has been developed for the independent Legal Advice sector. This Knowledge Unit supports the generic National Occupational Standards for Legal Advice.

To meet the National Standard, you must be able to:
a) Identify and explain the legislative framework affecting the provision of and entitlement to both private and social housing and describe how to access more detailed information
b) Describe the legal rights and responsibilities of landlords and tenants and explain how the rights of individual occupants may be affected by different forms of tenure
c) Explain the implications of legislation on environmental health and health and safety requirements as they relate to housing
d) Explain how to select housing options based on circumstances and eligibility, which are appropriate to the needs of individuals seeking advice

e) Explain definitions of homelessness, eligibility criteria in relation to it and the alternative options available

f) Explain the relationship between housing and entitlement to a broad range of benefits

g) Define the roles and responsibilities of individuals and agencies providing, regulating and monitoring housing

h) Describe the procedures for possession in both private and social housing

i) Explain the key principles of complaints procedures for housing organisations and when to apply them

Knowledge and Understanding

You must show that you know and understand:

1. The legislative framework affecting provision and entitlement to private and social housing with particular reference to:

- Types of tenure and their implications for tenants and landlords:
  - the difference between licences and tenancy
  - main forms of tenure and the rights that occupants have under each
  - rights and responsibilities of landlord and occupants
- Housing standards as they relate to residents:
  - terms of tenancy agreement relating to disrepair
    - expressed terms
    - implied terms (basic standards of repair)
  - environmental protection legislation, including local authority duties and powers
  - Health and Safety regulation
  - local authority powers and duties relating to the enforcement of housing standards

2. Statutory housing allocation, including:

- Eligibility
  - statutory scheme
  - local scheme
  - local arrangements for access and eligibility
- Help with applications
- Right to a written decision and time limits for challenge

3. Rights and entitlements in relation to harassment and eviction:

- Harassment/illegal eviction by landlord
- Security of tenure (e.g. exclusive occupation) in relation to harassment and illegal eviction

4. The implications of environmental, health and safety requirements and their impact on housing

5. Housing options available based on circumstances and eligibility, with particular
reference to:

- Residency status of the client
- Recognising emergency situations
- Giving options to clients:
  - private
    - private rental

- home ownership
- shared ownership
- friends and family
- housing options for specific client groups

LA45 First Line Employment Legal Advice

Summary

This Unit is designed to equip you with a broad understanding of the knowledge required to provide clients with employment information and advice at the point of initial contact with the service and to decide when to refer a client on to more specialist sources of advice.

This is a new Knowledge Unit that has been developed for the independent Legal Advice sector. This Knowledge Unit supports the generic National Occupational Standards for Legal Advice.

To meet the National Standard, you must be able to:
a)   Identify and explain the legislative framework relating to employment
b)   Describe the categories of employment status and explain where to find the detail of the tests to determine this
c)   Describe the main statutory rights determined by employment status and the specific rights protecting different clients or client groups.
d)   Define the difference between statutory and contractual rights in employment and describe the sources of evidence for contractual terms
e)   Describe the main contractual issues at work
f)   Describe the framework of legislation relating to discrimination in employment in terms of eligibility and scope
g)   Explain where to find the detail of the tests for discrimination in employment and describe the responsibilities of employers in relation to disability
h)   Describe the eligibility criteria for different forms of dismissal and the main statutory rights on termination of contract
i)   Explain how to draft straightforward documentation in support of simple cases
j)   Describe the key statutory procedures relating to employment actions
k)   Explain the different forms of employment proceedings, their jurisdictions and time limits
l)   Describe the potential outcomes from the range of available options for redress
m) Describe the sources of available funding and consultancy and referral

Knowledge and Understanding

You must show that you know and understand:
1. The legislative framework relating to employment
2. The categories of employment status, including:
- Employee
- Worker
- Self-employed
- Contract worker

- Agency worker
- Apprentice

3. That there are tests for employment status, what they are and where to find the detail

4. The specific statutory rights protecting different clients or client groups, including part-time workers, migrant workers, young people

5. The main statutory rights in work and how they are affected by status, including those relating to:

- Minimum wage
- Time off and holidays
- Deductions from wages
- Transfer of Undertakings (Protection of Employees) (TUPE)
- Written statement of terms and conditions of work
- Sickness
- Disciplinary and grievance
- Family and parental
- Working time
- Health & safety
- Not to be discriminated against

6. The difference between statutory and contractual rights in employment and the sources of evidence for contractual terms

7. The main contractual issues at work, including:

- Pay
- Contract variations
- Hours of work
- Time off/holidays
- Place of work
- Absence
- Notice
- Contract variations

8. The framework of legislation relating to discrimination in employment in terms of eligibility and scope, including:

- Sex
- Race
- Sexual orientation
- Disability
- Religion
- Age
- Part-time workers/fixed-term employees
- Trade union membership
- Public interest disclosure
- Health and Safety/asserting statutory rights
- Parental rights
- Equal pay

9. That there are tests for discrimination, what they are and where to find the detail in cases of:

- Direct discrimination
- Indirect discrimination
- Victimisation

- Harassment
- Vicarious responsibility

10. The key responsibilities of employers in relation to disabilities, including:
- Reasonable adjustments
- Health and safety

11. The eligibility criteria for different forms of dismissal:
- Wrongful dismissal
- Unfair dismissal
- Constructive dismissal
- Automatic unfair dismissal

12. The main statutory rights on termination of work, including:
- Redundancy
- Notice
- Dismissal
- Retirement
- Transfer of business
- Insolvency

13. How to draft relevant documentation in simple cases, including:
- Grievances
- Appeal letters
- Tribunal claims

14. The range of statutory procedures, including:
- Grievance procedure (GP)
- Disciplinary and dismissal procedure (DDP)
- Statutory questionnaire procedure
- Dispute resolution

15. Relevant time limits and how to record them

16. The different forms of relevant tribunals and courts, together with the appropriate jurisdictions and time limits, and how time limits may be affected by statutory dispute resolution procedures

17. The potential outcomes from the range of available options for redress

18. The sources of available funding and the range of external resources available for consultancy or referral

Index

349

Employment Tribunal Claims:
tactics and precedents
Second edition
Naomi Cunningham and Michael Reed

Reviews of the first edition:

'I would have given my eye teeth for this book as a newly qualified employment lawyer representing claimants.'
SCOLAG

'Naomi Cunningham's book ... is a rare gem; it is the 'flesh that clothes the bones' of the employment tribunal system.'
New Law Journal

'The text races along and the examples and anecdotes are so entertaining that it is truly a book you will not want your colleagues to borrow.' *Adviser*

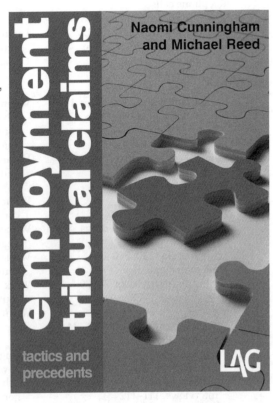

Naomi Cunningham and Michael Reed

employment tribunal claims

tactics and precedents

Pb 978 1 903307 55 7 464pp September 2007 £30

www.lag.org.uk/books

lag.org.uk

◜ Read sample chapters of our titles.

◜ Access the *Legal Action* editorial archive.

◜ Read the news stories from the latest issue of *Legal Action*.

◜ Register your interests to receive free e-mail bulletins
on relevant LAG products and policy.

◜ Find out more details on our full range of training courses.

◜ Use the new simplified ordering process for secure online
purchases of our products.

◜ Find out more about the LAG membership scheme and donate
money to help fund our campaigns.

◜ Get access to our full policy archives: discussion papers, press
releases, consultation responses and parliamentary briefings.

Legal Action Group | working with lawyers and advisers
to promote equal access to justice